Hong Kong, China

Hong Kong, China

香港中國

A Political History of the
British Crown Colony's
Transfer to Chinese Rule

by Steve Shipp

McFarland & Company, Inc., Publishers
Jefferson, North Carolina, and London

All photographs are courtesy of the Hong Kong Tourist Association
(maps are credited individually).

British Library Cataloguing-in-Publication data are available

Library of Congress Cataloguing-in-Publication Data

Shipp, Steve, 1937–
    Hong Kong, China : a political history of the British Crown
Colony's transfer to Chinese rule / by Steve Shipp.
        p. cm.
    Includes bibliographical references and index.
    ISBN 0-7864-0115-X (lib. bdg. : 50# alk. paper) ∞
    1. Hong Kong–Politics and government. 2. China–Politics
and government–1976–   3. Hong Kong–History. I. Title.
DS796.H757S56 1995
951.2505–dc20   95-14161
                                                                         CIP

Manufactured in the United States of America

McFarland & Company, Inc., Publishers
  Box 611, Jefferson, North Carolina 28640

To
Sylvia, Stephen and Ron

Contents

Preface

A historically rare non-violent transfer of property and people from one country to another will occur on July 1, 1997, with the negotiated handover of Hong Kong from the United Kingdom to China. This momentous event also portends a high degree of uncertainty for Hong Kong's 6 million residents, many of whom fled Communist rule in China, thinking they would be forever safe in the protective arms of Great Britain.

At stake for China is resumption of sovereignty over the British Crown Colony of Hong Kong, a 415 square mile piece of territory on the southern coast of mainland China. At stake for Britain is giving up (with honor) its most vibrant colonial possession after more than 150 years of watching it grow from a few thousand people to several million and become a powerful international financial center and one of the world's most famous ports.

After two years of negotiation, without participation from Hong Kong, Britain and China agreed on the wording of the 1984 Joint Declaration, which guaranteed certain personal rights for the people of Hong Kong and continuation of legal, social and other systems beyond expiration of the British lease in 1997. This was followed in 1990 by the Basic Law for Hong Kong, which detailed the rights and systems to be guaranteed after 1997, with assurances of continued capitalistic practices for another 50 years. Analysis of the Basic Law is a regular exercise of interpretation among journalists, lawyers and politicians of both China and Britain, and will continue to demand attention through midnight on June 30, 1997, and beyond.

This book draws heavily on day-to-day journalistic dispatches published in magazines and newspapers in Hong Kong, England, the United States and China. To some degree, it also considers the weight of editorial persuasion in those same magazines and newspapers, plus discussion and commentary carried on television programs focusing on

Map of Hong Kong.

Hong Kong, especially when that discussion relates to the 1997 transition. In addition, there is strong reliance on points of view in books relating to Hong Kong's history, along with more recent books on political and economic circumstances facing Hong Kong in the future.

My own acquaintance with Hong Kong began in 1978, when the territory seemed ready to burst at its economic seams. As my journalistic hosts suggested at the time, there was nowhere to go but up, and everybody was heading upward together, achieving economic dreams beyond expectation. Others could look around and see that such dreams were possible, albeit through hard work and optimism. By 1979, as I followed this most exciting and adventurous story unfolding on a tiny island, a bit of mainland and some 235 adjacent small islands, Britain began seriously discussing the uncertain future of Hong Kong. Its 99-year lease was coming to an end. Long-range investors and landholders wanted assurances they could continue to invest and lease land after 1997. By 1980, most realized that all they could rely on was their optimism. There would be no assurances of a secure future for Hong Kong except from appointed government officials, most of whom would soon be returning to Britain.

Negotiations on the Joint Declaration began in 1982 and continued until 1984, culminating in an assurance that China would indeed resume sovereignty over Hong Kong in 1997. In one form of response, emigration from Hong Kong became rampant, rising to more than 1,000 a week by the late 1980s. Those leaving included some of Hong Kong's most talented professionals (whose departure created what was dubbed a "brain drain"), who hoped to evade living under Chinese Communist rule by rebuilding their lives and lifestyles in Canada, Australia, the United States and other countries. The exodus became even more intense following China's June 4, 1989, violent crackdown against democratic protesters in Beijing's Tiananmen Square.

Attitudes about the changeover to Chinese rule became both more firm and more passive beginning in 1992. Emigration continued, but was given less attention by the media. Jobs opened up, and were often taken by young professionals who were reasonably confident of continuing their careers beyond 1997. Political beliefs and concerns were set aside, except by a few outspoken individuals determined to fully prepare Hong Kong for the handover and hoping to raise the level of its political readiness.

By 1994, a small percentage of the early emigrants were returning to Hong Kong, apparently concerned about recessions in other countries and lured by the belief they could do better in their former home. They would worry later about changing conditions under pending Chinese rule.

The purpose of this book is to present the transition of Hong Kong to Hong Kong, China, in a sequential series of events, situations, and negotiated changes. Some events recounted are historical in nature, such as Britain's early colonization, while others relate to agreements, such as the Joint Declaration and the Basic Law. Interested readers are encouraged to explore these events in greater detail by referring to books listed in the Bibliography.

An overview of Hong Kong's past, present and future is summarized in the Introduction, while Chapter 1 outlines its first 100 years as a British Crown Colony. Chapter 2 shows how Hong Kong recovered from Japanese occupation during World War II, advancing (despite setbacks caused by the Communist victory in China and economic sanctions against China because of its involvement in the Korean War) to the late 1970s when the United Kingdom decided to formally discuss with China what would occur upon expiration of the 99-year British lease. Chapters 3 through 18 examine in depth the period since 1979, when discussion of Hong Kong's future began in earnest between China and the United Kingdom.

In conclusion, the book shows how people and institutions in Hong Kong are preparing for the changeover to Chinese rule, including some personal views on what lies ahead for Hong Kong.

Appendices contain the complete texts of the 1984 Joint Declaration, the Basic Law, the Hong Kong Bill of Rights, and a June 5, 1989, statement by British Foreign Secretary Geoffrey Howe to the House of Commons. A final appendix presents a chronology of political events relating to Hong Kong.

A Word About Orthography

The introduction of pinyin in 1958 was intended to help Chinese schoolchildren learn the Chinese language in a phonetic manner. It has since gained widespread use outside China, gradually replacing the Wade-Giles method, which was intended to help foreigners pronounce Chinese names. This book reflects the currently accepted names of people and places. For example, this book uses Beijing for the city formerly known as Peking. On occasion, quoted historical material will refer by necessity to a proper name that is now not commonly used (Nanking instead of Nanjing, Canton instead of Guangzhou, Mao Tse-tung instead of Mao Zedong). Other proper names will be spelled the same throughout the text.

Introduction

Hong Kong leaves the twentieth century with apprehension, concern and mixed emotions pending its July 1st, 1997, metamorphosis into a city of mainland China after more than a century and a half of British rule. The international community, from capitalism to communism, is monitoring the transition intently, trying to follow the change from "Hong Kong" to "Hong Kong, China," while also watching carefully for potential (profitable) benefits. In one of the most unusual agreements in history, Great Britain formally consented in 1984 to return Hong Kong, Kowloon and the New Territories (plus 235 surrounding small islands) to the People's Republic of China at midnight on June 30, 1997. The 1984 Joint Declaration, signed in Beijing by British Prime Minister Margaret Thatcher and Chinese Prime Minister Deng Xiaoping, sealed the fate of Hong Kong and its nearly 6 million inhabitants, who realized it had to happen but were quietly hopeful that a different solution might be reached—one that would allow Hong Kong to avoid an abrupt change to Chinese rule.

Since the mid–1800s, China has maintained that its Hong Kong treaties with Great Britain were illegal, or at least "unequal," because they were made under duress. Prime Minister Thatcher, irked by China's claims, voiced concern that anyone who failed to honor one treaty might also fail to honor other treaties. However, her criticism may have been intended to raise the consciousness of Hong Kong residents about the coming transition. Through it all, Great Britain certainly realized it would be futile to continue its administration of Hong Kong, but (like other countries) also wanted to protect future economic relations with mainland China—a vastly larger and more profitable market than Hong Kong.

Great Britain initially acquired the island of Hong Kong in 1842, followed by Stonecutters Island and a 6.8 square mile area of Kowloon, the tip of the peninsula, in 1860. Finally, in 1898 Britain negotiated the

1

99-year lease of 235 islands and the New Territories, which adjoined
the extreme southeastern edge of mainland China. Altogether, Hong
Kong, Kowloon, the New Territories and the 235 islands cover 415
square miles of land, or less than one-third the area of Rhode Island.
Most unusual is that the 99-year lease between Britain and China involves *only* the New Territories. Britain's possession of Hong Kong and
the Kowloon Peninsula resulted from permanent cessions, not from any
lease agreement requiring their eventual return to China.

There are other unusual aspects of the Hong Kong transfer:

- No country has ever handed over to another country a flourishing society with such advance notice and without violence or
  threat of violence.

- Great Britain has never given up a possession that it created.

- The alternative of self-government, which Great Britain has
  allowed in the past (for Jamaica, Solomon Islands, Tuvalu,
  Ghana and India) was never considered for Hong Kong.

- Hong Kong will be allowed to continue its successful capitalistic
  system for another 50 years, until 2047, under the "one country, two systems" concept put forth by Deng Xiaoping (virtually forcing Communist China to preside over an economic
  system which is contrary to mainland policy).

As author Kevin Rafferty writes, "the most remarkable of Hong
Kong's miracles is the political one—how a tiny crowded territory on the
end of Communist China has not only avoided being absorbed by China
but has developed a flourishing lifestyle that seems to mock everything
that Communist China stands for."[1]

Hong Kong residents have had little authority or influence over
changes affecting their lives and future. Their main form of local participation has been limited to writing letters to newspaper editors, voic-
ing opinions on radio talk shows and (more recently) responding to
public surveys. Even negotiations leading to the 1984 Joint Declaration
involved only representatives of Britain and China, without direct
representation from Hong Kong.

When the Joint Declaration was announced in 1984, many
residents of Hong Kong wanted to believe that the agreement would
mean continuation of their successful economic system and social
lifestyle, without undue interference from mainland China. And that is
what both China and Britain wanted them to believe, thus reducing the

This map of the Pearl River Delta shows Hong Kong Island, Kowloon, Lantau Island and the New Territories, along with the Shenzhen Economic Zone in southern China. Also note the tiny Portuguese enclave of Macau, across the Pearl River Estuary from Hong Kong. Reprinted by permission of Lonely Planet Publications, Hawthorn, Victoria, Australia, from Hong Kong, Macau & Canton, *1989.*

strain and stress of the transition. However, the high outflow of the
middle and upper class from Hong Kong, along with high-ranking corporate officials, during the 1980s and 1990s, indicated a distrust of
China's implied promise to allow continuation without domination.
Even Jardine Matheson, whose presence had dominated Hong Kong
business for 150 years, moved its headquarters to Bermuda in 1984 and
announced in March 1994 that it would stop trading its shares on the
Hong Kong Stock Exchange effective December 31, 1994.

Anticipated leadership changes in China in 1995 continued to fuel
tensions in Hong Kong, sometimes reflected in the reactionary ups and
downs of the Hong Kong stock market. An early indication of the successor to Deng Xiaoping as the country's paramount leader occurred
on January 31, when President Jiang Zemin appeared at the end of the
traditional Lunar New Year's Eve nationwide television broadcast. It
was a symbolic privilege which had been exercised for many years by
the 90-year-old Deng, whose declining health in 1994 raised both
speculation and concern in Hong Kong about who would become
China's main leader and how the change would affect their lives and
lifestyles after the July 1, 1997, handover.

During his reign, Deng Xiaoping had acknowledged his pride in
achieving the negotiated agreements to regain Chinese sovereignty over
Hong Kong in 1997 and Macau in 1999, though he was disappointed
in efforts for similar success regarding Taiwan, the island home of the
Republic of China.

President Jiang, general-secretary of China's Communist Party,
had been appointed personally by Deng to be his successor, and the
choice was generally supported by other top Chinese leaders, at least
initially. In his Lunar New Year's Eve appearance on television, seen
by hundreds of millions of Chinese, Jiang was accompanied by Premier
Li Peng and National People's Congress Chairman Qiao Shi.

By far the strongest move to preserve dignity and self-confidence
in Hong Kong has been influenced by Chris Patten, appointed as governor in 1992 by British Prime Minister John Major. Patten quickly pro-
ceeded to upset Beijing by trying to introduce "a bit of democracy"
before the 1997 handover, including a widening of the voter base in
direct elections for some of the seats in Hong Kong's Legislative Council. The Chinese leadership responded by threatening to disband all of
Hong Kong's democratic reforms in 1997 and reviewing all of its laws
to determine which should remain in force after 1997.

Hong Kong's best hope for "prosperity and stability" in the twenty-first century is to establish firm institutional changes (such as greater eligibility in voting for legislators and local council seats) and to have faith in China's historic record of honoring international agreements. Meanwhile, preparing for the 1997 handover, China designated Hong Kong as a "Special Administrative Region" and developed the Basic Law, a constitution-like document for the post–1997 period. One significant concern in Hong Kong is the eventual interpretation of the Basic Law for Hong Kong: Will it be used to define the rights of the state or guarantee the rights of the people?

CHAPTER 1

"Barren Island" to International Entrepôt

"The island of Hong Kong is ceded for ever to Her Britannic Majesty."
London Times, November 1842

Hong Kong, in the 1840s, was an island sparsely settled by a few thousand villagers and fishermen, some living on land, some on their boats. Through subsequent treaties and the 1898 New Territories lease, Hong Kong became an important British colony with nearly 6 million people and a welcome refuge through the twentieth century for hundreds of thousands of mainland Chinese seeking safety from wars, revolutions and political oppression. More than 85 percent of Hong Kong's land was unsuitable for agriculture, leaving the area without any other natural resources—except for the magnificent sheltered harbor between Hong Kong Island and Kowloon. Hong Kong's most important status, however, has been as an international pawn—affecting the past, current and future politics of the world's most powerful countries and the economies of countries large and small.

Portugal had already staked out Macao, about 40 miles from Hong Kong across the Pearl River estuary, opening a major settlement there in 1557. The Portuguese monopolized trade routes from China to Europe for the next two and one-half centuries, except for some low-level British expeditions up the Pearl River to Canton (Guangzhou) during the mid-seventeenth century. The British even occupied Macao for a time in 1808, supposedly to "protect" the enclave from a possible attack by the French, but China objected to the British presence and joined with Portugal to persuade Britain to leave Macao.

Britain had strengthened its foothold in the area in the late 1700s, mostly by trading English silver, cotton, woolens, furs and other goods

7

for Chinese silks and teas – and gradually adding a steady flow of opium from India into China through the East India Company (the only trading firm authorized by China). East India would license "country traders" for the opium shipments from India to China and sell the opium in Canton for silver, which then would be used to purchase silks, teas and other products for shipment to England. In 1796, China's ruling Ch'ing leaders banned the use, sale and importation of opium, which nevertheless continued through smuggling. East India's monopoly on trading with China was ended in 1833, after which other British companies could make their own trading arrangements. British merchant firms legally operating in Canton totaled 66 in 1834 and 156 by 1837.

Foreign trading, however, was carried out under unusually restrictive conditions. China permitted foreigners to conduct their trading only at Canton, only during the winter, only within their authorized compounds, and only with the Co-hong (the officially designated import authorities). Traders spent their summers downriver at Macao, administered with China's approval since the mid-sixteenth century by Portugal.

Meanwhile, opium traffic continued to grow, rising from about 2,000 chests (150 pounds each) in 1800 to more than 26,000 chests in 1836. It was more than China's leaders could accept, since it was smuggled (thus bypassing customs revenue) and was causing a high amount of silver outflow from a country that was on the silver standard.

Taking action in 1839, the emperor of China named Lin Tse Hsu (governor general of Hu-Kuang Province) as Canton's imperial commissioner, directing him to halt the opium traffic. Lin immediately issued an order demanding surrender of all opium in Canton warehouses and on British ships at Macao. He also said traders would be subject to punishment by death if they brought in any more opium. The crackdown was sudden and strong – and there was more. Lin also ordered all foreign traders in Canton to remain in their compounds until all the opium then in warehouses and on ships had been satisfactorily delivered to his agents.

The British government decided to challenge the order under its responsibility to protect British citizens. Captain Charles Elliot, appointed by Britain in 1836 as Chief Superintendent of Trade, directed British merchant ships (under protection of two Royal Navy ships) to take refuge in the harbor between mainland China and the Hong Kong Island.

Elliot then sailed for Canton, where he found Chinese soldiers surrounding the British compound. He quickly arranged to surrender more than 20,000 chests (1,500 tons) of stored opium, telling traders they would be reimbursed for their losses, and directed the merchants to sign a bond, as ordered by Lin, that they would cease trafficking in opium. The six-week siege was over. Lin destroyed the opium. The merchants did what they were told, and were released.

But Britain decided it was time to increase the "protection" of British citizens, sending an army on a fleet of ships from India to "uphold British honor" and bring about more access to trading in China. Arriving in June 1840, the British military force of 16 vessels and 4,000 soldiers began moving from Hong Kong up the southeastern China coast. Britain's decision to go to war with China was made by the British foreign minister, Henry John Temple Palmerston, who later was prime minister when China ceded Kowloon Peninsula and Stonecutters Island to Britain after the Second Opium War ended in 1860. Lord Palmerston, in his frequently quoted assessment, described Hong Kong as "a barren island with hardly a house upon it."

The display of force led to a series of confrontations (the First Opium War), an 1841 agreement (the Treaty of Chuanpi) which wasn't good enough for either side, and finally ended with the 1842 Treaty of Nanking, which awarded Hong Kong Island to Great Britain. The treaty also included provisions for trading in five Chinese ports, plus compensation for the costs of the military expedition. Hong Kong at that time was home for fewer than 5,000 people in some two dozen tiny villages and another 2,000 or so fisherman who lived on their boats.

In February 1841, less than a month after the first agreement between China and Britain, James Matheson, business partner of William Jardine, built a warehouse on Hong Kong Island. In June 1841, Charles Elliot conducted a summer land sale involving 50 lots. The first lot auctioned was located on the two-block-long Ice House Street, which now runs along the west side of the top-rated Mandarin Hotel. George Pottinger arrived in December 1841 to replace Elliot as superintendent of trade, and quickly summed up the situation by saying Hong Kong had "already advanced too far to admit of its ever being restored to the Emperor."[1] Pottinger went on to command the British military force in a confrontation with China which led to the Treaty of Nanking in 1842. He was then appointed the first administrator of the British Crown Colony of Hong Kong.

A dispute in 1858 led to another British military incursion and another treaty ceding land from China to Britain. This dispute, variously known as the Second Opium War and the Arrow War, was sparked by China's decision to search a ship, the *Arrow*, which was flying a British flag in a Chinese port. Lord Elgin, whose father, the Earl of Elgin, had acquired for Britain the famous "Elgin Marbles" from Greece, commanded a force aided by French troops which entered Beijing in October 1858, sacking and burning the emperor's summer palace. The conclusion was the 1860 Treaty of Peking, permanently ceding to Britain the tip of Kowloon Peninsula (about 3.5 square miles) for "the maintenance of law and order in and about the harbour of Hong Kong."[2]

Great Britain officially took control of Kowloon on January 19, 1861, and the division was ceremoniously marked by China with the construction of an eight-foot-high bamboo fence extending along the entire border between China and the ceded portion of the peninsula. Traditional colonial trappings had already become established in the tiny colony, including the exclusive Hong Kong Club, built in 1846; a cathedral; religious schools for the local population; and a downtown cricket pitch. Government House, the official residence of presiding Hong Kong governors, was a construction project that took three years from 1852 to 1855.

Colonial pride expanded after the Second Opium War and cession of the tip of Kowloon Peninsula. The business firm of Kelly & Walsh, in an 1893 handbook, stated that Hong Kong "stands forth before the world with its City of Victoria and a permanent population of over two hundred thousand souls – a noble monument to British pluck and enterprise. . . . No stranger, however unsympathetic, can pass along the roads and streets of Hongkong without a feeling of wonder and admiration at the almost magical influence, which in so few years, could transform the barren granite mountain sides of the island of Hongkong into one of the most pleasant cities of the earth."[3]

China's problems continued through the end of the nineteenth century. Japan soundly defeated China in the war of 1894–95, forcing it to give up the island of Formosa (later known as Taiwan). A weakened China then opened the door for Germany, France, Russia and Britain to acquire treaties for "leasing" ports along the China seacoast.

Finally, in April 1898, Britain's representative in Peking, Claude MacDonald, told Chinese leaders that Hong Kong's boundaries should be expanded "for defensive purposes." In May 1898, MacDonald sent London an explanation: "The question of the nature of our title to the extension of the territory was more troublesome. I tried to obtain an absolute cession, but could not resist the force of argument that all other nations who have obtained leases of territory would follow suit, which might be inconvenient for ourselves. The principle of a lease having been admitted, a term of 99 years seemed sufficient."[4]

Thus, in June 1898, the "Convention Respecting an Extension of the Hong Kong Territory" was signed in Peking, adding the New Territories (bordering Guangdong Province) and 235 islands (about 370 square miles of land) to the already ceded British holdings of Hong Kong Island, Kowloon Peninsula and Stonecutters Island. The document declared that the expansion was "necessary for the proper defence and protection of the Colony."

The question of land leases in the New Territories was raised early in the twentieth century by Cecil Clementi, who became governor of Hong Kong in 1925. Clementi's concerns were similar to those presented in 1979 by Governor Murray MacLehose: Investors needed assurances that their leases would continue beyond the 1898 treaty stipulation of three days before July 1, 1997.

Clementi offered two possible courses to resolve the matter. First, he proposed that Britain demand permanent cession of the New Territories, saying the area's eventual return to China would be "fatal to this colony." Second, he said that if Britain were forced to protect its interests through "war-like action," the result should include ceding of the New Territories as a "condition of the resumption of friendly relations" with China.[5] London, however, took a more pragmatic view of the situation, cautioning Clementi against upsetting China in any way, and particularly by calling attention to the 1898 lease.

Clementi made another attempt to resolve lease questions during a 1927 trip to London, but again was cautioned by the Foreign Office's deputy under-secretary of state, Victor Wellesley, against "encouraging Hong Kong to think we were going to keep the New Territories forever."[6] Wellesley's remarks were supported in an unsigned note in the Colonial Office's 1927 Hong Kong file which said: "It is unthinkable that we should ever consent to return Hong Kong or the New Territories to China."[7]

CHAPTER 2

Postwar Hong Kong Rises Again

"It is better to keep Hong Kong the way it is. We are in no hurry to take it back. It is useful to us right now."

Mao Zedong (1959)[1]

Hong Kong, never historically in control of its own destiny, faced an uncertain future after World War II. Even during the war, while under Japanese occupation, its postwar future was being planned by British officials in London as well as by Chiang Kai-shek in China. The postwar administration of the British Crown Colony might have been in serious doubt had it not been for Franklin Gimson, the colonial secretary who had arrived in Hong Kong two weeks before the Japanese took control and was interned throughout the Japanese occupation. Gimson was freed in August 1945 and immediately raised the British Union Jack over Government House, retaining British colonial rule over Hong Kong.

Britain had announced that its military representatives would officially receive the Japanese surrender of Hong Kong. Chiang Kai-shek of China announced on August 25, 1945, that he would not send Chinese troops to formally accept the surrender, but protested against sole British acceptance for what he considered Chinese territory. Thus, the surrender ceremony in Hong Kong on August 30, 1945, was received by the British, but on behalf of both the Chinese and British governments.

Restoration of British administration in Hong Kong was effective with the May 1, 1946, return of Governor Mark Young. In a radio broadcast filled with promises, Young said:

> His Majesty's Government has under consideration the means by which in Hong Kong, as elsewhere in the Colonial Empire, the inhabitants of the

Territory can be given a fuller and more responsible share in the management of their own affairs. One possible method of achieving this end would be by handing over certain functions of internal administration, hitherto exercised by the Government, to a Municipal Council constituted on a fully representative basis.

The establishment of such a council and the transference to it of important functions of government might, it is believed, be an appropriate and acceptable means of affording to all communities in Hong Kong opportunity of more active participation, through their responsible representatives, in the administration of the Territory. But before a decision is taken on the methods of giving effect to the intentions of His Majesty's Government, it is considered essential that the important issues involved should be thoroughly examined in Hong Kong itself, the fullest account being taken of the views and wishes of the inhabitants.

Young said he had "accordingly been instructed to examine the whole question, in consultation with the representatives of the community, and to submit a report at an early date, bearing in mind the policy of His Majesty's Government that the constitution should be revised on a more liberal basis as soon as possible. The aim will be to settle and to announce not later than the end of the year the principles on which that revision should be based."[2]

Despite numerous plans, proposals and petitions from interest groups and individuals, the Young Plan never got off the ground. Hong Kong's Legislative Council was unable to agree on the proposals, one of which was direct elections for a majority of its own members. Young was succeeded as governor in 1947 by Alexander Grantham, who took no action other than forwarding all of the proposals to London.

Consideration of reforms for Hong Kong was further set aside during the Chinese Civil War, which raged until 1949, when Chiang Kai-shek and his nationalist Kuomintang Party followers were driven from the mainland by Mao Tse-tung (Mao Zedong) and his Communism movement. Chiang fled in defeat to the island of Taiwan, established the nationalist Republic of China in 1950 and achieved recognition by the United States and other countries.

The only true natural resource of Hong Kong, after Victoria Harbor, has always been its people. The colony's population under Japanese occupation of World War II had dropped to about 600,000 as a result of deportations and fleeing civilians. Most returned after the war's end, increasing Hong Kong's population to 1.8 million by the end of 1947. The colony's government had to deal with further overcrowding during

1949-50, as more than 775,000 Chinese refugees fleeing the Communist regime crossed the border to settle in Hong Kong. The massive influx included talented professionals, entrepreneurs and experienced managers and workers, all of whom contributed to Hong Kong's success as an international trading and financial center.

Relations between mainland China and Hong Kong were seriously interrupted in 1950 when China supported North Korea in its war against South Korea. The 1951 United Nations trade embargo against China meant Hong Kong had to ignore its main trading partner. The result was a major change for the colony from its 150-year traditional function as an entrepôt, moving goods in and out of China, to a new function as a producer of goods for the world. By 1951, the population of Hong Kong, swelled by the tremendous influx of refugees from Red China, had climbed to 2.02 million. The vast numbers of new people, combined with the postwar return of old residents, also provided the foundation for the colony's evolvement from trading center to manufacturing center. Domestic production accounted for 15 percent of Hong Kong's total exports in 1950, rising to more than 70 percent within 10 years. It was a remarkable record of personal and collective flexibility, contributing to an equally remarkable capacity for growth.

Hong Kong's international status and importance to the United States were demonstrated in 1969 with the establishment there of the American Chamber of Commerce. Its declared purpose was to develop, promote and otherwise encourage trade and commerce between the United States and Hong Kong. American participation in Hong Kong trade, already considerable, increased by 1970 to 42 percent of the colony's exports and 13 percent of its imports.

Greater local participation in Hong Kong's present and future was encouraged in the early 1970s through the Community Involvement Plan, which promoted leadership by area groups comprised of people from all levels, rather than the previous practice of indirect control by community leaders. For the first time, Hong Kongers felt they were being consulted and listened to by their own government. The Community Involvement Plan divided Kowloon and Hong Kong into 74 areas, each with about 45,000 people. Each area had a 20-member committee, which dealt directly with an unofficial member of the Legislative Council. "Unofficial" members of the Legislative (Legco) and Executive councils (Exco), as non-government delegates appointed by the governor, reviewed government policies, made recommendations for changes and considered grievances regarding governmental activities.

The language in Hong Kong has always been Chinese. But English was the official language of Hong Kong, from the early days of traders and merchants and colonial administrators appointed by the British government. In the 1950s, however, letters to the government written in Chinese began sometimes to be answered in Chinese, a departure from the previous practice of all official correspondence being written in English. The language situation finally began to fall into order in the early 1970s.

Under pressure from organizations, individuals and publications, Hong Kong's colonial secretary announced on October 9, 1970, the formation of a committee "to examine the use of Chinese in official business." The committee also was asked "to advise on practicable ways and means in which the use of Chinese might be further extended in the interests of good administration and for the convenience of the public." Four reports were developed by the committee, after which the government approved the Official Languages Act in 1974. The act, in part, allowed for continued use of English as the official language for laws, but permitted Chinese to be an equal official language in other governmental activities and functions. Another campaign began in 1978 to encourage the teaching of the Chinese language in schools.[3]

Murray MacLehose, one of the most popular governors in the history of Hong Kong, took office in November 1971 and presided over a decade of economic prosperity, improved social programs and political stability. He came to Hong Kong after a diplomatic career background which included assignments in Denmark, Vietnam, Malaysia and China, plus a three-year stint (1959–62) in Hong Kong as a political adviser to Governor Robert Black.

When MacLehose became governor, Hong Kong's population had climbed past 5 million, of whom 98 percent were Chinese. Seventy percent of the colony's residents lived on Hong Kong Island and Kowloon, where in the most crowded sections the population density was 6,500 per square acre, one of the highest rates in the world. In some areas, garbage collection was required eight times a day.[4]

Hong Kong's status was given worldwide attention in March 1972, when China's ambassador to the United Nations, Huang Hua, raised questions about the enclaves of Hong Kong and Macau in a letter to the U.N. Committee on Decolonization. In his letter, Huang said: "As is known to all, the questions of Hong Kong and Macau belong to the category of questions resulting from the series of unequal treaties left over by history, treaties which the imperialists imposed on China." As such, he said, "they should not be included in the list of colonial territories covered by the Declaration on the Granting of Independence to Colonial Countries and People."

Huang said Hong Kong and Macau "are part of the Chinese territory, occupied by the British and Portuguese authorities," and should be "immediately removed" from United Nations documents. Continuing, he said, "The settlement of the questions of Hong Kong and Macau is entirely within China's sovereign right." Also, in an often-quoted remark, Huang said: "With regard to the questions of Hong Kong and Macau, the Chinese government has consistently held that they should be settled in an appropriate way when conditions are ripe." Britain responded with a brief note to the U.N. secretary-general, stating its disagreement with China's claim but adding that "in no way" did it affect "the legal status of Hong Kong."[5]

Even before Huang's complaint to the United Nations, "colonial" references began disappearing from official Hong Kong, evolving to its frequent designation as a "dependent territory." Responsibilities of the Colonial Office were assumed in 1967 by Britain's Foreign and Commonwealth Office. In 1976, almost as significant, Hong Kong's colonial secretary became chief secretary, a position second to the governor in administering affairs of the territory.

Hong Kong's gross domestic product growth averaged more than 9 percent a year during the 1970s, adversely affected only slightly by the 1974-75 worldwide recession. It was one of Hong Kong's most glorious periods of growth, allowing businessmen and investors to become almost complacent about the longer-term concern over the colony's 1997 lease. That was followed by China's sudden economic openness to the world in 1978, which resulted in positive changes for Hong Kong, especially regarding links with its nearest mainland neighbor, Guangzhou (Canton). New air service was permitted between the two cities, along with hydrofoil service on the Pearl River. Border restrictions were relaxed to allow faster shipment of goods transported by trucks. Later, the border town of Shenzhen, southeast of Guangzhou, was designated by China as a "special economic zone," bringing mutual economic benefits for both Hong Kong and China.

In a historic incident in 1978, MacLehose, in his personal pursuit of internal "normalization" with mainland China, exchanged toasts with Wang Kuang, then director of the New China News Agency, commemorating China's National Day in a Hong Kong ceremony sponsored by the NCNA.[6]

CHAPTER 3

The Final Political Battle Begins

"My recent declarations in favour of holding a National Convention of the People of China and abolishing the unequal treaties should be carried into effect as soon as possible."
Kuomintang founder Sun Yat-sen (1925)[1]

The future of Hong Kong, even before Sino-British negotiations began, was almost entirely a matter of sovereignty over a tiny area which China had wanted to settle for decades. China maintained that Britain's possession of Hong Kong resulted from "unequal treaties" and was therefore "illegal" and "null and void." For the People's Republic of China, sovereignty over Hong Kong would have to be settled first. Only then could meaningful negotiations about the future of Hong Kong be held between China and Great Britain.

Relations between Hong Kong and China were generally cordial during the 1970s. Thus, when Governor Murray MacLehose was invited by Deng Xiaoping to visit Beijing in March of 1979, he eagerly accepted, marking the first official visit to China by any Hong Kong governor since the Communist Party took control in 1949. He opened his 11-day trip by journeying from Hong Kong to Guangzhou (Canton) by train, and then continuing to Beijing to meet with Chinese leaders.

The visit by MacLehose turned out to be the opening bell of the final political battle over Hong Kong, one which the once mighty empire of Great Britain would lose to the great patient bear of mainland China. One of the issues brought up by MacLehose, under pressure from business interests in the colony, was the matter of land leases. Would they still be valid after Britain's lease for Kowloon and the New Territories ended in 1997? Could they legally be extended past 1997?

17

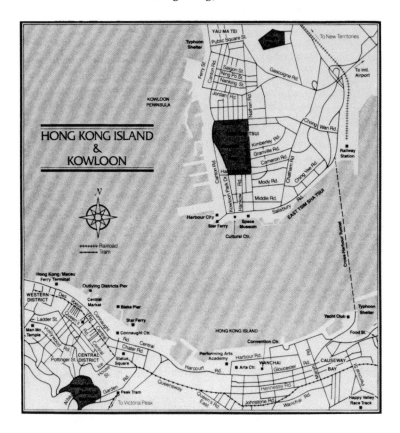

Hong Kong Island and the tip of Kowloon. Hong Kong's Central District is at bottom left. Courtesy Hong Kong Tourist Association.

Virtually all of the land in Hong Kong was owned by the government, which in turn negotiated leases to business concerns in varied terms. Although some early leases had been issued for 75, 99 and even 999 years, leases in the New Territories were held to a maximum 15 years, with options for renewal. Land leases in Hong Kong were acquired by auction, often for a very substantial premium (perhaps justifying the purchaser-lessee generally being called the "owner" of the land).[2] Rent fees were nominal, and leases were generally renewed automatically, for the same amounts and without additional premiums. By 1982, leaseholders wanted to know if their leases were valid, or would be renewed when Britain's lease on the region ended on June 30, 1997.

Many types of watercraft operate in the "fragrant waters" of Victoria Harbor between Kowloon Peninsula and Hong Kong's Central District.

It was time for the Hong Kong government to get some answers, realizing that worried land-lease holders might be inclined to move elsewhere before their leases expired.

In Beijing, MacLehose anxiously submitted the land-lease question directly to Deng Xiaoping, hoping the concerns could be resolved with a few calming words and perhaps some official approval in the form of written documents. However, once MacLehose raised the land-lease question, Deng decided it would be best to conduct formal talks to resolve the situation. And the situation, Deng said, was actually a matter of sovereignty—who would really be in control of Hong Kong after 1997. MacLehose, like others, realized there could only be one outcome: whatever China wanted. Also, like others, he thought Britain could hold back on conceding sovereignty in exchange for other demands that might benefit Hong Kong in the long run.

MacLehose returned to Hong Kong in the same way he had left 11 days before, on a train from Guangzhou, a dramatic and symbolic demonstration that the Guangzhou–Hong Kong train journey was now direct. Passengers would no longer have to change trains at the border, which had required six hours to make the 90-mile trip. At the same time, MacLehose returned to Hong Kong with what he characterized as good news. Deng, he said, had told him to tell investors in Hong Kong to "put their hearts at ease."[3] What MacLehose failed to report was that Deng implied that Great Britain's lease of Hong Kong would not be renewed, though a timetable was not discussed during their one-hour meeting.

Anxiety Grows

The Prosperous '70s seemed almost too quickly to move into the Anxious '80s. What was to become of Hong Kong? More important, how should people and companies prepare for 1997?

Former British Prime Minister James Callaghan, trying to assess the situation, visited Beijing in May 1980. He returned to London with a personal view that China had backed off on its public interest in Hong Kong, suggesting that the issue of Hong Kong was now on the back burner. Prime Minister Margaret Thatcher, who succeeded Callaghan in 1979, was more concerned with domestic problems than with dealing with a colony halfway around the world that was scheduled to leave the Commonwealth.

Hong Kong needed reassurances, and some were offered by Mac-Lehose, who told the Legislative Council in his 1980 policy speech: "There is nothing in this rapidly evolving situation which we have to fear. But naturally it involves new problems as well as new benefits. It is therefore important that we should keep in close touch with the Provincial Government of Guangdong and find ways by which any new problems can be solved by mutual cooperation. This we are doing."[4]

MacLehose offered the same sort of assurances in his annual speech to the Legislative Council in October 1981, saying:

> Sino-British relations continue to be excellent in themselves and over Hong Kong. In Hong Kong, the relations of our officials with those of the Central Government and the Guangdong Provincial Government are friendly, practical and constructive. I note with satisfaction the steady development of economic cooperation between agencies of the Chinese Government and Hong Kong businessmen in Hong Kong, in Guangdong and other parts of China. I am convinced that at this time the best contribution we can make to our own future is the fostering of the growing economic links that exist with our neighbor. These are complementary to our very large economic interests in other parts of the world."[5]

Britain's Foreign Office, under Foreign Secretary Lord Carrington, continued to press ahead with resolving what now was considered "the Hong Kong question." By now, though, the British proposal of allowing land leases to continue beyond 1997 had been solidly rejected by China, leaving no room to pursue alternative actions without approval by the Chinese leadership.

Lord Carrington decided to follow up with his own effort, traveling to Beijing in April 1981 to meet again with Chinese Foreign Minister Huang Hua. Carrington had met 14 months earlier with Huang in London, and found him at least receptive to discussion about Hong Kong. Huang, for the most part, simply repeated the general Chinese position that Deng Xiaoping's "authoritative statement" on Hong Kong should be "sufficient" for both Britain and China. Nevertheless, Carrington met again with Huang in Beijing and tried to discuss Hong Kong. This time, however, Huang politely declined to respond about anything to do with Hong Kong. Undaunted, Carrington met the following day with Deng Xiaoping, who insisted on discussing plans for returning Taiwan to Chinese rule. Deng's only response to the Hong Kong question was to say again, as in 1979, that investors should "set their hearts at ease."

Preparing for Negotiations on the Future of Hong Kong

There was a distinct and noticeable difference in attitude throughout Hong Kong at the beginning of 1982. Change was in the air, and many residents wanted to believe that any change would be positive. In fact, however, one of the most pressing problems became even more pressing. The problem was land, or more specifically, the leasing of land in the New Territories. By law, leases in the New Territories were limited to 15 years and could be renewed, but only until three days before the end of June 1997. Leaseholders and prospective leasebidders wanted to know what to expect after expiration of Britain's 99-year lease on the New Territories.

Another worrisome factor affecting Hong Kong in 1982 was the worldwide economic recession. Hong Kong's annual economic growth rate was a very attractive 11.9 percent from 1976 to 1981, but hopes for sustaining the high growth rate were disrupted in 1982, largely because of a sharp decline in the volume of domestic exports.

Pressure began to build, especially after British Deputy Foreign Minister Humphrey Atkins went to China to arrange for a possible visit by British Prime Minister Margaret Thatcher later in the year. Chinese Prime Minister Zhao Ziyang had been approached previously, in and out of diplomatic channels, about discussing the future of Hong Kong after the end of the British lease on July 1, 1997. Just as regularly, Zhao and other Chinese leaders generally declined to entertain any serious discussion about the colony.

After a seemingly spontaneous, cordial meeting with Zhao, Atkins said the question of British rule over Hong Kong would be on the agenda, quietly informing the Chinese leadership that Britain would not seek renewal of its 99-year lease of the New Territories. Atkins was surprised to discover that Zhao was quite willing to discuss Hong Kong, and especially any preparations for the post–1997 period, assuring Atkins that China wanted Hong Kong to maintain its status as a free port and continue to be one of the world's major financial and commercial centers. He said that, in any event, Hong Kong should be reassured of continued prosperity. At the same time, Zhao cautioned that China wanted to safeguard its claim to sovereignty over Hong Kong.

Atkins was more than pleased. It was far more than he expected to hear from Zhao. He quickly arranged with Zhao to plan for a visit later in the year by Prime Minister Thatcher, thereby fulfilling his main purpose for the Beijing trip. Thatcher's journey would be a diplomatic follow-up to Chinese Communist Party leader Hua Guofeng's visit to Thatcher in London in November 1976.

On the evening of January 6, almost immediately following the meeting between Zhao and Atkins, a formal announcement was issued in Beijing saying that Mrs. Thatcher would visit Beijing in the autumn of 1982. The announcement did not mention Hong Kong, nor did it need to—everyone knew that the future of Hong Kong was finally going to receive some serious attention between the leaders of China and Britain.

Optimism was overflowing when Atkins left Beijing and went on to Hong Kong. Speaking openly to reporters in the colony, Atkins said he was convinced the Chinese leadership realized that "confidence will be endangered" without some sort of agreement by 1997.[6]

Still brimming with confidence, Atkins also talked about his discussion with Zhao in a private meeting with members of the Legislative and Executive councils. "It was quite clear when Humphrey got back that this was the beginning of the negotiating process," one Exco member said later.[7]

After the visit by Atkins to Beijing, China organized its policy on the matter and assured Great Britain that it would be ready to open formal talks on the future of Hong Kong in September 1982. A series of diplomatic talks between the two countries during the spring and summer preceded the pending visit by Mrs. Thatcher. China also announced the formation of a special committee to study the issue of post–1997 Hong Kong, though its immediate purpose would be to prepare for the opening of diplomatic discussion on Hong Kong's future during Mrs. Thatcher's September visit to Beijing.

MacLehose Retires as Governor of Hong Kong

A number of important developments occurred over the next few weeks and months of 1982, particularly for Hong Kong and Great Britain. Edward Youde, a career British diplomat and former ambassador to Beijing, was sworn in on May 21 as the new governor of Hong Kong, replacing Murray MacLehose.

Youde, the British Foreign Office's leading China expert, knew he had assumed the governorship of the colony at a delicate time, but declared he was ready for the challenge and accepted it with full realization of what lay ahead. The future of Hong Kong and its residents, whose number was now approaching 5.3 million, would come under intense discussion which would especially be watched by anxious businessmen fearful about what might follow the expiration of Britain's lease of the New Territories in 1997.

MacLehose had been a popular governor, and the longest-serving administrator in the history of Hong Kong. He had presided over the colony, through several term extensions, since November 1971. MacLehose had overseen the growth and changes in Hong Kong in more than one way during his eleven years as governor. Standing 6 feet 6 inches, the slender Scotsman towered over members of the Legislative and Executive councils and was easily visible whenever he made a public appearance or simply walked informally outside Government House. Reasons for MacLehose's popularity in the colony included his initiation of long-ignored social reforms and educational improvements and the development of welfare and medical facilities. During his terms, the government of Hong Kong began developing public housing intended to provide inexpensive living quarters for 1.8 million people over a 10-year period. Many of the intended occupants were homeless; others needed homes to replace rundown apartment buildings which had either burned or been torn down to make way for new commercial development projects.

Under the guidance of MacLehose, three new towns were developed in the New Territories, and three other market towns were expanded. He also improved lines of informal communication with China through the Hong Kong branch of the New China News Agency. (Britain had refused, since the mid–1950s, to permit official diplomatic status for China in Hong Kong.) Education improvements included provisions for at least three years of secondary education for everyone by 1978, along with availability of further education at university, polytechnic and vocational levels. MacLehose also had a five-year plan ("the way ahead") for social services which led to more health and medical facilities, pollution control, family planning and general improvement of quality of life for the population of Hong Kong.

MacLehose enjoyed his years as governor, took his responsibilities seriously and initiated a welcome change of administrative style. As one example, he usually walked from Government House to the Legislative Council Chambers instead of riding the short distance in the official limousine. He frequently strolled into residential areas of Hong Kong, easily recognized because of his height and his casual clothing, often short-sleeved shirts and slacks.

Under his persistent prodding, the Hong Kong government and the Urban Council developed swimming pools, sports stadiums, running tracks, small sports fields, concert halls, auditoriums, cultural centers, a planetarium and the Hong Kong Arts Centre. MacLehose also supported development of a subway system for mass transit under Victoria Harbor and road tunnels through the hills of Kowloon and Hong Kong Island.

Other improvements during his time as governor included the electrifying and double-tracking of the Kowloon-Guangzhou Railway and expansion of Hong Kong's container port, vital to the trade and economic growth of the colony. As one journalist noted: "To the people, he (MacLehose) was a relaxed, smiling, informal and benevolent governor, anxious to go out into the streets to learn of problems, and then do something about solving them."[8]

MacLehose, who suffered a mild stroke in April 1982, was 65 years old when his governorship of Hong Kong came to an end. His departure had the outward appearance of a traditional ocean liner ceremony, plans

Hong Kong's tram system has operated since 1904 and is a popular mode of transportation among local residents and tourists.

for a more elaborate farewell having been abandoned because of his stroke and recovery. Thousands of people gathered at the pier at Victoria, openly displaying "the genuine wave of concern and affection which the formal ceremonies would have largely concealed"[9] as MacLehose and his wife boarded a ferry which would transport them across the bay to Kowloon's Kai Tak Airport.

Even at 65, and despite complications from his stroke, MacLehose still had plenty of expertise which could be invaluable to the British leadership. According to Derek Davies, correspondent for the *Far Eastern Economic Review*, MacLehose was expected to become Prime Minister Thatcher's chief personal assistant.[10] Davies also described MacLehose as Hong Kong's "most successful governor."

Another major event in 1982 was Britain's war with Argentina to retake the Falkland Islands. Argentina, deciding to take action in its long-simmering claims over the Falklands, invaded the dependency of South Georgia on March 25th, moving on to the Falklands on April 2. The invasion was characterized as a surprise by the British, although there had been ample warning signs. One specific warning came in a March 3 telegram to London from the British ambassador in Buenos

Aires, who suggested strongly that threats were building towards some kind of forceful action by Argentina against the Falkland Islands. But the invasion produced immediate action at 10 Downing Street. Britain's House of Commons was summoned to emergency session on April 3 to deal with the Argentinean incursion of the Falkland Islands. Their subsequent recovery came nearly 10 weeks later, with the formal surrender on June 14. Britain's overwhelming military action, aided by satellite intelligence reports from the United States, had resulted in a future under British rule for the 1,800 residents of the Falklands who preferred that form of security and protection rather than to be ruled by Argentina. The military incursion and aftermath had fully occupied the attention of Prime Minister Thatcher and her government. There was little time during April, May, June and July for dealing with the question of Hong Kong.

Thatcher Prepares for Hong Kong Visit

Finally, on July 28, only two months before her scheduled visit to Beijing, Mrs. Thatcher held her first comprehensive preparation meeting to review the British position on Hong Kong and how it might be presented to the Chinese leadership. As it turned out, Governor Edward Youde had worked on development of the British position over the summer, during the Falklands war. This was not an easy task. Thatcher's time had been consumed by the Falklands war, and then by the glory of the British triumph. But Youde, realizing the present and future importance of the Hong Kong question, persisted in his efforts, even managing to bypass newly installed British Foreign Secretary Francis Pym, whose communication with Thatcher was always at a low level.

One government insider said Youde was the one person who brought reality to a situation that Britain wasn't quite ready to face. He said the idea of a "Proposal to Divest Sovereignty over Hong Kong to Foreigners" being placed "under Mrs. Thatcher's nose in her hour of triumph was more than any foreign secretary could bear. It was Teddy Youde who finally got things moving, going back to London and cranking the Prime Minister up."[11] Thus, it was Youde's preparation and persistence that led to the July 28 meeting at 10 Downing Street, presided over by Prime Minister Thatcher. Percy Cradock, Britain's ambassador to China, flew in from Beijing for the meeting. Also on hand was Alan Donald, the British foreign office's under-secretary for Asian and Pacific Affairs.

Although the British leadership would have liked to solidify its diplomatic stance on Hong Kong, it was forced instead to consider a response to China's position. The latest Chinese view on Hong Kong had been known since early April (12 days after Argentina's invasion of the Falklands) but had been set aside until the July 28 meeting in London. Chinese intentions for Hong Kong were personally submitted to Edward Heath, Britain's prime minister in the early 1970s, who had met with Deng Xiaoping in Beijing on April 6.

Deng told Heath that China would reclaim sovereignty over Hong Kong, ending all administration of the colony by Great Britain. He said Hong Kong would continue as a financial center and free port, with no change in its economic and social systems. In addition, it would be administered by its own government, the basis of a Beijing campaign which stressed "Hong Kong run by Hong Kong people." Heath's report on his meeting with Deng, with the clearly specified Chinese intentions, was reviewed at the July 6 meeting at 10 Downing Street. Another consideration was a report from the January meeting in Beijing between Deputy Foreign Minister Humphrey Atkins and Chinese Premier Zhao Ziyang which signaled China's readiness to consider discussing the future of Hong Kong.

The feeling among residents of Great Britain was always somewhat detached, though many felt it would be proper to continue treating Hong Kong as a colony, even if it meant a change in the arrangement between China and Britain. In a survey conducted during the summer of 1982 by the London-based Reform Club of Hong Kong, a business group fashioned after British political organizations of the 1800s, 70 percent of respondents favored continuation of British administration over the colony after 1997. This response supported the Reform Club's proposal that London give up all claims to Hong Kong in 1997, but continue to administer the colony as a British trust territory for 20 years or longer, depending on a 10-year notice by Beijing for recovering control. Reform Club representatives began discussing their proposal in April 1982 with members of Parliament, but their efforts were set aside when Britain began dealing with the Falklands war.[12]

Meanwhile, the people of Hong Kong had little official means to participate in the most important event in their history. The best they could do was try to indicate their feelings through opinion polls. Some of these surveys were conducted during 1982, when Britain's attention was diverted to recovering the Falkland Islands.

One detailed survey was made during May and June of 1982 by a civic organization known as the Hong Kong Observers. Interviewers sought opinions on five possible solutions regarding the future of Hong Kong. These possibilities included:

1) Return of Hong Kong to China.
2) Development of Hong Kong as a special economic zone within China.
3) Maintenance of the status quo.
4) Independence.
5) Maintenance of British administration in Hong Kong under Chinese sovereignty.

The survey showed that 26 percent favored the return of Hong Kong to China; 42 percent favored designating Hong Kong as a special economic zone within China; 95 percent preferred maintenance of the status quo; 37 percent favored independence for Hong Kong; and 64 percent favored continued British administration over Hong Kong under Chinese sovereignty.

At the same time, the survey by the Hong Kong Observers confirmed that a majority of people in Hong Kong lacked sufficient understanding of the problem, and thus were unable to fully determine how they might be affected by the outcome. Responses showed that 53 percent hadn't discussed the question of Hong Kong's future, while 28 percent said they seldom talked about it, and 19 percent said they discussed the issue only occasionally.[13]

A sense of helplessness also surfaced in questioning by the Hong Kong Observers about the future of Hong Kong. The survey showed that 97 percent of those responding had made no preparations whatsoever in connection with the pending changes for Hong Kong. When asked why, 33 percent said they lacked capability; 30 percent said their future was a matter of fate; and 21 percent admitted they simply didn't know how to prepare.[14]

Generally, most people in Hong Kong, at all levels of society and business, believed the future of Hong Kong would be easily resolved by Great Britain and China, and probably, like most Hong Kong deals, within two or three days. After all, didn't everyone talk about continued "prosperity and stability" for the colony?

Beijing Seeks Opinions about Hong Kong's Future

China's expectations about the future of Hong Kong evolved through a series of meetings with a variety of prominent figures from the colony during the early summer of 1982. Although characterized as opinion-gathering sessions, they actually helped provide a not-so-subtle manner of revealing the basic intentions of the Chinese leadership. In one such meeting, Deng Xiaoping summoned a group of 12 business leaders from Hong Kong and Macau to Beijing on June 15 – the day after Britain formally accepted Argentina's surrender and its return of the Falkland Islands after 10 weeks of battle. Gathering in the Great Hall of the People, Deng requested suggestions about Hong Kong from the visiting businessmen, but reminded them of his two requirements: sovereignty for China and continued prosperity for Hong Kong.

A *Pai Shing* writer said Deng had stressed that "China will regain sovereignty over Hong Kong and will devise a workable method for maintaining stability and prosperity in hong Kong, enabling the free port to continue to give full play to its role." The writer called the situation involving Hong Kong "a question left over from history," adding: "Not only the people of Hong Kong brood about the time limit of 1997, the PRC leaders also take it to heart. At the very least, a line has to be drawn at this date."[15]

Another political magazine in Hong Kong, *Cheng Ming*, also published an article on the June 15 meeting, listing what it called "principles and policies of the Chinese authorities for solving the Hong Kong issue."[16] Even more specifically, unnamed Chinese officials outlined their plans for Hong Kong in a Chinese-language magazine article published in mid–August (six weeks before Prime Minister Thatcher arrived in Beijing to formally open negotiations on the future of Hong Kong).

Nearly all of the eventual main elements in the 1984 Joint Declaration were outlined in the August 16 issue of *Wide Angle*, particularly noting preparation of a "detailed solution" based on the idea of China's "one country, two systems" policy over Hong Kong after its reversion to Chinese rule. A *Wide Angle* writer, quoting "some well-informed people in Beijing and Hong Kong," said it was "clear that China is determined to recover the sovereignty of Hong Kong." There would be continuation of Hong Kong's status as an international financial center and free port, continuation of "current economic and legal systems and the lifestyle of the people" and continuation of international trade agreements.

At the same time, Hong Kong's defense matters and external affairs would become the responsibility of China. "In brief," the writer said, "after Hong Kong has returned to China, there will be no change other than a five-star flag and a Chinese Governor taking the place of the Union Jack and the British Governor of Hong Kong. Hong Kong will remain as it is, able to indulge in its speculative gold, stock and real estate markets, as well as its colorful night-life."[17]

Meanwhile, one of Hong Kong's most sensitive barometers of change, the Hang Seng Index of blue-chip stocks, plunged dramatically in August 1982 following disclosure that the Hong Kong government had approved the sale of a prime parcel of real estate in Hong Kong's central business district to China for unusually low terms. That transaction followed another controversial deal announced a week earlier in which Hong Kong agreed to purchase from China a parcel of land in the New Territories for what was considered an unusually high price.

Hong Kong Financial Secretary John Brembridge responded to critics of the central district sale by describing it as "a good thing for Hong Kong," adding: "Every person in Hong Kong thinks that any real estate deal with China is cheap. They should realize that this is a good deal, and the market should interpret it positively."

CHAPTER 4

Thatcher Goes to Beijing to Open Talks

"Hong Kong is the last truly capitalist place on earth."
Jimmy McGregor, Director, Hong Kong
General Chamber of Commerce (1982)

Prime Minister Thatcher, unlike some of her fellow British officials, always seemed somewhat cool in dealing with China. In her only previous visit (in 1977 as leader of the opposition), she was said to have found China not very attractive. One observer described her as "a great exception to the general rule among political and business leaders" and said she regarded China as "a rather unpleasant place governed by rather unpleasant people."[1]

That chilly attitude never thawed over the next five years, for either side. One indication was the main radio news in Beijing on the evening of September 22. Thatcher's arrival to open talks on Hong Kong followed a news commentary on the recent national congress of the Communist Party, a news report on reactions to the congress by coal miners in Henan Province and a brief report on the arrival in the Chinese town of Xi'an of North Korean President Kim Il-Sung.[2] Despite the public's near nonrecognition of her visit, she was greeted at the Beijing airport with a welcoming ceremony, including chanting school children and a military honor guard.

Officials from both Britain and Hong Kong accompanied Mrs. Thatcher on her trip to Beijing, including Hong Kong Governor Edward Youde. Her arrival was preceded by a deluge of Beijing-supplied newspaper reports, published in Hong Kong on September 21 and 22, thoroughly outlining Chinese intentions for the Crown Colony. There seemed little more to discuss. It appeared the deal was done; all that remained was for Mrs. Thatcher to add her signature to the Chinese proposal.

Negotiations were ready to begin, and China held the firm hand. However, there was little to negotiate until two major demands raised by China were settled: sovereignty over Hong Kong and the completion of an agreement by September of 1984. The matter of sovereignty, for China, affected more than Hong Kong. China still had to resolve the return of Macau from possession by Portugal. Another issue was Taiwan, the island home of the Republic of China since 1949, when the National Chinese government moved there to escape the Communist uprising. The Chinese were fully aware that giving up sovereignty of Hong Kong might lead to a similar result in recovering Taiwan.

In addition, historically, China still had a dispute with Russia over "unequal treaties" forced upon the Chinese during land expansions of the Russian czars in the nineteenth century. There was no possibility of reaching any agreement without giving sovereignty to China, and if an agreement were not reached by September 1984, China suggested it would make its own decision on the future of Hong Kong.

Asked to assess Mrs. Thatcher's state of mind going into the discussions in Beijing, one British source said:

> Her strength as a politician was that she could see quickly the key issues that were important from her own point of view. Hong Kong was no exception. . . . I think what was in her mind was that a solution had to be found which would have the effect of substantially preserving what Hong Kong people valued about Hong Kong, so that the bulk of the population would want to stay there. She also wanted to protect Hong Kong from coming under the direct control of a Communist politburo, and that was a factor which pulled in the same direction.
>
> I don't think she had a preconceived idea, at this stage, of what had to be done in order to achieve these objectives. She just knew that you did not start by playing the only card of significance in your hand [willingness to consider transfer of sovereignty]. She thought you always had to be reasonably tough if you were going to achieve your objectives. So there were moral factors at work, and practical ones. They marched in the same direction, which was the direction of not allowing Hong Kong to become a political disaster for a British prime minister.[3]

Negotiations officially began with a "warm and friendly" two-hour afternoon meeting on world affairs between Prime Minister Thatcher and Chinese Prime Minister Zhao Ziyang. At an official state banquet that evening, Zhao mentioned (in a *mao-tai* toast)[4] the "problems left over from history" in Chinese-British relations, but said they would be "not difficult to solve" through good faith on both sides. Mrs. Thatcher responded briefly, trying to play down Zhao's obvious inferences, saying: "We have not yet begun our discussions on Hong Kong. I look forward to pursuing this important matter with you tomorrow."[5] She also emphasized Britain's large capital investments in Hong Kong's banking, insurance and industry, with important mutual benefits through access to markets in China.

In addition, Mrs. Thatcher said British industry "stands ready to help China's ambitious modernization program, especially in . . . energy, including oil and coal mining, in communications building, port construction, aviation and telecommunications, and in agricultural science and consultative services."[6] Her proposed assistance apparently led to China's approval in 1983 of the first oil-exploration contract in the South China Sea to a consortium headed by British Petroleum.

The next day, as Thatcher approached the meeting room in the Great Hall of the People, Zhao was already there, telling journalists, "China will certainly take back its sovereignty over Hong Kong. However, in my opinion, the problem of sovereignty will not affect Hong Kong's stability and prosperity. Hong Kong should not worry about its future."[7] When questioned on that point, Zhao said: "Why should they worry? China will certainly take a series of policies and measures to guarantee Hong Kong's prosperity and stability." He then gave reporters a printed outline of China's plans—similar to his offering the previous April to Edward Heath.

Despite being tired and recovering from a cold which came on during a hectic four days in Japan before coming to Beijing, Mrs. Thatcher met as scheduled with Zhao for two hours. One British official said a half-hour was devoted to trade, but declined to give other details, saying, "We don't propose to negotiate through the media."[8] She then attended an afternoon concert at the Beijing Conservatory, toured the Central Academy of Fine Arts, stopped in briefly to a book display sponsored by the British Council and finished the evening by attending a dinner with British businessmen in a Beijing hotel.

The most important discussion of the Beijing visit came on Friday morning, when Prime Minister Thatcher met with Deng Xiaoping, China's most important leader. Deng got right to the point in his opening statement, saying China's basic intention was "to resume the exercise of sovereignty over Hong Kong while maintaining its prosperity," an issue which he described as two parts of an inseparable whole. "In preserving Hong Kong's prosperity, China hopes to enjoy Britain's cooperation," he said. "Fundamentally speaking, the territory's ability to maintain its prosperity depends upon the adoption of policies suited to Hong Kong's circumstances upon China's resuming the exercise of sovereignty over, and administration of, Hong Kong."[9]

Mrs. Thatcher, displaying her best-rehearsed façade of firmness, said she realized that sovereignty was important to China, but insisted that China must also realize that the three existing treaties involving Hong Kong, two of which were permanent cessions, were valid in international law. She said Britain felt responsible for Hong Kong's continued prosperity, stability and future administration, which would have to be resolved before considering the question of sovereignty.

One of Mrs. Thatcher's most embarrassing moments, captured on live television, occurred during the lunch break of her meeting with Deng. She had stepped outside the Great Hall of the People and, distracted by a reporter's question, tripped on the steps and fell forward on her hands and knees. It was a clear demonstration of her near exhaustion from the combination of her cold and her long trip to the Orient. The embarrassing moment was captured on television and viewed around the world.

The incident led to a number of humorous responses, including the frequently repeated remark, "She has decided to kowtow to Chairman Mao at last!"[10] Later, in Hong Kong, she had to endure comments such as getting "off on the wrong foot" in opening the talks on the future of Hong Kong.[11]

After concluding her meeting with Deng, Thatcher, apparently unhurt by her fall, met with journalists to read a brief joint statement regarding the discussion: "Today, the two leaders of both countries held far-reaching talks in a friendly atmosphere on the future of Hong Kong. Both leaders made clear their respective positions on the subject. They agreed to enter talks through diplomatic channels following the visit, with the common aim of maintaining the stability and prosperity of Hong Kong."[12] Her voice, husky from her cold at the beginning of the news conference, grew worse during the news conference, forcing those present to strain to hear her words.

Journalists asked Mrs. Thatcher about her discussions with Chinese officials, but she declined to provide any details, saying, "I think the people of Hong Kong will recognize that to maintain confidence, you must also maintain confidentiality." Apparently, the Chinese leadership didn't adhere to the same guarded sense of confidentiality. The joint statement that Thatcher read to journalists was also issued by Beijing, with one additional sentence: "The Chinese Government's position on the recovery of the sovereignty of the whole region in Hong Kong is unequivocal and known to all."[13]

When a reporter with a copy of the Chinese version asked for her reaction, Thatcher first said she could not respond because she had not seen the Chinese statement, but then said, "There are three treaties in existence. We stick by our treaties unless we decide on something else. At the moment, we stick by our treaties."[14] Noting the seriousness of future negotiations on Hong Kong's future, Thatcher said, "The whole thing must now be speeded up and discussed more intensely and in much greater detail than it has been before." She also added her personal assurances: "My responsibility as Prime Minister of Her Majesty's Government is to the people of Hong Kong, and that is how I tackle it."[15]

On Friday evening, with Zhao Ziyang as guest of honor, Thatcher presided over her farewell banquet in the Great Hall of the People. Zhao was the only senior leader at the "curiously subdued affair," as Deng and others had opted to attend another formal dinner in the same building, hosted by Kim Il-Sung of North Korea.[16]

Undaunted, though tired, Thatcher addressed Zhao and her dinner guests in a somewhat conciliatory tone, saying: "Our conversations have enabled me to attain a clearer insight into China's affairs, and a close personal understanding of the Chinese government's point of view."[17]

In a staged event intended to symbolize improved relations between Britain, China and Hong Kong, Thatcher traveled outside of Beijing on September 25 to christen a ship for Hong Kong billionaire Yue-kong Pao at a shipyard in Shanghai, China's largest city. After lunch with Yue-kong, who fled from Shanghai in 1949 and became head of the Worldwide Shipping Group in Hong Kong, she went to the Jiangman shipyard for a ceremony naming his 27,000-ton freighter *World Goodwill*. In comments to Shanghai Mayor Wang Daohan, Thatcher said, "This ship is a symbol of the close relationship between China, Britain and Hong Kong. What could be more fitting than a Hong Kong ship launched by a British Prime Minister in China's most famous port?"[18]

Even at a well-planned event such as a ship launching, the unexpected continued to plague the prime minister. An interpreter introduced her as "The Quite Honorable Margaret Thatcher," and the champagne bottle selected for the christening refused to break at the appropriate launch moment.[19] Using the traditional British formula for launching ships, she declared: "I name this ship *World Goodwill*. May God bless her and all who sail in her." Her remarks were translated, after which the attending crowd broke into applause.[20]

Thatcher's visit to Shanghai came a few weeks after the British government announced it would reopen a consulate in the city. The last British mission in Shanghai was withdrawn in 1966, at the start of Mao Zedong's Cultural Revolution, because the staff was harassed by Red Guards. In a dinner speech the night before, she described the reopening of the consulate as a sign of improved relations between China and Britain. "It will enable us to make further efforts to promote Sino-British trade and other forms of economic cooperation, particularly in Shanghai and central China," she said.[21]

Prime Minister Thatcher, reflecting her image of firmness, issued a news release in Beijing at the end of her visit, emphasizing mainly that both sides entered the talks "with the common aim of maintaining the stability and prosperity of Hong Kong." She also repeated earlier statements about Britain's "moral responsibility" to the Hong Kong people. A senior British diplomat, who asked not to be identified, told one reporter: "It is all very delicate. Not that we think the Chinese are about to overrun the place or anything like that. But one false step could cause confidence to collapse in Hong Kong itself, and Hong Kong is built on confidence."[22]

Hoping for the best, Thatcher insisted that negotiators for Great Britain maintain pressure for legally settling the issue of Hong Kong and for assurance of a continuation of British rights derived from the three treaties under which it had gained possession of the Hong Kong area. Beijing quickly rejected London's demand for British presence in Hong Kong after 1997 as a condition for stability and prosperity, maintaining that such presence would represent a "de facto renewal of the unequal treaties" that in China's view simply could not be allowed. Continued British presence in Hong Kong after July 1, 1997, just like sovereignty, would not be negotiated. China's position on the future of Hong Kong was simple and direct, based fully on its intentions to finally end its long adherence to three "unequal" treaties. As Premier Zhao Ziyang cautioned, "No country can put prosperity ahead of sovereignty."[23]

CHAPTER 5

Negotiations Stall Over Sovereignty Issue

"The issue of the future of Hong Kong far transcends the intrinsic importance of that spectacular bit of landscape and real estate."
Brian Crozier, *National Review* (1982)

The long-anticipated negotiations between China and Great Britain on the future of Hong Kong appeared to be fizzling almost as soon as Prime Minister Thatcher departed from the Crown Colony in late September of 1982. She left behind considerably reduced confidence in Hong Kong, reflected by immediate sharp declines in the Hang Seng Index and the Hong Kong dollar. Nearly all of the pre–September optimism was suddenly gone, replaced by even greater fears, trepidation and concern by the Hong Kong people, especially those with businesses.

Chinese rhetoric was strong, swift and intimidating, which added to the general concern. On September 30, Xinhua, China's official news agency, declared:

> Hong Kong is a part of Chinese territory. The relevant treaties regarding the Hong Kong areas as concluded and signed by the British government and China's Qing dynasty are unequal treaties and have never been accepted by the Chinese people. If today some people still adhere to these unequal treaties, this can only remind the Chinese people, the British people and the people of the whole world of the history of British imperialism's aggression against China.

In conclusion, Xinhua said: "We maintain that the matter of Hong Kong is a matter of primary importance to the state sovereignty and national interests of the thousand million Chinese people, including Chinese residents of Hong Kong. It is only the government of the People's

Republic of China which has the right to say that, as a sovereign state, it has responsibility for the Chinese residents of Hong Kong."[1]

The Question of Sovereignty

For the People's Republic of China, sovereignty over Hong Kong would have to be settled first. Only then could meaningful negotiations about the future of Hong Kong be held between China and Great Britain. The question of sovereignty weighed heavily for the nearly 5.5 million residents of Hong Kong in 1982, worried by the apparent distressing flow of events which would place them under control of mainland China in 1997.

It was all the more worrisome for the hundreds of thousands of Chinese who fled mainland China during the Cultural Revolution for what they had perceived as a life of freedom in Hong Kong. In addition, it was worrisome for the more than 2.6 million residents born in Hong Kong who had grown up in the protective arms of Great Britain, which governed their lives and well-being while they pursued their personal fortunes and lifestyles. Despite strong economic and family ties to China, these native Hong Kongers probably never believed they would eventually grow into maturity under control of a Communist country.

The first stage of talks on Hong Kong, involving representatives of Great Britain and the People's Republic of China, got under way early in October of 1982 in Beijing. Direct representation from Hong Kong was excluded from the beginning, another key condition set by Beijing.

In addition, China and Britain agreed to complete secrecy in the negotiations. No details were to be released until final settlement. Britain, as might be expected, adhered to the condition of secrecy throughout the negotiations, but China occasionally leaked hints of the talks, when it benefited China and to put pressure on the British side, through the Hong Kong office of Xinhua, the "official" news outlet for the Chinese government.

Negotiations plodded along for months, primarily because China wanted sovereignty and Britain resisted conceding it, maintaining that some form of British presence should continue in Hong Kong after 1997. As a result, the first year of talks centered mostly on procedure and various technical aspects of the post–1997 administrative guidelines for Hong Kong.

Just one week after the visit of Prime Minister Thatcher, on October 6,

Located at one end of Repulse Bay Beach on the south side of Hong Kong Island is a small park which contains statues of Taoist and Buddhist deities.

the pro–Beijing *Wen Wei Po* newspaper in Hong Kong issued a strong editorial: "On Chinese soil, British Prime Minister Mrs. Thatcher repeatedly declared that the 'Treaty of Nanking' and the other two treaties 'must be respected' and 'cannot be abrogated.' Naturally this fallacy imbued with colonialism has aroused the indignation of Hong Kong compatriots and has once again recalled to the one billion Chinese people the history of aggression against China by the British Empire."

The editorial said terms of the treaties had "all been dropped into the Pacific Ocean by the Chinese people since the five-star flag was first hoisted in 1949. And yet Mrs. Thatcher wants the Chinese government to abide by those treaties today. Is it not, then, that she wishes to enjoy once more the aggressions of the past?"[2] More articles and editorials were published during October, focusing on the origins of the Hong Kong problem, the Opium Wars of the nineteenth century and "a treaty signed at the muzzle of a gun" (alluding to the Treaty of Nanking).[3]

Governor Edward Youde, trying to offset the propaganda, falling markets and declining dollar, told his Legislative Council on October 6 that China and Britain had officially begun meetings to develop an agreement for Hong Kong's future. "The contents of the talks must necessarily remain confidential," he said. "The aim will be to complete them as soon as possible."[4]

What Youde didn't say was that the "meetings" were in fact one session between China's vice minister for foreign affairs, Zhang Wenjin, and Britain's ambassador to Beijing, Percy Cradock. And the meeting was little more than a submission by Cradock of Prime Minister Thatcher's previously stated proposals for Hong Kong. Giving the appearance of appeasement, Cradock's submission said Britain would accept a document recognizing China's sovereignty over the territory if China would approve a "transitional" British administration continuing in Hong Kong beyond 1997.[5]

The lack of any further news about meetings in Beijing soon produced a sense of despair among residents of Hong Kong, mostly because of the absence of anything to give them hope for their futures and for the future of their home city. Trade unions in Hong Kong, a place previously known for its unlimited opportunities to work, estimated that unemployment had gone up in 1982 to between 6 and 7 percent, and that many companies reported a high rate of part-time workers. Also, figures showed 452 firms in Hong Kong had filed for bankruptcy in 1982.

In other economic indicators, the Hang Seng Index of blue-chip stocks had fallen by late October to 772, after hitting 1,300 in July. The Hong Kong dollar had dropped in a year's time from HK$5.83 to HK$6.83 to the American dollar—its lowest point in a quarter century.

A writer for London's *Financial Times* summed up the period by saying: "Hong Kong's summer of frayed nerves has given way to autumn of depression and uncertainty."[6] A Chinese-language newspaper in Hong Kong philosophized even more succinctly: "The cruelest form of death in China is death by a thousand cuts, in which the victim's skin is slowly peeled off, scrap by scrap. After a time, the victim comes to crave that he may died instantly, so that his slow and painful torture may be ended."[7]

Britain's stance in October 1982 seemed to be putting up a strong front for continued British administration after 1997 and withholding agreement to allow China's sovereignty over the colony. Beijing's propaganda explosion in October, focusing mostly on the words of Prime Minister Thatcher, did little more than increase anxiety in Hong Kong, as reflected in the decline of the Hang Seng Index and the drop in the Hong Kong dollar.

China Promotes "Hong Kong People Ruling Hong Kong"

China increased the rhetoric pressure on November 1 when the National People's Congress vice chairman, Xi Zhongxun, told a visiting group from Hong Kong: "We want to solve this issue through diplomatic channels. A plan on how to solve this issue should be worked out within one or two years."[8]

. Three weeks later, on November 20, the notion of "Hong Kong people ruling Hong Kong" was projected in Beijing to visiting members of the Hong Kong Factory Owners Association by Liao Chengzhi, China's main strategist for Hong Kong, Macao and Taiwan affairs. Liao said that China expected to resume sovereignty over Hong Kong by 1997, but that Hong Kong would be ruled by its own people. Also, there would be no change in Hong Kong's legal and judicial systems, the Hong Kong dollar would continue as the territory's currency, passports would say "China–Hong Kong" and the word "Royal" would be removed from the Royal Hong Kong Jockey Club.[9]

Britain complained meekly that the Chinese pronouncements were openly violating the agreed-upon confidentiality supposedly surrounding negotiations between the two countries. But Chinese officials dismissed complaints about confidentiality, saying their purpose was to present their position on the matter and to outline their own policies. Nevertheless, references to the negotiations continued to figure into the propaganda. Xinhua quoted a businessman after a meeting with Chinese officials as saying: "We asked them why, if Beijing had made up its mind what to do about Hong Kong, Sino-British negotiations were being held at all. The official said that China recognized the role the British had played in building up Hong Kong to what it is now. The object of the talks was therefore to draw up a suitably ceremonious departure for the governor. And he wasn't joking."[10] Finally, Chinese spokesmen made themselves available to British journalists, openly declaring an ultimatum: "Deng Xiaoping, China's leader, is insisting that Britain publicly agrees to relinquish sovereignty over Hong Kong Island and Kowloon in 1997, when the lease on the New Territories expires, before talks on the future of the colony are opened."[11]

CHAPTER 6

Second Phase of Talks

"Hong Kong's strength has always been its ability to respond quickly to opportunities, and the present situation is no exception. The adjustment process is not hindered in any way by government intervention. Market forces are allowed to play their part."

Eric T. Lo, Hong Kong Secretary
for Trade and Industry (1983)[1]

When talks between China and Britain in October 1982 failed to produce a satisfactory agreement on agenda and procedures, the negotiations quickly dissolved to a level of diplomatic discussions. Occasional meetings between Chinese and British diplomats were held, but with no apparent progress towards development of the Sino-British Agreement on Hong Kong. Surrounded in secrecy, the months of diplomatic discussions had naturally generated considerable anxiety and concern in Hong Kong. Business executives were making arrangements to leave, while similar plans were being made by technicians, scientists, lawyers and other professionals who knew they could qualify to live in other countries. Finally, in the spring of 1983, the Chinese finally were assured they would soon achieve the breakthrough they wanted in their basic condition in the negotiating battle over the future of Hong Kong—concession of sovereignty from Great Britain.

Signs of progress began showing up, coinciding with the second phase of talks. Queen Elizabeth II, in her annual speech to the British Parliament in June 1983, expressed her own personal sort of optimism, saying the British government would "continue talks with China on the future of Hong Kong, with the aim of reaching a solution acceptable to this Parliament, to China and to the people of Hong Kong."[2]

Prime Minister Thatcher told the British House of Commons in July 1983 that the negotiations were going ahead and offered her assurance that the views of Hong Kong and its people were "taken into account."

Finally, the negotiations could resume, with China firmly in control and confident that continued patient optimism would produce a settlement acceptable to Britain, China, Hong Kong and the rest of the world. However, in truth, China had given Britain an ultimatum during the September 1982 visit by Prime Minister Thatcher. According to the American magazine *Newsweek*, Deng Xiaoping threatened during "an acrimonious private meeting" that China would "impose its own solution" if an agreement were not reached by the end of 1984. The conversation between Deng and Thatcher was described by Communist Party General Hu Yaobang during a rare two-hour interview with Parris Change, a China scholar from Penn State University.[3]

The second phase of talks began in July 1983, but only after China and Britain agreed to a temporary suspension on the dispute over sovereignty. Deng admitted later he had allowed suspension of discussion on sovereignty to help get Prime Minister Thatcher "out of an embarrassing situation."[4] However, it was soon realized by negotiation watchers that Britain had sent a broad signal to the Chinese leadership in Beijing, hinting that it would eventually accept China's claim for sovereignty over Hong Kong.

Anxiety Heightens from Months of Secret Negotiations

Hong Kong's domestic situation worsened in 1983. Trade union officials estimated a decrease of between 10 and 30 percent in the income of workers in manufacturing and building. The Hong Kong dollar fell to a new low against the U.S. dollar (US$1=HK$7.82) in July, at which time the government permanently fixed the Hong Kong dollar at $HK7.80. By September, the gloominess of an unknown and uncertain future caused much upheaval in the day-to-day activities of both individuals and business. Another sign of despair was the hoarding of rice, toilet paper and liquor, generally considered in Hong Kong as "the three staples of life."[5]

When formal talks on Hong Kong reopened in July 1983, the Chinese negotiators were led by Yao Guang, China's deputy foreign minister and former Chinese ambassador to France. (Yao had succeeded Liao Chengzhi, who died of a heart attack in June 1983, one week before he was expected to be elected vice president of China by the National People's Congress.) Following the mid–July talks Yao declined to provide any details about progress, reminding reporters that both sides had agreed to maintain confidentiality regarding the discussions, adding: "All I can say is that the talks are useful and constructive, and we'll resume our talks on July 25th and 26th in Peking."[6]

Britain's team was headed by Percy Cradock, the British ambassador to China, with assistance by Edward Youde, who had become governor of Hong Kong in 1982. Youde's presence raised optimism that progress was finally occurring. Also, he was already familiar with negotiating policies of the mainland Chinese, gaining that experience from his many years as a career diplomat.

As an example to demonstrate the almost absolute control of the Chinese over events surrounding the negotiations, Youde caused some upset in July 1983 when he told reporters that he represented Hong Kong's 5.5 million residents in the talks. The Chinese Foreign Ministry quickly responded that Youde could not represent Hong Kong because he was a member of the British delegation and could "only represent the British Government at the talks." Soon after, Youde returned to Hong Kong following a meeting in London with Prime Minister Thatcher, saying at a news conference that Britain and China had "gained a better understanding of each other's positions."

A Letter to the Chinese Leadership

The "breakthrough" was implied by negotiators in October of 1983, just before the fifth round of talks, when reports surfaced that Cradock had delivered a letter to the Chinese leadership from Prime Minister Thatcher which essentially said that Britain would accept the Chinese demand for sovereignty over Hong Kong after 1997.

Changes in mood and attitude were immediate, for both sides. A joint statement was issued in Beijing in early October, characterizing the talks as "useful and constructive." It was apparent that new life had been given to the talks after Britain's concession to China over who would control Hong Kong after 1997. Although Britain had kept its promise of secrecy regarding the talks, the Chinese occasionally leaked details in an effort to maintain pressure on the British negotiators. Attempting to justify the leaks, a *People's Daily* article said: "The Chinese leaders and the Chinese press have every right to explain and publicize to the Chinese people, including the compatriots in Hong Kong, the basic stand of the Chinese Government. How can this be interpreted as 'negotiating in public'?"[7]

Demonstrating a brief emotional flare-up about the issue during a mid–1983 meeting with American journalists, Thatcher said (in remarks published October 6 in the Manchester *Guardian*): "But for the 19th-century lease under which Britain holds most of Hong Kong, it would have been independent years ago."[8]

An example of comments on the pending agreement from Chinese officials was contained in a January 1984 interview with Ji Pengfei, head of China's Hong Kong and Macau Affairs Office. In the interview, published in the English-language *China Daily*, Ji said Hong Kong could expect to retain its status as a free port, and could enter into agreements with foreign countries as long as there was no conflict with Chinese security or foreign policy. He also said Hong Kong's legal system would continue with little change, government officials would be chosen from the local population, and its citizens would enjoy "a high degree of autonomy."[9]

On January 13, unrest gave way to an outbreak of violence in Kowloon, the most congested section of Hong Kong, across the harbor from Victoria. Journalist Clare Hollingworth described the situation as "the worst unrest since the Cultural Revolution in the 1960s."[10] Events leading to the unrest, for the most part, could be attributed to anxiety from the blanket of secrecy in negotiations over Hong Kong's future. Most residents, already concerned about their future, had to continue going about their day-to-day lives and business, which was threatened further by downturns in property values and the stock market. Their very security was in danger.

United States Avoids Direct Role in Talks

Chinese Premier Zhao Ziyang made an official visit to the United States in January 1984, attempting to improve relations between America and China. The United States, fully aware of significant and growing American investment in Hong Kong, had successfully avoided any direct role in the negotiations between China and Britain, although it was kept informed about their progress.

However, in an unusual public comment on the matter, Eugene Lawson, a senior official of the U.S. State Department's East Asian Bureau, said:

> While we have a considerable interest in how these talks progress, we have no intention of inserting ourselves and our views when they are going

on. We accept that a peaceful and satisfactory solution is possible to preserve the investment climate and the political and economic freedom that makes Hong Kong what it is. Hong Kong is unique in the world. We appreciate that it will not take too much to change that climate and bring about economic disaster. We have an interest in how the talks progress, but we have no intention of interposing our views at the present time. We look at it as strictly an issue between the U.K. and the People's Republic of China.[11]

A few months later, Burton Levin, the United States' consul-general in Hong Kong, reviewed important American economic interests in Hong Kong and gave special attention to U.S. concerns about its cultural and human relations.

As a prosperous and creative society, we have attracted thousands of students from Hong Kong to our universities and hundreds of thousands of Hong Kong tourists and businessmen to our cities and towns. Many of the three-quarters of a million Chinese living in the States have family ties in Hong Kong. Millions of Americans have visited Hong Kong. Over the past few decades the people of the United States and Hong Kong have gotten to know each other much better. Americans come away from this relationship with respect and admiration for a group of people who have worked hard, endured many hardships over the decades and have contributed in many ways to the world community. We believe they deserve a secure future.[12]

Levin also repeated previous references to the cautious stance and lack of active participation by the United States in connection with the negotiations. "The United States does not see a role for itself in the present negotiations," he said. "We have made clear our interest in a settlement that preserves Hong Kong's prosperity and stability, and our pleasure that both the U.K. and the P.R.C. share and are working toward this objective. We will be supportive in any appropriate way we can."[13]

Hints of Progress in the Negotiations

About this time, signs of apparent progress were reflected by Prime Minister Thatcher's decision to send Foreign Secretary Geoffrey Howe to Beijing at least three times in the spring and early summer of 1984. In April, Howe also went to Hong Kong, where he publicly announced that "it would not be realistic to think of an agreement that provides for continued British administration of Hong Kong after 1997."[14] Howe's statement quickly deflated the hopes of the people of Hong Kong, who had been somewhat optimistic that Britain would be able to negotiate conditions that would allow extending of land leases and continue British administrative control over the area in the twenty-first century.

Little information about the negotiations was made public until the summer of 1984, when the government of Hong Kong was allowed to establish a working group to conduct "shadow talks" of the formal negotiations, headed by David Wilson, who would later succeed Edward Youde as governor of Hong Kong. The quickened pace of progress in the talks was evident in August 1984, when Deng Xiaoping cut short his summer vacation to meet with Howe in Beijing. Commenting informally after their meeting, Deng said: "General De Gaulle ended French colonialism. Now we can also say that Prime Minister Thatcher and you are going to end British colonial rule."[15]

Further optimism, mixed with pessimism, was shown in September 1984, when political commentator T.L. Tsim said in Hong Kong: "The destiny of Hong Kong is now the same as the destiny of China. There is no escaping. For Britain, the need to resolve the problem of Hong Kong is paramount. London will do nothing else now but serve as an agent for the Chinese Communists."[16]

Meanwhile, the Hong Kong government began making its own preparations for the 1997 transition. In July, two months before the initialing of the Draft Joint Declaration, a Green Paper entitled "The Future Development of Representative Government in Hong Kong" was issued.[17] The government stressed its goal "to develop progressively a system of government, the authority for which is firmly rooted in Hong Kong, which is able to represent authoritatively the views of the people of Hong Kong, and which is more directly accountable to the people of Hong Kong."

The Green Paper also focused on democratic reforms for Hong Kong, such as direct elections for members of the Legislative Council. The proposal said "suggestions have been made that direct elections to the Legislative Council, based on a universal franchise, should be introduced as soon as possible," adding that "such arrangements are a standard feature of many democratic systems of government." All of this raised the spirits of the majority of Hong Kong Chinese, who believed that the Green Paper was actually developing a method for directly electing legislators, and that this method was truly essential for the ultimate success of the Joint Declaration.

This belief was strengthened in Britain on July 18, when British Foreign Secretary Geoffrey Howe discussed the Green Paper during an appearance before the House of Commons, saying, "Those proposals are well designed to enhance the representative status of Hong Kong's Central Government institutions and to give the Hong Kong people a stronger voice in the administration of the territory in the years to come." Howe also said, "The people of Hong Kong will now be putting forward their views, which will be taken into account in a subsequent White Paper." In addition, he made specific references, without elaboration, to Legislative Council elections in 1988 and 1991.

Finally, by September 18 negotiators let it be known that only a few minor points remained to be settled. China and Britain had finally reached agreement on the Joint Declaration, a blueprint for Hong Kong under Chinese rule and the foundation for conditions after 1997.

CHAPTER 7

Signing of the Joint Declaration

"*We expect the American business communities, both in the United States and Hong Kong, will see in this agreement good reason for sustained confidence in the future of Hong Kong as an attractive and thriving commercial center.*"

George P. Shultz, U.S. Secretary of State (1984)[1]

The most ceremonial occasion between China and Britain since the September 1982 opening of talks on Hong Kong occurred in Beijing on September 26, 1984: the formal initialing of the Draft Joint Declaration, a basic blueprint designed to maintain Hong Kong's "prosperity and stability" after its 1997 transition to Chinese rule. The event contained almost all of the exuberance and grandeur expected of the formal signing ceremony (scheduled for December), except for the absence of Chinese leader Deng Xiaoping and British Prime Minister Margaret Thatcher.

After nearly two years of secret discussion, argument and negotiation, the Draft Joint Declaration for Hong Kong was initialed by Zhou Nan, China's chief negotiator, and Richard Evans, the British ambassador to China. Their audience in Beijing's Great Hall of the People included numerous Chinese and British diplomats, along with Hong Kong Governor Edward Youde and several specially invited prominent figures from Hong Kong.

"We have together traversed a course of decisive significance," Zhou told Evans during the ceremony. "We believe that the agreement fully conforms to the fundamental interests of the one billion Chinese people, including our compatriots in Hong Kong, and those of the British people, and will win their endorsement and support."[2] Evans responded by describing the Joint Declaration as "the practical embodiment of the imaginative concept of one country, two systems." Taking a cue from previous Chinese remarks, he also said the agreement "demonstrates that peaceful negotiation is the best way to resolve problems left over from history."[3]

The formal initialing occurred on September 26, just prior to China's National Day on October 1st. After attending the initialing ceremony, Youde returned to Hong Kong to describe the document during a special session of the Legislative Council, noting that the agreement had been endorsed by the Executive Council (which had been briefed regularly during the secret discussions) and by the Thatcher government in London. Youde stressed the idea of a legislature "constituted by elections," which he said was promised by the Joint Declaration. He also said the agreement would "allow scope for the development of Hong Kong's governmental system as the years progress." Continuing to look forward in an optimistic and positive manner, Youde focused on positive aspects of the document. "As you know," he said, "our objective in the years immediately ahead is to use that process to root political power in the community where it belongs."[4]

But the people of Hong Kong, who had been anxiously awaiting the agreement for two years, seemed almost stunned by mixed relief and resignation, a mood reflected by the drizzling rain that prevailed that evening while Youde was meeting with the Legislative Council. Their feeling was characterized by political commentator T.L. Tsim: "The destiny of Hong Kong is now the same as the destiny of China. There is no escaping."[5]

That same night the official government printer began distributing more than a million Chinese-language copies of the 46-page agreement, plus 250,000 English-language copies. The free copies were snapped up as quickly as they could be printed, most by people who had waited for hours in the rain. Everyone wanted to know what lay ahead. Meanwhile, British Foreign Secretary Geoffrey Howe told journalists in New York City that Hong Kong really had no choice in the matter—it was "between this agreement and no agreement."[6] The *London Times* offered a similar assessment: "Given the limits on what could be achieved, it comes close to being as good as Britain and Hong Kong can expect to get. And, as such, it should be judged a success."[7]

The United States, mostly quiet throughout the two years of negotiations between China and Britain, had restrained praise for the Joint Declaration. Secretary of State George Shultz said in Washington that the United States welcomed the agreement, calling it "a solid foundation for Hong Kong's enduring future."[8] A *New York Times* editorial said the "Hong Kong bargain struck by China and Britain seems a salutary triumph for common sense."[9]

The Joint Declaration for Hong Kong defined a number of basic changes effective when the British lease expires July 1, 1997. One significant change was the designation of Hong Kong as a "Special Administrative Region" within China, with retention of its status as a free port and international financial center. Laws already in force would remain unchanged, and local government authorities would maintain public order. The agreement pledged continuation of Hong Kong's social and economic systems and "lifestyle" until the year 2047, including the right to strike and freedom of speech, assembly, travel, press, correspondence, occupation, association and religion. Residents of Hong Kong would not be taxed by China. In addition, the agreement provided for establishment of the Sino-British Joint Liaison Group (to ensure the "smooth transfer" of government in 1997), consideration of Hong Kong land leases extending beyond 1997 and development of the Basic Law, a constitution-like document defining rights and policies of post–1997 Hong Kong. Hong Kong's business sector optimistically supported the Joint Declaration, and the agreement was promptly approved by the Chinese General Chamber of Commerce, representing more than 3,000 companies in Hong Kong. Support continued flowing in from virtually all Hong Kong institutions and organizations. Among the few critics to speak up was T.S. Lo, a long-time member of Hong Kong's Executive and Legislative councils, who immediately resigned from both councils and donated money to establish a nonprofit group to provide emigration information for Hong Kong Chinese.

The Hong Kong Assessment Office then decided to survey public sentiment on the agreement, apparently hoping to get at least simple "yes" or "no" responses, but the effort was a major disappointment. Only about 2,500 people submitted responses, perhaps because they feared repercussions later from the Chinese leadership. After determining the people's basic fear over the confidentiality in responses, the government declared it would burn all of the submissions following the scheduled ratification of the Joint Declaration in 1985. Responses increased to some degree, and the Assessment Office announced in November 1984, "After the most careful analysis and consideration of all the information received, the office has concluded that most people of Hong Kong find the draft agreement acceptable."

There were other reasons for the lack of initial response to the Joint Declaration. First, many in Hong Kong probably hoped for an agreement that would simply allow them to continue their lives and lifestyles without significant change after 1997. Second, they had been permitted virtually no participation in the decision-making process; the negotiations on their behalf were conducted in Beijing by officials from China and Britain. Third, the discussions were kept secret, by mutual agreement of China and Britain. (Members of the Hong Kong Executive Council were kept informed on progress of the talks, but only after being sworn to secrecy.)

Therefore, residents of Hong Kong had no input into their own future, and the secret talks resulted in a form of anxious limbo that had lasted nearly two years. Details of the agreement were thrust upon them without any preparation or education. They simply were not sure what to think, and did not want to endanger their personal and professional futures until they knew more about what was going on.

Even though they were not outspoken, there was general support from most residents in Hong Kong for the Joint Declaration. After all, it appeared to assure them of certain protections that they already had under British rule. They also welcomed the promise of "a high degree of autonomy" after 1997 and were delighted with the idea of "Hong Kong people ruling Hong Kong" after 1997. In addition, they accepted Britain's explanation that there was no alternative, and no way to amend the agreement. In other words, everyone was happy. Hong Kong would continue to be Hong Kong, and the governments of Hong Kong, Britain and China could safely say that the agreement was satisfactory to the residents of Hong Kong.

The subsequent White Paper on "The Further Development of Representative Government in Hong Kong" was published in November 1984, just before a British House of Commons debate on the Joint Declaration. Although the White Paper was accompanied by governmental praise, it was actually somewhat watered down from the previous Green Paper. In particular, it affirmed the need for prompt democratic reform, but noted "considerable general public concern" that "too rapid progress toward direct elections could place the future stability and prosperity of Hong Kong in jeopardy."

Endorsement followed with expected ease in both China and Britain. Beijing's Standing Committee of the National People's Congress debated and endorsed the Joint Declaration on November 14, 1984, and London's House of Commons debated and endorsed the agreement on December 5, 1984. Prime Minister Thatcher then returned to Beijing on the morning of December 19, 1984, to formally sign the Joint Declaration in an elaborate ceremony with Chinese Premier Zhao Ziyang.

Thatcher and Deng Xiaoping had a discussion that same afternoon, a meeting which some described as considerably more amicable than two years before.[10] Deng, obviously proud of the outcome and his personal contribution of the "one country, two systems" philosophy, described the Joint Declaration as a combination of "dialectical Marxism and historical materialism."[11] Prime Minister Thatcher was somewhat more reserved in her comments, characterizing the agreement as "an ingenious idea."[12]

Thatcher went on to Hong Kong on December 21, taking part in a news conference which she may have expected would be routine. Unfortunately, some of her responses about key details were not entirely accurate, causing Governor Edward Youde to offer corrections to certain answers. One reporter's challenge even led to a frustrated outburst by Thatcher that was quoted and recalled frequently after the occasion. Journalist Emily Lau (later named to the Legislative Council) asked her to comment on the "morality" of handing over more than 5 million people to control of a Communist regime. (Lau's own family had fled from China following the Communist takeover in 1949 and had known Chinese persecution firsthand.)

Thatcher's knee-jerk response seemed comparable to a reprimand. "Can I say this to you? What do you think would have happened if we had not attempted to get an agreement?" she said, adding that in 1997, "ninety-two percent of the territory would automatically have returned to China without reassurances." Then came the chiding, directed at Emily Lau: "I think you would have had great cause to complain had the government of Great Britain done nothing until 1997, and I believe that most of the people, indeed the overwhelming number of people, in Hong Kong think the same. You may be a solitary exception."[13]

A few minutes later, Thatcher, the internationally renowned "Iron Lady," departed from the Legislative Council chambers, entered a waiting automobile and left Hong Kong to continue wondering about an uncertain future.[14]

CHAPTER 8

Aftermath of the Agreement

"If current trends continue, it's plain that after 1997 we will only get as much freedom of maneuver as China believes is good for us, regardless of the wishes of the people of Hong Kong."

Martin Lee, member of
Hong Kong Legislative Council (1986)[1]

An event occurred in May 1985 which had great significance in Hong Kong and great repercussions in China. The Hong Kong soccer team unexpectedly defeated China's national team in preliminary World Cup competition. The loss led to a night of rioting which Chinese officials described as Beijing's worst sports violence in 30 years. Beijing's *People's Daily* reported 30 policemen beaten (4 seriously injured), 127 people detained, 25 vehicles damaged (including 5 taxis and 11 buses) and the injury of a taxi driver whose vehicle was overturned by the rioters. A *China Daily* editorial described the rioting as "disgraceful behavior," saying: "Though the rioters amounted to only a rotten apple in the barrel, this is totally alien to the image of the Chinese nation, long noted for its politeness and courtesy. It also shows the neglect of education, particularly civic education, during the decade of the Cultural Revolution."[2]

Foreign journalists were quick to note that the eruption of violence over a soccer defeat clearly violated the revered Maoist policy of "friendship first, competition second."[3] Residents of Hong Kong expressed "shock and disbelief" over the rioting, and were especially concerned by reports of hostility to foreigners and Hong Kong Chinese. Top Chinese officials in Beijing called the rioters "ignorant and barbaric" and promised "due punishment," adding that the riot showed "serious weakness in the party's ideological work and in the work of educating people, particularly young people, in the necessity of abiding by the law."[4] China's soccer team was subsequently withdrawn from Beijing's Great Wall Cup competition in June because it "failed to live up to the expectations of the party."

Meanwhile, the 1984 Sino-British Joint Declaration took effect in May 1985 with an exchange of ratification documents between China and Great Britain. Coinciding with the Joint Declaration was the formation of the Sino-British Joint Liaison Group (JLG) to continue discussions on the smooth transition of Hong Kong to China in 1997. Members of the JLG were announced simultaneously on May 21 in London, Hong Kong and Beijing.

The British delegation was headed by David Wilson, the Foreign Office's assistant under-secretary for Asian affairs who had led Britain's negotiators working on the Joint Declaration. Others in the British group included John Boyd, political adviser to the Hong Kong government; Eric Ho, Hong Kong's secretary for trade and industry; Tony Galsworthy, director of the Hong Kong department at the Foreign and Commonwealth Office (FCO); and Peter Thompson, counselor at the British Embassy in Beijing.

The Chinese delegation was led by Ke Zai Shuo, the Beijing director of the Hong Kong and Macau Affairs Office. Others included Chen Ziying, counselor at the Chinese Embassy in London; Zheng Weirong and Ye Shoukeng, both with the Hong Kong and Macau Affairs Office; and Qiao Zong Huai, deputy secretary general of the Hong Kong branch of Xinhua, China's official news agency.

Following approval of the Joint Declaration, China's leaders frequently suggested that direct elections to Hong Kong's Legislative Council should be delayed until after the Basic Law took effect in 1990, to avoid any constitutional conflict. Ji Pengfei of the Hong Kong and Macau Affairs Office specifically cautioned in October 1985 that significant changes, such as direct voting for council members, should definitely not occur during the transitional period.

The point was further strengthened in November 1985, when Xinhua director Xu Jiatun held his first news conference in his two and one-half years in office, proclaiming that changes "relating to political systems are changes of fundamental significance." Xu said the changes "should be carried out in accordance with the contents and principles laid down in the Sino-British declaration."[5] Xu's public remarks both upset and surprised British negotiators, who expected that any disputes would be discussed in secret by the Joint Liaison Group.

China's attitude towards the transfer of Hong Kong to Chinese rule was explored, examined and evaluated during a trip to Beijing in January 1986 by Timothy Renton, Britain's minister of state with responsibility for Hong Kong. Renton returned to London with a conciliatory response: "Britain and China had agreed that the territory should undergo a period of consolidation, during which the recently introduced system of indirect elections to the Legislative Council would be allowed to settle."[6]

Martin Lee, Hong Kong's leading pro-democratic advocate, assessed the situation in a more concise manner, saying, "The British view and the Chinese view have converged every time so far, and it is particularly sad that every time there is convergence of views between the British and Chinese governments, it is always the Chinese government which takes the lead."[7] Lee was a leading member of the Joint Committee for the Promotion of Democratic Government (JCPDG), organized in 1986 to promote discussion on Hong Kong's political system. The committee developed several proposals concerning constitutional changes, but focused primarily on achieving direct voting for at least some members of the Legislative Council in the 1988 elections.

The JCPDG also invited public opinion by setting up a survey office, eventually determining that 96 percent of submissions concerned the question of voting in 1988. "The people of Hong Kong have chosen to concentrate on the issue of direct elections in 1988," said Martin Lee in a Joint Committee report published in November 1986.[8]

Nearly 200 local organizations participated in the JCPDG, including such influential groups as the Hong Kong Affairs Society, the Federation of Civil Servants Association and the Professional Teachers Union. During 1987 the group continued taking polls which also reflected support for direct elections in 1988. One JCPDG signature campaign produced 220,000 names, "all of whom supplied their identity cards numbers, a significant development in a society which had traditional avoided personal identification with a particular course of political action."[9]

Queen Elizabeth II made a visit to Beijing in October 1986 that included a lavish 10-course banquet in the Great Hall of the People given in her honor. For the dinner, the Queen, regally adorned in a dress highlighted by peonies (China's national flower) and wearing her familiar tiara, was seated between Chinese Prime Minister Zhao Ziyang and President Li Xiannian, an arrangement which some regarded as an "unusual honor."[10]

During the banquet, Queen Elizabeth offered optimism for Hong Kong's future under provisions of the 1984 Joint Declaration. "Today, relations between the United Kingdom and the People's Republic of China are closer than they have ever been," she said "This owes much to the settlement worked out between us for the future of Hong Kong. Both our countries are committed to doing everything possible to maintain Hong Kong's continued stability and prosperity."[11]

Chinese President Li Xiannian said the visit by Queen Elizabeth to Beijing was "an important milestone in the annals of Sino-British relations."[12] Li had made the same comment earlier in the day during an official welcoming ceremony in Tiananmen Square, a ceremony which local citizens were not allowed to participate in or witness. Another highlight was the Queen's gift of 1 million pounds to finance research work by Chinese scientists in British laboratories over a three-year period. The award would provide one-year "Royal Fellowships" to 30 postdoctoral scientists, designed to improve science relations and bilateral trade between China and Britain.[13] Queen Elizabeth II stayed six days in China before going on to Hong Kong where she spent an afternoon at the Shatin horse racing track, watching the races and an elaborate fireworks display that drew more than 600,000 people.

American influence in Hong Kong was becoming more visible during the 1980s, both in numbers and images. By 1986, about 60 percent of the English-language television programs were produced in America. Also, Hong Kong residents and visitors could choose among 3 Kentucky Fried Chicken outlets, 6 Pizza Huts, 28 McDonald's restaurants and 168 Seven-Eleven convenience stores.[14] The number of American residents in Hong Kong in 1986 totaled 16,400, compared with 14,800 British residents (not counting 5,500 military servicemen and dependents). Britons had peaked at 23,400 in 1979.[15]

Illegal Chinese immigrants remained a daily problem in Hong Kong during 1986. The problem was ritualized by a daily 2:45 P.M. siren, after which buses moved slowly from British authority to Chinese authority, transporting illegals back to China where they were subject to fines equaling US$90 and prison sentences ranging up to three months, a measure designed to deter illegal immigration by skilled workers.

Hong Kong officials said about 17,000 illegal immigrants from China were arrested and returned during the first 10 months of 1986, exceeding the number for all of 1985. Joseph Cheung, the top Hong Kong policeman at the Man Kam To border, said returning the illegal immigrants was a responsibility, but not a pleasant one. "We sympathize with them," he said. "But if we allowed them in, we would have many thousands coming in, and we cannot accommodate them all."[16]

One of Hong Kong's most popular governors, Edward Youde, died in December 1986 while on a trade visit to Beijing. Youde, a leading British specialist on China, had helped negotiate the 1984 Joint Declaration on Hong Kong between Britain and China. He had been governor of Hong Kong since May 1982, and was the first to die in office.

Youde, who was 62, died in his sleep after participating in a Beijing exhibition of Hong Kong products, the opening of a Hong Kong trade office in Beijing and a formal dinner with Chinese officials. His death was apparently the result of heart problems (he had a heart bypass operation in 1981). The announcement in Hong Kong of Youde's death by Acting Governor David Akers-Jones was followed by a sharp decline in Hong Kong's stock market and subsequent suspension of trading out of respect to Youde.

CHAPTER 9

New Governor David Wilson Offers Strained Assurances

"If there is to be change, it should be prudent and gradual. It must not disrupt the steady progress we have been making, nor the stability which we prize."

Hong Kong Governor David Wilson (1987)[1]

One of the first surprises of 1987 was the forced resignation of Hu Yaobang as general secretary of the Chinese Communist Party on January 16. An advocate of political change in China, Hu had risen through the vagaries of China's political system to become, within the relatively short period of ten years, one of the most powerful political figures in the country—second in importance only to senior leader Deng Xiaoping.

Hu had been appointed as general secretary in 1980 by Deng Xiaoping and was expected to succeed Deng as the supreme head of China. His resignation raised the tension level in Hong Kong, where many regarded him as sympathetic to efforts toward political reforms before 1997. As noted by Martin Lee, a member of the Legislative Council and a pro-democracy leader, "Any change of this kind is bound to have repercussions in Hong Kong and affect our confidence."[2]

The evening news in China on January 16 led off with a two-minute announcement of Hu's resignation, its acceptance by the Politburo and the immediate election of Chinese Premier Zhao Ziyang as the new general secretary. In addition, a brief news release about the resignation was issued by Xinhua stating that Hu had appeared before an "enlarged meeting" of the Politburo and "made a self-criticism of his mistakes on major issues of political principles in violation of the party's

principles of collective leadership."[3] Besides accepting Hu's resignation
and electing Zhao Ziyang as his replacement, the Politburo also urged
continued opposition of "bourgeois liberalization" by the 44 million
members of China's Communist Party.[4]

Hong Kong's stock market duly reflected the immediate concern
and uncertainty following Hu's departure. The Hang Seng Index of
blue-chip stocks declined sharply on January 19, then alarmed investors by continuing to fall the next day. A midweek recovery followed
assurances at a January 20 luncheon by Xu Jiatun, head of the Hong
Kong branch of Xinhua, that the change in top leadership would not
affect development in China.

Ironically, Hu's resignation was announced on the same day that
Britain announced the appointment of David Wilson as the next governor of Hong Kong. Wilson declined to offer extensive comment on the
resignation of Hu, remarking: "We have to expect change in political
leaderships."[5]

Wilson told journalists he was confident Beijing would respect conditions of the 1984 Joint Declaration on Hong Kong, an agreement
which he had helped develop. Wilson also said he planned to spend his
first year as governor of Hong Kong "familiarizing himself with his administrative duties."[6] Upon becoming governor, Wilson would relinquish his post with the British delegation to the Joint Liaison Group, the
Sino-British committee which met twice yearly to discuss the future of
Hong Kong.

A significant change of a different sort was announced in
mid–January of 1987. The Hong Kong government announced that the
infamous Kowloon Walled City would be torn down and replaced with
a park. The Walled City had long had the dubious distinction of being
the world's worst slum, with more than 40,000 people crammed into
7 acres of tall buildings (up to 15 stories) separated only by narrow
alleys. Hong Kong officials said arrangements would be made to move
residents of the Walled City to other living facilities, adding that the
residents would be compensated for their forced relocation.

Hong Kongers expressed the usual cautious concern for their own
uncertain future in a late January public opinion survey, taken by the
South China Morning Post, Hong Kong's largest circulation English-
language newspaper, which showed 52 percent opposing any direct
voting for members of the Legislative Council (Legco). In the survey
only 6 percent supported directing voting for Legco, while 34 percent
supported direct voting for some members and 9 percent offered no

opinion. The same survey showed 43 percent as "slightly interested" in any form of voting system, 39 percent as "not at all interested" and only 3 percent as "very interested."[7]

Controversy of a milder sort arose in February 1987 over the Chinese name of Governor David Wilson. The problem was in the sound of his Chinese name Ngai Tak-ngai—it was too similar to a Cantonese dialect phrase which meant "hypocrisy to the extent of being dangerous." Even worse, his Chinese name included brushstrokes suggesting "1,800 female ghosts"—an unfavorable suggestion immediately recognized by anyone reading the name.

Choosing the "right" Chinese name was generally the responsibility of translators with large companies, though sometimes the assignment was given (for a $45 fee) to one of Hong Kong's many fortunetellers. "It's always a problem in this part of the world," said Simon Murray, head of Hutchison Whampoa Ltd. in Hong Kong. "Names can get you in a lot of trouble."[8] The problem was quickly resolved when Wilson agreed to adopt the Chinese name of Wai Yik-shun, which carried the meaning of a "man of glamour and trust."

During the 1980s and 1990s, Hong Kong was sometimes called "the gateway to China." By early 1987, the "gateway" nickname was reflected in strong evidence showing Hong Kong's economic influence over China, which many analysts considered favorable in Hong Kong's transition to Chinese rule. Hong Kong government figures in February 1987 showed that Hong Kong accounted for 22 percent of China's foreign trade and 79 percent of foreign investment in China. Much of Hong Kong's large percentage involvement in foreign trade and investment with the Chinese mainland was the result of improved investment opportunities in China, often developed and secured through contacts in Hong Kong.

Many were optimistic that Hong Kong would continue its "gateway" reputation into the twenty-first century, apparently not realizing that after July 1, 1997, Hong Kong would no longer be a gateway to China, but part of China and under Chinese rule. Its official designation as a special administrative region enjoyed the support of optimists, though many realized inwardly that even an SAR would be under Chinese rule and control. China's economic influence in Hong Kong was becoming more visible in 1987 through the growing presence of the Bank of China and its 13 Hong Kong affiliated branches, and the controversial purchase of 12.6 percent of Hong Kong–based Cathay Pacific Airways by the China International Trust and Investment Corporation.

Visitors and residents alike spend time at the popular Stanley Main Beach, on the south side of Hong Kong Island.

It was disclosed in March 1987 that the Hong Kong government had for 34 years allowed China undue influence by censoring theatrical films that might offend the Beijing government. The disclosure noted that some movies were even screened and assessed by Xinhua, which served as an unofficial representative for China in Hong Kong. The Hong Kong government proposed legislation to define its authority for film censorship, even though its unauthorized censorship had already influenced a generation of Hong Kongers.

Meanwhile, in April 1987, Deng Xiaoping laid out Chinese intentions for pre–1997 control of Hong Kong in a significant speech to members of the Basic Law Drafting Committee, saying: "There are certain things which can hardly be solved without the central authorities taking the matter up." Deng also disclosed what could be expected after Chinese rule began: "After 1997, if there are certain people in Hong Kong who curse the Chinese Communist Party and China, we shall allow them to do so. However, it is not allowed to turn curses into actions and turn Hong Kong into a base for opposing the mainland under the cloak of 'democracy.' In that case, we shall have to interfere. We do not necessarily have to call out the garrison troops. Only when great turmoil happens will the garrison troops be called out."[9]

In July 1987, the Hong Kong Observers, a civic and business group, issued a statement on the question of direct elections: "The freedom to choose one's government is a basic human right. The onus should not be on the Hong Kong people to show why it should enjoy that right, but on the Hong Kong Government to show what extraordinary circumstance could justify withholding it."[10] The organization maintained the 1984 Joint Declaration allowed "a legislature constituted by elections" and noted that if most of the people were silent, "by definition, their opinion is not known."[11]

Meanwhile, the money-making confidence in Hong Kong's stock exchange was shaken in late 1987, reflecting the alarming worldwide downturn affecting all stock markets. The Hang Seng Index plunged by one-third on October 26, one of the world's worst-ever one-day stock market declines. Many analysts and business experts feared the worst—that the Hang Seng decline was indicative of tremendous investor uncertainty about Hong Kong's future.

Deng's remarks made clear that China's eventual sovereignty over Hong Kong meant intervention in Hong Kong matters could occur during the transition period before 1997, whenever the Chinese leadership determined that China's interests might be involved. In addition, Deng told a visiting group of Hong Kong business leaders: "The political system in Hong Kong cannot copy that in the West. The present system has gone through one and a half centuries. It is not proper to copy completely the parliamentary system in Britain or the United States and to judge whether this is democracy or not."[12] On another occasion, the chairman of a Hong Kong company said: "Hong Kong might be the only place in the world where, in a free election, the population conceivably would vote not to have a democracy."[13]

In May 1987, one month after David Wilson officially became governor, the Hong Kong government published another Green Paper, this one seeking responses to a variety of confusing and complex political options. Descriptions of some options were so technical that most people simply could not figure out the answers, or for that matter interpret the questions. Specifically, the Green Paper requested public comment on possible adjustments to Hong Kong's political system, included in 26 main proposals and 14 sub-options. The proposals and options covered all political levels, from local districts to the Legislative · Council.

Government-sponsored surveys based on the wording and options of the Green Paper found that fewer than 15 percent of the people favored direct elections by 1988. This was an unusual determination, since a specific question about direct elections was not even in the Green Paper. Instead, references to voting were buried deep in the proposals and sub-options of the document. Some participants managed to wade through the confusion, as reflected later in a Hong Kong Assessment Office poll, which showed more than 265,000 favoring direct elections, just under 95,000 against and less than 1,800 expressing no opinion. That result was played down, however, when the Assessment Office said most of the support for elections came from petitions, and was thus unacceptable as "individual" submissions. At the same time, "individual" pre-printed form letters against direct elections were found to be acceptable by the Assessment Office.[14]

The Assessment Office poll sharply conflicted with nearly a dozen opinion polls made by other groups during the same period which showed considerable interest and support for direct voting by 1988 for at least some members of the Legislative Council. The outflow of professional people from Hong Kong became more even more prevalent in 1987, with emigration exceeding 10,000 for the year.

China's intentions for the transition period were further proclaimed in June 1987, when Li Hou, secretary general of the Basic Law Drafting Committee, maintained there was little real evidence in Hong Kong, despite opinion polls to the contrary, that anyone wanted changes in the political system, such as direct voting for Legislative Council members. Li also said, somewhat contradictorily, that China did not object to democracy, but that democratic participation had many forms.[15]

CHAPTER 10

China and Hong Kong Move Towards "Convergence"

"The British confer, but it is the Chinese who decide."
Political analyst in Hong Kong[1]

Pro-democracy groups in Hong Kong rallied in February 1988 to protest political conclusions outlined in a government White Paper which focused on stability instead of introducing some degree of direct legislative voting in the 1988 elections. Government officials said the decision was based on results of opinion polls which indicated Hong Kong residents had little interest in direct elections. Despite growing political awareness among a growing number of residents, most still preferred their old ways of quietly allowing the government to proceed as always—without expressing their collective voice one way or the other.

Political demonstrations in Hong Kong were almost nonexistent before the 1980s, so political analysts proclaimed a turning point in political awareness when 500 people marched to Government House on a clear Sunday afternoon in February to protest the conclusions of the White Paper and submit a petition for immediate direct elections. "Four years ago, nobody would march to Government House for political reasons," noted a British university professor. "And certainly no poll four years ago would have found, as many current polls have been finding, that thirty to sixty percent of the general population here favor direct elections of legislative representatives."[2]

Analysts said the people of Hong Kong were beginning to realize that post–1997 democracy, for them, was going to be limited. The White Paper was regarded as the probable political scenario, suggesting direct voting for only a few of the 59 members of Hong Kong's Legislative

65

Council. Others realized that it might be the last formal effort to influence change in Hong Kong's political system.

Political scientist Joseph Y.S. Cheng of the Chinese University of Hong Kong was among those aware of Britain's timidity in preparing the colony for change, saying, "Clearly the British administration has given up all initiatives for political reform in the transition period. The White Paper is significant because it shows that Beijing is now calling the tune here."[3] Pro-democracy activist Martin Lee, a member of the Legislative Council, said it "simply means we will turn our attention now to Beijing. We must keep up the pressure so they cannot ignore us in writing the Basic Law."[4]

By the late 1980s, Hong Kong, a pinpoint on the southeastern tip of mainland China, had become one of the most densely populated places in the world, with 5.8 million people crammed into 415 square miles—less than one-third the size of Rhode Island, and more than five times its population. By comparison, Hong Kong's total land area, including newly reclaimed land, comprised one nine thousandth the size of mainland China, and its population was only one-half of 1 percent of the more than 1 billion people living in the People's Republic of China. Macau topped all countries of the world in population density with 69,500 per square mile, followed by Monaco at 41,000, Hong Kong at 14,000 and Singapore at nearly 11,000.[5] Although the population density for all of Hong Kong was just over 14,000 per square mile, it jumped to more than 20,000 per square mile in the central business areas of Hong Kong and Kowloon.

Apparently attracted by economic opportunity, the Republic of China in Taiwan announced a significant change of policy in early 1988, stating that it would make "large-scale" investments in Hong Kong, mostly involving hotels, theaters and a variety of cultural areas. Taiwan, which Beijing claimed should be returned to mainland Chinese rule, had long resisted direct investment in Hong Kong, allowing Beijing to capitalize on its absence.

On April 28, strengthening its pressure for "convergence," China issued its first draft version of the Basic Law for Hong Kong, ending a three-year process to develop a "mini-constitution" outlining considerable autonomy for Hong Kong during five decades beyond 1997 in trade, cultural, economic and political affairs. The document was developed by a committee of 59, including 23 members from Hong Kong, all chosen by China. In a statement accompanying the release of the Draft Basic Law, Xinhua said, "The region shall not practice the socialist system and policies, and will maintain the current capitalist system and life style for 50 years."[6]

Not everyone saw it that way, especially Martin Lee, who maintained that provisions of the document would give China the power to revoke or change any laws approved by Legco. "It's supposed to be a mini-constitution for the new administrative district of Hong Kong," Lee said. "I'm not happy with it at the moment. A great majority of the articles are all right, but about ten percent are not all right. But you're not marking an examination paper, so that ninety percent means high marks. If you're doing a constitution, if you get one thing wrong you can make the whole thing unworkable."[7]

Publication of the Draft Basic Law failed to slow down the rush of emigration by thousands of Hong Kong's most talented, best educated and most polished professionals. Applications for emigration climbed in the late 1980s to more than 1,000 a week, mainly to Canada and Australia. Subsequent changes in American immigration policies led to thousands of applications from Hong Kongers for residence in the United States. Great Britain was never among the leading destinations for the new emigrants.

Most of the Hong Kong residents resettling in Canada were attracted to Vancouver and Toronto, cities that already had large Chinese populations The influx led to a welcome upsurge in real estate activity in both cities, along with talented business management people, many of whom had studied in Canadian and American universities. Some of the incoming Hong Kong Chinese, assured of Canadian residence, returned to Hong Kong under lucrative contracts to fill the growing number of important job vacancies. Other immigrants meanwhile invested in Canadian firms or started up their own businesses, thus creating new jobs in their adopted cities.

Martin Lee said the overwhelming number of emigrating Hong Kong residents was a clear indication of their distrust of China and concern for their personal lives and future under Chinese control after 1997. He also said the Draft Basic Law failed to provide the assurances they needed to stay in Hong Kong. "I'm afraid this will add to the sense of unease," Lee said. "People go away because they don't see any possible future in Hong Kong. Under the formula advocated by the People's Republic itself, it is 'one country, two systems.' That means Hong Kong people ruling Hong Kong. Beijing should not send its people down to rule because they don't know anything about Hong Kong."[8]

After consistently maintaining that emigration patterns were normal, the Hong Kong government in May 1988 announced the formation of a task force to investigate reports that key professionals and middle-class residents were leaving to avoid the post–1997 Chinese rule. The task force was established about two weeks after Hong Kong Governor David Wilson acknowledged, "We have to face the fact that there is a problem, because even though the figures have not gone up enormously, there are more people from the key middle management sector leaving."[9] Wilson said an estimated 27,000 Hong Kong residents emigrated in 1987, or nearly double the figure of 1986.

Amnesty International added its opposition to Hong Kong's Draft Basic Law, claiming in July 1988 that it failed to guarantee human rights. In a report, the watchdog organization said it was particularly concerned about a provision that Hong Kong "shall prohibit by law any act designed to undermine national unity or subvert the Central People's Government." Amnesty International said this provision threatened freedom of expression and minority rights by allowing the possibility that such cases could be transferred to China's Supreme People's Court in Beijing.

By 1989, "convergence" was becoming more than a convenient word for Hong Kong's transition into China. Millions of Hong Kong Chinese crossed the border to the mainland each year to take vacations, visit relatives, consult doctors and a variety of other reasons. It worked both ways, with several hundred thousand mainland Chinese crossing into Hong Kong either as tourists or to conduct business.

Convergence also worked in other ways, especially near the border, where much of Hong Kong's television programming was popular among residents in neighboring Guangdong Province of southern China. Hong Kong songs, movies and books were growing in popularity throughout much of mainland China. In addition, about 2 million people in Guangdong Province worked directly or indirectly for companies in Hong Kong. Perhaps the most important sign of convergence was financial—Hong Kong in 1989 was the largest foreign investor in China, just as China was the largest foreign investor in Hong Kong.[10] One assessment which characterized convergence came from businessman Gordon Y.S. Wu, head of Hong Kong's Hopewell Holdings (which was investing heavily in China), who said, "We see no boundaries. It's basically an enlargement of Hong Kong."[11]

Language in Hong Kong was really an unusual and forced mix of two languages. Official English was still required in courts, government business and schools, and everyone was surrounded by English language radio, television, movies and newspapers. As mentioned earlier, however, the unofficial language within families and business circles was Chinese, generally Mandarin or Cantonese dialects. After all, 98 percent of the residents of Hong Kong were Chinese. By the late 1980s, Chinese was becoming more dominant in day-to-day activities, though most professional workers realized that English would be important in the day-to-day business dealings with other countries.

One of the most impassioned pleas on behalf of Hong Kong residents worried about a future under Chinese rule was made in April 1989 by Dame Lydia Dunn, a senior member of Hong Kong's Legislative Council. Appearing before a British Parliament committee considering Hong Kong's future, Dame Lydia voiced concern that even though Hong Kong's residents were British subjects, they had no right to work and live in Britain. "I sometimes wonder what the British people feel when they read about Hong Kong British subjects scurrying around the world to find somewhere else to take them in," Dame Lydia told the committee. "It would do so much to help families commit themselves to a future here if they could be guaranteed a hope of last resort in Britain."[12]

The continuing upward economic trend for Hong Kong in the late 1980s was dramatically reflected in a record budget surplus of US$1.82 million for fiscal year 1988-89, marking the third straight year of a budget surplus for Hong Kong at a time when many countries were battling budget deficits. Hong Kong financial officials, somewhat humbled by the surplus, responded by increasing spending and approving limited tax cuts to a community already enjoying one of the lowest tax rates in the world. In addition, officials predicted another budget surplus for the 1989-90 fiscal year.

Ironically, the government was unable to consider improving services in Hong Kong, because so many of its professional people had emigrated to other countries. Government figures showed about 45,000 Hong Kongers, many of them managers and professionals, emigrated in 1988 to establish new homes and futures in Australia, Canada and the United States. The Hongkong and Shanghai Banking Corporation's chief economist, V.H.C. Cheng, said it would be nearly impossible to improve services, "even when you are rich." As Cheng noted: "There is a labor shortage here, so even if they budgeted millions they could not find the doctors, social workers, nurses, construction workers."[13]

CHAPTER 11

Chinese Credibility and the Tiananmen Square Massacre

"This storm was bound to happen sooner or later. As determined by the international and domestic climate, it was bound to happen and was independent of man's will. It was just a matter of time and scale."

Deng Xiaoping, on the
Tiananmen Square crackdown (1989)[1]

China's unexpected forceful suppression of pro-democracy protesters on June 4, 1989, when troops opened fire and killed hundreds of demonstrators in Tiananmen Square, shook the emotions of Hong Kong residents, giving them a real-life dramatic preview of what life might be like under control of the People's Republic of China. Reaction was swift and emotional. One million people, most draped in the traditional Chinese black and white mourning colors, marched through the streets of Hong Kong on June 4. Britain immediately suspended its participation with the Joint Liaison Group, which was preparing for the 1997 transition of Hong Kong to China. Hong Kong's Hang Seng Index, reflecting the mood of the moment, plunged 22 percent on June 5, the day after the Tiananmen crackdown.

In related action, British Foreign Secretary Geoffrey Howe, addressing Britain's House of Commons, announced the suspension of high-level military contacts, arms sales to China and all diplomatic exchanges. However, his message also affirmed that Hong Kong residents would not be welcome in England as a means of escaping Chinese rule. Howe said Britain had an interest in enhancing "the security of the people of Hong Kong," but "could not easily contemplate a massive new immigration commitment which could more than double the ethnic minority population of the United Kingdom." In other words, the objection focused on race rather than the number of people.[2]

British government figures showed that fewer than 1,000 Hong Kong Chinese had immigrated to the United Kingdom each year from 1985 through 1988, compared with 49,000 immigrants from all countries in 1988 alone. However, British sympathy was never especially strong for an influx of Hong Kong Chinese. In a Gallup Poll of British residents published just after the June 1989 Beijing crackdown, 46 percent opposed granting residency rights to Hong Kong citizens, 42 percent were in favor and 12 percent were undecided. A similar Gallup Poll in November 1983 had produced almost the same result.

Much of Hong Kong was closed down by strikes on June 7, and police had to use tear gas to control crowds attacking Chinese-owned shops and banks. Governor David Wilson flew to London the same day to request residency rights in Britain for Hong Kong citizens. (There was a time when colonial citizens had residency rights in Britain, but these rights were gradually restricted or removed in provisions of four nationality acts passed between 1962 and 1981 by the British Parliament.)

Governor David Wilson met on June 9 in London with Prime Minister Margaret Thatcher, who offered him "more than tea and sympathy" but rejected his request to grant right-of-residency permits to Hong Kong's 3.25 million British passport holders.[3] About the only tangible result of Wilson's pleading in London was an announcement that British Foreign Secretary Geoffrey Howe would visit Hong Kong in early July to "assess" the situation.

Howe arrived in Hong Kong on July 2 to face jeering crowds and protesters shouting "shame!" as his limousine carried him from Kai Tak Airport to Government House. He attempted to reassure anxious residents about their future, saying on arrival: "You have no stauncher friend than Britain."[4] Instead, he confirmed what many already realized — that Britain would not be taking them in. "There is simply no way that a British government could grant to several million people the right to come and live in Britain," Howe said. "It dismays me that some have suggested that this is a matter of race. It is nothing of the sort — it is a practical problem on an enormous scale."[5]

Some of those attending the midday speech walked out in protest to Howe's remarks, including eight members of Hong Kong district boards. He then tried to smooth over his message, saying that Britain would speed up democratic reforms in Hong Kong and would pressure China to keep its promises.

Several prominent financial institutions are located in the famed Central District.

Howe defended concerns of Britain's government and residents of the United Kingdom about allowing residency for the 3.25 million Hong Kongers with British passports, saying, "We would never know how many of those might present themselves for settlement as a matter of right, not just in the next eight years, but over the coming decades." As a final glimmer of hope, he said the door would not be closed if the situation became intolerable, promising to "mobilize the international community to help us if the number leaving Hong Kong were larger than we could deal with alone."[6]

Before departing, Howe said it was important for China to help restore confidence in the "one country, two systems" focus of the 1984 Joint Declaration. "One of the central messages to get through the Chinese leadership is [that] they need to apply themselves from now on to an active agenda of deeds, not words, to begin restoring that confidence," he said. "I understand the extent to which people in Hong Kong are concerned with citizenship, the 'right-of-abode' issue, but I believe that the people of Hong Kong now have a clearer and better understanding of the impossibility of Britain offering a blank check for three, four or five million people."[7]

In August, political commentator R. Emmett Tyrrell, writing from London, summed up the thoughts of many with the question, "What is going to happen to Hong Kong?" His answer: "Well, what happens to a jewel left unguarded on a park bench in the sun?" Tyrrell wrote that "the fate of the Hong Kong people appears to be grimmer than that of almost any other people on earth" and proposed that "all Western governments should draft plans to accept Hong Kong residents fleeing Communist oppression."[8]

John Major, who replaced Geoffrey Howe as British foreign secretary in the last week of July 1989, began a delicate task of pursuing a more honorable course of action. Major addressed the United Nations General Assembly on September 27, proposing to speed up introduction of direct elections in Hong Kong, develop a bill of rights for Hong Kong and expand the rights of certain key Hong Kong citizens. He said it was necessary to restore confidence in Hong Kong and maintain pressure on China to keep its promises regarding the future of Hong Kong. Major said Britain intended to grant residency rights in the United Kingdom to "essential" Hong Kong people, though he didn't elaborate on how those people would be selected.

Hong Kong, already uneasy from the emotional ups and downs of the 1980s, moved into 1990 with even more reason to be worried:

Britain's decision to grant full passports to only 50,000 Hong Kong families. The plan, announced at 11:45 P.M. Hong Kong time on December 21, 1989, was intended to provide a "sense of security" for about 225,000 people, out of 3.25 million holders of British Dependent Territories Citizen passports and British National Overseas passports. Although designated "British," those two special passports did not grant the right to live and work in Great Britain. They were primarily used as travel documents.

The new passport plan would grant full citizenship for up to 50,000 heads of households, mostly businessmen, professional people and government workers. The passports would be issued on a point system, with criteria including length of service with British institutions, knowledge of English, emigration analysis and the value of an individual's services. In addition, some provision would be made for those threatened by the political situation. Part of the reasoning behind the passport plan was that most people would actually continue residing in Hong Kong, knowing they could move to Britain if conditions were undesirable after China's takeover in 1997.

British Foreign Secretary Douglas Hurd told the House of Commons in London that the main purpose of the "safety net" was not to encourage immigration into Great Britain, but "to persuade to remain in Hong Kong those whom we need to retain there, if our last substantial colony is to pass successfully through the final eight years of British rule."[9]

Hurd acknowledged that the mood of Hong Kong was "at a low ebb," particularly after the violent June 1989 Tiananmen crackdown. "The problem of confidence," he said, "is shown by increasing emigration from the territory, and increasing numbers of people who contemplate leaving. A growing proportion of these people are those whom Hong Kong can least afford to lose."[10] He said 42,000 had left Hong Kong in 1989, with another 55,000 expected to leave in 1990. "We have eventually worked out what we believe to be the most sensible balance between our desire for good race relations and harmony in our cities and our very strong feeling that we have a continuing sense of responsibility to people in Hong Kong."[11]

Many residents of Britain, as reflected in surveys at the time, voiced concern about a great influx of Hong Kong Chinese, even though ethnic minorities (mostly Asians and Afro-Caribbeans) constituted fewer than 5 percent of the country's 56 million inhabitants. More specifically, about 350,000 Chinese people were living in Great Britain in 1990, according to Lydia Lee of the Chinese Information and Advice Center in London.[12]

Although clearly unsatisfactory to nearly everyone in Hong Kong, to some individuals the package was characterized as "a step in the right direction."[13] Lo Lung-Kwong of the Hong Kong People Saving Hong Kong movement said the British passport plan was the first step, optimistically adding, "and so we need a second step, with the numbers enlarged."[14] Tony Halmos, campaign coordinator of Honour Hong Kong, a group supported by local business firms, said: "When the package is announced, that's when the intensive lobbying really begins."[15] Honour Hong Kong had been pressing for Britain to grant passports to 318,000 families, involving between 700,000 and 800,000 people.

Albert Cheng of the Right of Abode Delegation, a citizens' lobby, called the package "totally disappointing." Cheng said: "Fifty thousand is a very small number and it is too small to have any impact on the confidence of Hong Kong."[16] Still another group, British Citizens for Hong Kong, involving some 800 expatriate Britons living in Hong Kong, strongly criticized the British passport package, describing it as "a divisive and dishonorable gesture of dismissal."[17] Rosanna Tam, a member of Hong Kong's Legislative Council, also was disappointed. "The number falls far short of our request," she said. "We remain committed to pressing the case for all Hong Kong British subjects."[18]

Attempting to explain the decision, Governor David Wilson said, "Of course, in an ideal world we would prefer to have passports, full passports for all the British nationals in Hong Kong, but it has been clear for some time that was not going to be politically possible."[19] The Hong Kong government also issued an official statement containing no significant expression of either disappointment or criticism, saying the plan "will help re-establish confidence and stability." The statement also stressed that the plan was designed especially to "help people in both the public and private sectors who are important to the efficient working of the territory and who are currently most vulnerable to emigration." At the same time, the statement said the passport package "should not be seen as elitist."[20]

Just over a week later, China officially issued a strong complaint about the British passport plan granting residency rights to 50,000 Hong Kong families, saying it was "greatly surprised at this action of the British government" and describing the plan as "a gross violation of its own solemn commitment."[21] China's Foreign Ministry said Britain's decision had violated a previous memorandum agreement to permit use of British passports without granting right-of-abode. The British "about-face," the statement said, represented "disregard of the relevant agreement" and "will inevitably create contradictions leading to divisions and confrontations among Hong Kong citizens." China said issuance of the passports would be "detrimental to the stability and prosperity of Hong Kong" and warned that Britain should reverse its decision or "bear a series of consequences arising therefrom."[22]

Geoffrey Howe, then leader of Britain's House of Commons, said the passport plan, despite Beijing's criticisms, would be a positive factor in maintaining the prosperity and stability of Hong Kong, which he described as the "over-riding purpose" of the Joint Declaration. "What the Chinese sometimes overlook," he said, "is that some forty to fifty thousand people have been leaving Hong Kong each year, going to countries such as the United States or Canada or Australia, and going there to settle in order to acquire the right to stay there as citizens. We tell them, 'Look, you may become citizens of the United Kingdom, but you do not need to come here to achieve that.'"

Howe, Britain's foreign secretary during development of the 1984 Joint Declaration, also rejected fears of an influx of Hong Kong Chinese into Britain. "Some of them may come, but we don't think they are all likely to come, by any means," he said. "We are offering the prospect of citizenship with a right to come here, but on the basis that will encourage people to stay in Hong Kong."[23]

Meanwhile, Robert Adley, a member of Parliament and consistent supporter of smooth China-Britain relations, said he had cautioned Britain's Foreign Office that the passport plan would upset the Chinese. "This action by Britain is a clear abuse of both the spirit and letter of the 1984 agreement," Adley said. "It is one of the most serious mistakes the Foreign Office has made for a long time. What we, the British and Hong Kong governments, are silently telling the Chinese is that we trust neither the ability, nor the good intentions of the Chinese to honor their part of the 1984 agreement."[24]

Other members of the British Parliament, including those in the Conservative Party of Prime Minister Margaret Thatcher, also voiced opposition to the passport plan. The leader of the revolt in the House of Commons was Norman Tebbit, Conservative Party chairman during 1986-87. "The public feels that they were never asked their opinion about whether these people should come here. They were foisted on them," Tebbit said. "It's a dangerous thing to issue an insurance policy that would bankrupt you if the event occurred. That's not proper underwriting."[25] Tony Marlow, a Conservative Party member from the Midlands, reflected some of the general feeling in Britain: "We've had a massive amount of immigration for thirty years, and people have had enough. Most people are uneasy."[26]

Hong Kong's Governor David Wilson visited Beijing for three days beginning January 10, 1990—his first visit since the massacre at Tiananmen Square in June of 1989. The trip was especially designed to provide some calmness in the flurry of exchanges between China and Britain, and to ease the uncertainty in Hong Kong. "I've been explaining the views that people in Hong Kong have, both on short-term political developments and the hopes that people have for long-term development, for steady and continued development of the political structure," Wilson said. He characterized the three days of talks as "useful," but acknowledged that no progress had been made to ease tensions between Beijing and Hong Kong.

Wilson said he also tried to explain the reasoning behind London's proposal to grant passports to 50,000 Hong Kong Chinese and their families. "I can't say that in these discussions we have solved every problem, but I do think that as a result of these meetings, it has been possible to increase understanding on both sides and get back to resuming the sort of practical dialogue which we need if we're to deal with practical issues in Hong Kong at the moment," he said. "We in Hong Kong have no wish, we have no intention, that Hong Kong should be used as a base for subversion against China. In particular, we don't want people from outside Hong Kong to come to Hong Kong to use it as a battlefield against China. At the same time, we treasure our own liberties and freedoms in Hong Kong."[27]

British Foreign Secretary Douglas Hurd went to Hong Kong on January 12 to meet with Wilson and others regarding political reforms. Little noteworthy progress was announced during Hurd's four-day visit, but he repeated a previous goal that "the first prize" would be development of a political framework in Hong Kong that would continue after its July 1, 1997, handover to China. Hurd's promise may have had its roots in his novel *The Smile on the Face of the Tiger*, written some years before, which focused on China's takeover of Hong Kong—with a happy ending.

Stepping up its pressure against Britain's new passport plan, Beijing announced in mid–January that it would exclude holders of foreign passports from all top government positions in Hong Kong after July 1, 1997, and would probably extend the exclusion to other governmental positions. Related statements specified that the restrictions would apply to future chief executives and judges, along with directors of immigration and customs.

The issue of special residency documents was raised in Washington during a January 29 meeting between British Foreign Secretary Douglas Hurd and U.S. Secretary of State James Baker. Hurd formally requested that the United States grant passports to Hong Kong residents employed by American firms. His request, however, failed to achieve any immediate response from American government officials, including President George Bush.

Two small concessions in Hong Kong's future political system were made by China in mid–February: an increase in the number of directly elected legislative seats from 18 to 20 and an increase from 15 to 20 percent in the number of foreign passport holders allowed to serve in Hong Kong's Legislative Council after 1997.

The Chinese stance quickly changed, however, and became even more restrictive regarding foreign passport holders in Hong Kong. China's Foreign Ministry announced on March 1 that since Hong Kong was Chinese territory, Hong Kong Chinese were Chinese nationals — and therefore unable to hold foreign passports after July 1, 1997. The decision was apparently intended to counter Britain's plan to issue full British passports to 50,000 Hong Kong families, or about 255,000 people. Political analysts said the announcement would probably increase the emigration rate from Hong Kong, then running about 1,000 people a week. China's announcement against recognizing foreign passport holders in Hong Kong was greeted with a subdued response in London, where a British Foreign Office spokesman said the Chinese had not liked the nationality package when it was proposed in December 1989, "and they don't like it now."[28]

Meanwhile, London newspapers reported on March 1 that Britain had successfully persuaded seven countries to issue at least a limited number of passports to residents of Hong Kong seeking some degree of personal security after the 1997 Chinese takeover. The countries were identified as Singapore, Japan, Australia, Italy, France, Canada and the Netherlands. British Foreign Secretary Douglas Hurd called the newspaper reports premature, but said other countries were being approached to consider granting the passports. "We are, as you know, in touch with a number of governments, drawing attention to the need which we felt to encourage key personnel to stay in Hong Kong," he said. "That's all I can say at the present time."[29]

The 70-story Bank of China Tower, the tallest building in Hong Kong, was designed by Chinese-American architect I.M. Pei. It dominates the cluster of skyscrapers overlooking Victoria Harbor from Hong Kong's Central District.

China also responded to the newspaper reports about other countries granting passports, saying that any Chinese citizen seeking foreign citizenship would first have to acquire permission from China to "forfeit his Chinese citizenship."[30]

The reality of "convergence" became more evident in the early 1990s with the opening of the new 70-story Bank of China glass tower dominating Hong Kong's skyline from the downtown business district. The 1,209-foot tower, the tallest building in the world outside the United States, was designed by the noted Canton-born American architect I.M. Pei and intended to "celebrate the modernization of China."[31] Another bit of convergence affecting all Hong Kong residents was the pending ratification by the National People's Congress in Beijing of the Basic Law for Hong Kong, defining its rights and political policies after 1997.

CHAPTER 12

China Approves "Basic Law" for Post–1997 Hong Kong

"Since Hong Kong compatriots have accepted the premise that Hong Kong's future will be decided according to the guiding policy of 'one country, two systems,' it is natural for them to pay close attention to the question of how to design Hong Kong's future political structure."

Lian Xisheng, Professor of Constitution,
China University (1990)[1]

Hong Kong may have been concerned about its handover to Beijing, but much of its anger was directed towards Great Britain for failing to better prepare the territory for the years after the 1997 lease expiration. That failure to provide self-determination for Hong Kong was described by Anthony Rogers, chairman of the Hong Kong Bar Association, as "one of the biggest denials of human rights by Britain in this century."[2] Hong Kong's leading pro-democracy activist, lawyer and Legislative Council member Martin Lee, was even more direct: "The people of Hong Kong were led down the garden path by the British and Chinese governments."[3] The popular Hong Kong newsmagazine *Far Eastern Economic Review*, in an emotional cover story proclaiming "the surrender of Hong Kong," charged: "The perpetrators of 4 June 1989 were, in effect, given veto powers over liberty and democracy in Hong Kong."[4]

China's position against democratic reforms in Hong Kong was actually supported by Barrie Wiggham, secretary for civil service in Hong Kong, who said any changes would be counterproductive, since China would probably overturn those changes after assuming control in

1997.[5] "The reality is that we live alongside China, and so there are limits to how far we can travel down that road," Wiggham said. "It was a question of how much we could achieve in Hong Kong without upsetting the system or creating instability."[6] Under the Basic Law, a constitution-like document intended to regulate the Hong Kong Special Administrative Region beginning July 1, 1997, residents were assured of fundamental rights in such areas as religion, education, social services, trade, labor and commerce. Directly elected members of the Legislative Council would total 24 in 1995, rising to 30 in 2003, and would serve four-year terms. However, beginning in 1997, Beijing would appoint all "principal officials" of Hong Kong, including its chief executive. The Standing Committee of China's National People's Congress would have the authority to reject any Hong Kong laws (enacted before or after 1997) that did not conform with the Basic Law.

Two previous draft versions of the Basic Law had been worked out in 1988 and 1989 by the Basic Law Drafting Committee (BLDC), established by Beijing in 1985 and comprising 26 members from mainland China and 23 from Hong Kong. A related group, called the Basic Law Consultative Committee (BLCC), with 180 members (all Hong Kong residents), was set up by Beijing in late 1985 to consider and analyze public opinion in Hong Kong about provisions of the Basic Law.

Announcement of the final draft version of the Basic Law for Hong Kong in January 1990 was met with emotional concern—especially by the Hong Kong members of the BLDC, none of whom voted in favor of the document. Its approval was entirely dependent upon the larger number of mainland Chinese members on the committee. Raymond Wu, leader of the Hong Kong group, even refused to participate in a joint news conference to announce completion of work on the final version, telling journalists, "I am afraid I would not be able to control myself from breaking into tears."[7]

A spokesman for the Hong Kong lobbying group Joint Committee for the Promotion of a Democratic Government said the final draft of the Basic Law demonstrated that Hong Kong's consultation in the matter was "just a farce," adding, "The Chinese government didn't listen to the wishes of the people of Hong Kong."[8] One senior Hong Kong government official tried to soften the concern by calling the document "just a draft," adding, "It must make its way up through the Chinese hierarchy, and so there will be room for changes. As far as we are concerned, the development of democracy here is still being negotiated between the British and Chinese governments."[9]

Nevertheless, with only minor changes, the Basic Law for Hong Kong was approved on April 4 by delegates to China's National People's Congress in Beijing. Chinese Prime Minister Li Peng held a 90-minute news conference following formal approval of the Basic Law, although questions from journalists mostly concerned China's decision to fire on protesters in June 1989.

Offering an explanation of the Beijing crackdown, Li said: "At the beginning of the turmoil last spring, we didn't think of using force to solve the problem. It was only after a long period of tense waiting, and only when the fate of the People's Republic of China and the socialist system were in serious jeopardy and when Beijing was thrown in great anarchy, that the Chinese government was forced to take these measures." Li said he was convinced that the decision "had won the support of the overwhelming majority of Chinese."[10] In addition, Li said: "At that time, it was impossible to think of any alternative."[11]

The first anniversary of the June 1989 violent crackdown in Beijing's Tiananmen Square was marked in Hong Kong with a march involving more than 100,000 people, dressed mostly in black and white, the traditional Chinese mourning colors. Organizers of the march, who earlier predicted 30,000 people might participate, said they were surprised by the turnout, which they estimated at closer to 250,000. The march stretched for some two miles, under a consistent light rain, through Hong Kong's business district.

One of the leaders of the march, pro-democracy figure Martin Lee, said the number of people in the march reflected strong optimism for the future on the part of the Hong Kong Chinese. He said participants in the march realized they could be subject to later punishment, since photographs of demonstrations were taken by representatives of mainland China.

Absent from the march was a replica of the Goddess of Democracy statue, an enduring image from the June 1989 suppression in Beijing. The replica had been displayed in Hong Kong parks during the summer of 1989, stored for several months and then buried after Hong Kong's government refused to grant permission for permanent display. It was a telling example of efforts by the Hong Kong government to avoid upsetting the leadership in China.

Similar action occurred in July 1990 when five leading pro-democracy figures amazingly went on trial in Hong Kong for using hand-held megaphones without a permit. The charges were based on a public nuisance law enacted in 1900. The five had used megaphones during

A cross-harbor view of Hong Kong's Central District.

early 1990 rallies protesting provisions of the Basic Law. The charges carried maximum penalties of less than $10 and three months in jail.

Meanwhile, Britain's plan to grant 50,000 passports to Hong Kong heads of households and their families continued to be criticized by China's leadership, who maintained the action could lead to divisions between China and Britain. The legislation was approved 313 to 216 after a six-hour debate on April 20 in Britain's House of Commons and was followed immediately by an angry response from the Chinese leadership. In a statement issued April 20 through the Hong Kong office of Xinhua, a spokesman said,

> The Chinese government has time and time again made clear its solemn stand against the unilateral decision of Britain to change the nationality of some of the Hong Kong Chinese citizens. The Chinese memorandum of the Sino-British Joint Declaration states that under the nationality law of the People's Republic of China, all Hong Kong Chinese compatriots, whether they are holders of the British dependent territory citizen passports or not, are Chinese nationals. The nationality status of the Hong Kong Chinese compatriots can only be determined in accordance with China's nationality law. This is a matter within the scope of China's sovereignty.[12]

The statement maintained that British approval to grant passports to 50,000 heads of households in Hong Kong was "worked out unilaterally" by Britain without consultation with China, and could hasten the departure of professional people. It warned that China reserved the right to take "corresponding measures."

By voice vote on June 13 Britain's House of Commons gave final approval to the legislation granting passports to 50,000 heads of households from Hong Kong, sending the proposal to the House of Lords for consideration and expected approval. The House of Lords had the choice of approving the legislation without change, amending it (with approval of Commons) or rejecting it. Rejection, though unusual, would have required the British government to either reintroduce or abandon the proposal. As before, the Chinese government issued a formal objection to the legislation.

Britain's Parliament formally approved the British Nationality (Hong Kong) Act of 1990 on July 23, quickly bringing more objections from China to the effect that the legislation violated the spirit of the 1984 Chinese-British Joint Declaration on Hong Kong. In a statement issued through Xinhua, Beijing said: "The Chinese Government cannot but express regret over this. This move of the British side contravenes the spirit and essence of the Chinese-British Joint Declaration and impairs China's sovereignty. It is unacceptable to the Chinese government." In response, a Hong Kong government spokesman said: "There is nothing in the act which contravenes the Joint Declaration. The key point is that recipients of British citizenship under the act will have the absolute assurance of right of abode in the United Kingdom."[13]

Hong Kong emigrants in 1990 averaged more than 1,000 per week, or about double the numbers of 1986. Michael Rowse, head of Hong Kong's task force on emigration, estimated the outflow in 1990 at 62,000 and predicted it would level off at 60,000 in each of the next two years. Rowse admitted that many of the emigrants were skilled and educated professionals, characterizing the situation as "bad, but not a disaster."

Emigration from Hong Kong took on greater extremes in 1990 as hundreds of families tried to assure the futures of their children by arranging for their births in other countries, especially the United States and Canada. A foreign passport, they believed, was the most important legacy they could give to their children. Author and news columnist Frank Ching said, "In Hong Kong, when people ask you where you are going to have your baby, they don't mean which hospital—they mean which country."[14] The overwhelming interest in emigration from Hong Kong also led to the creation of counseling services on the subject, along with publication of several books and a popular new magazine entitled *The Emigrant.*

Queen Elizabeth's annual birthday list in June 1990 included a life peerage for Dame Lydia Dunn, executive director of Swire Pacific Ltd. and leading member of Hong Kong's Executive Council (Exco). Many viewed her appointment to Britain's House of Lords as strengthening Hong Kong's influence in Britain. Others noted that the appointment would preclude any chance of her becoming Hong Kong's chief executive after 1997.

The pending Legislative Council elections in Hong Kong required voter registration, a difficult task in a community not accustomed to voting. Officials estimated that fewer than half of the eligible 4 million voters were registered by August of 1990, and only 30 percent of those registered had actually cast ballots in previous district board elections. In 1991, for the first time, 18 of the 60 members of Hong Kong Kong's Legislative Council (Legco) would be subject to direct election. Previously, members of Legco were either appointed by the Hong Kong government or elected by constituency groups such as teachers, lawyers and businessmen.

A planned six-week voter registration drive was extended to ten weeks in October to increase the number of people eligible to vote in 1991. Author Joseph Cheng, a specialist in the politics of China and Hong Kong, said one problem in registering voters was that "people believe there will never be a meaningful system of representative government here, because Beijing will always have the final say."[15] A similar assessment was made by Norman Miners, also an author and political science instructor at the University of Hong Kong: "A great many people in Hong Kong are convinced that neither China nor the Hong Kong government will pay any attention to what they do or what they want."[16]

In a further example of convergence, mainland Chinese influence in Hong Kong journalism was becoming more pronounced in the early 1990s. Reporters acknowledged they were concerned about future punishment if they reported anything that displeased China. Newspapers were having problems keeping objective writers, and many newspaper writers talked of growing self-censorship. In a move to avoid eventual retribution from China, journalists in Hong Kong writing articles critical of Beijing used pen names for bylines.[17]

By October of 1990, China had control of five daily newspapers in Hong Kong and began publication of a new Hong Kong magazine entitled *Bauhinia,* named for the territory's official flower. Intimidation from China could take such forms as administrative action after 1997 against the fourteen other independent newspapers (including two English-language papers) or an order for advertisers to refrain from doing business with certain publications.

Hong Kong investment and interest in the United States received a large boost in November when President George Bush signed into law the Immigration Act of 1990. The legislation raised from 5,000 to 10,000 the annual number of immigrants from Hong Kong during 1991, 1992 and 1993; and to 25,000 in 1994 and thereafter. The bill also allowed the granting of 36,000 special visas to Hong Kong employees of American companies operating in Hong Kong.

CHAPTER 13

A New Airport:
Who Will Pay?

"We have an agreement with this project with the confidence and certainty we've been looking for. I don't think this is a bad deal for Hong Kong."

Hong Kong Governor David Wilson (1991)[1]

Plans for a new multi-billion-dollar airport and shipping port expansion for Hong Kong, first announced in October 1989, became in 1991 a major focus of attention for China, whose leaders claimed that its enormous cost would drain the financial resources of the territory and leave China with a large debt. The $16.3 billion project led to a series of nine secret meetings between Chinese and British officials in 1990 and 1991, along with a barrage of warnings and threats from Beijing over starting any work without Chinese consent and approval.

The Chinese claimed, with some justification, that Beijing had a right to approve or disapprove every project or policy involving post–1997 Hong Kong. However, many diplomats, analysts and government officials in Hong Kong suggested that China used the airport dispute as a convenient means of asserting control before the 1997 handover. Most people in Hong Kong, especially businesspersons, agreed that the project would help improve the future of the territory under Chinese rule. One banker said, "We have to make ourselves vital to China and the development of south China. Our very existence as a commercial center depends on this."[2] Robert Broadfoot, managing director of Political and Economic Risk Consultancy Ltd., was even more realistic: "The airport package will create the impression in the minds of businessmen that no matter what the political developments here, there will still be forward economic development, still be money to be made in

Hong Kong. The project will help counter the impression, the fear some people have, that Hong Kong will be a ghost town in 1997."[3]

The airport issue, like the 1984 Joint Declaration, was actually a diplomatic discussion between China and Britain, with no official participation by Hong Kong. As explained by Hong Kong educator Anthony Cheung: "The airport project is a matter of great importance to the Hong Kong people. But it seems that it has become an issue for the Chinese and the British to debate. No one has asked the Hong Kong people."[4] Another educator, T.L. Tsim of Hong Kong's Chinese University, said, "The issue is not over the airport. The Chinese are using it to get political control. They want it because they've got to control the place."[5]

The Chinese leadership, amid rising levels of public objection, began secret negotiations with Britain to resolve the question of financing the airport project. But the question and frequent objections also became a frustrating months-long test of words and wills between the two countries. In one instance, Hong Kong officials went to Beijing to discuss financial and technical details of the planned airport and were told to delay any action on the project until China's objections were resolved.

One member of China's airport negotiating team, Chen Zuoer of the Hong Kong and Macau Affairs Office, cautioned in January that any effort on the project without China's approval would result in "serious consequences." The Chinese position was clarified in a mid–January statement issued by Chinese Deputy Premier Wu Xueqian, who declared that "during the transition period, only the Central People's Government can, and is entitled to, speak on behalf of the people of Hong Kong."[6] One political observer characterized Wu's statement as "astonishing."

Martin C.M. Lee, pro-democracy leader, lawyer and member of Hong Kong's Legislative Council, said, "China says it isn't asking for a veto, but if the two sides can't agree on something, nothing will go ahead, and that's effectively a veto, isn't it? This would render the Hong Kong government into a puppet government. It would no longer be a lame-duck government, but a puppet government."[7] Writer George L. Hicks described the dispute as "a big fight at the moment" and Hong Kong's "moment of truth," saying, "If Hong Kong gives in to it, it's a de facto takeover."[8]

Hong Kong Governor David Wilson traveled to Beijing in late January to formally notify Chinese authorities that the project would proceed, despite their objections. Wilson tried to play down his visit, insisting that his primary objective was to promote "a sensible relationship, a good relationship with China."[9]

Beijing had agreed that a new airport was necessary for Hong Kong, whose Kai Tak Airport—second busiest in Asia after Tokyo's Narita Airport—was handling nearly 20 million passengers annually and expected to reach its capacity of 24 million before 1997. But China's objections and insistence on being involved in decisions regarding the new airport contributed to the triple problems of issuing contracts, attracting private capital and hiring the thousands of workers required to develop the project.

The matter was finally resolved in July 1991 when China and Britain announced a seven-point Memorandum of Understanding, allowing Beijing to be consulted on decisions involving the new airport and promising that Hong Kong would have cash reserves totaling at least $3.2 billion when China assumed control on July 1, 1997. The announcement was welcomed by Governor David Wilson and quickly praised by the Hong Kong General Chamber of Commerce.

During the 18 months leading to the agreement, more than $20 million had been spent on site preparation, environmental studies and engineering for the airport on nearby Chek Lap Kok, a small area of land adjacent to Lantau Island. Initial work included expensive sea reclamation for the terminal, parallel runways and adjacent area on the 2,500-acre site. Officials said the first runway, 12,470 feet long, might be completed after 1997, accommodating a maximum of 35 million passengers yearly. The new airport would be linked to Hong Kong by high-speed trains, a tunnel, a mile-long suspension bridge and a six-lane highway. Construction of a second runway would begin in 1999, raising capacity to 87 million passengers upon completion.

The agreement was formally signed in September by Chinese Premier Li Peng and British Prime Minister John Major, the first Western European leader to visit Beijing since the 1989 Tiananmen Square crackdown. During his visit, Major confidently declared the return to "a general normalization of relations" between China and Britain. At the same time, Major cautioned that Britain had not withdrawn concerns "about past events that caused such a rupture in our relationship in 1989 or the human rights or arms sales problems that have been the subject of frequent discussions between our two countries."[10]

Following John Major's concern about human rights, Li Peng authorized a response by Wu Jianmin of China's Foreign Ministry:

"China and Britain have different social systems, and their value systems, ideologies and historical traditions are different. So, regarding the problem of human rights, the two sides definitely will have differences here and there. This is natural. However, the two sides can exchange opinions on this and can enhance mutual understanding."[11] Wu also said a Chinese historian had reminded Li Peng that China had been "bullied and humiliated" for more than 100 years by foreign powers who "totally disregarded the human rights of the Chinese people."

Optimism in Hong Kong reached new levels following the airport agreement. The Hang Seng Index of blue-chip stocks closed at a record-high 4,019 on July 23, followed by another record of 4,028 the following day. Officials also estimated that housing prices rose 10 percent within three weeks after the agreement was announced. Meanwhile, the people of Hong Kong continued with their favorite activity: making money and more money.

Nearly two years after the June 1989 Beijing crackdown, Hong Kong's Legislative Council approved a draft version of a Bill of Rights, intended to adhere to the International Covenant on Civil and Political Rights. Two significant provisions, however, were excluded: the right to elect political representatives and the right to self-determination.

At the same time, many believed Hong Kong's Bill of Rights would have little authority after the handover in 1997. China did not participate in the International Covenant and therefore was not required to submit reports to the United Nations' Human Rights Committee. In other words, it was a document without any guarantee for the rights of Hong Kong residents.

Meanwhile, Britain continued with its two-phase plan to issue passports to 50,000 heads of households from Hong Kong, with 43,500 to be distributed in 1991 and the remaining 6,500 after 1993. The British government, with smug optimism, printed one million application forms for the passports, expecting a deluge of applications before the February 28, 1991, deadline. But the first phase of the passport plan attracted only 60,000 applications, or about 20 percent of the 300,000 that were expected.

Some government officials suggested that most Hong Kong residents decided against applying because they believed they probably would not meet the qualifications of the complex plan. According to Paul C.K. Kwong, a demographer specializing in emigration trends, "Anyone who could fill out the 32-page application for the British plan, and make his way through all its thick, pseudo-legal language, would be educated enough to go to the United States or Canada or Australia, which are the preferred destinations of Hong Kong people." Kwong also said the United States, Canada and Australia are "places people think of as open, fair, full of opportunity, and Britain is just not seen that way."[12]

Robert Broadfoot, head of Hong Kong's Political and Economic Risk Consultancy, described the low number of applicants as "a classic case of Hong Kong civil servants misreading the Hong Kong people." As Broadfoot explained, "There were people with good hearts, saying we have to help people here who face a future under the Communists. But the thing is, Hong Kong people have never longed to live in Britain. They don't like its economy or its weather, and if they want to escape the Communists, there are plenty of places they would rather go than Britain."[13]

Hong Kong businessman Simon Murray, head of the conglomerate Hutchison Whampoa and a pressure group called Honour Hong Kong, characterized as "sublime conceit" the worries of British citizens that Hong Kong citizens would want to move to Great Britain.

Meanwhile, in a history-making event, Hong Kong residents were preparing to choose 18 members of the 60-member Legislative Council by direct vote. Fifty-four candidates competed for the 18 Legco seats, campaigning mostly by knocking on doors, shaking hands and handing out leaflets, since the Hong Kong government did not allow political commercials on television and radio. Also, broadcast news programs in Hong Kong declined to cover the election campaigns because of restrictive government equal-time regulations.

CHAPTER 14

Pro-Democracy Candidates Dominate First Direct Elections

"The people here have clearly shown they want democracy, and not only that, they want it knowing they run the risk of offending China."

Martin Lee, leading vote-getter in first
Legislative Council elections (1991)[1]

The first-ever direct legislative elections in Hong Kong offered something for everyone – opinions, rhetoric, campaigning, confrontation, arguments and, most of all, participation. Sixteen of the eighteen elected seats were won by pro-democracy proponents, with the other two won by an independent and a pro-business candidate. The remaining 40 seats in the Legislative Council would either be appointed by the Hong Kong governor or indirectly elected by constituency groups relating to legal, medical and education professions, as well as banking, tourism and other business concerns.

Many of the candidates were openly supported by China, and the campaign included firm warnings in China-controlled newspapers against supporting pro-democratic candidates. Xinhua routinely reported on the election without calling attention to the fact that China-supported candidates were soundly defeated. Also, there was no immediate post-election response by the Chinese leadership.

Analysts were quick to maintain that election results reflected the desire of Hong Kong residents to choose their own political leaders, although the turnout of 39.2 percent of the 1.9 million registered voters was considerably lighter than desired. (Another 2 million eligible voters failed to register.) Government officials had projected that the elections would attract at least 50 percent of the registered voters.

One of Hong Kong's most outspoken pro-democracy leaders, 53-year-old lawyer Martin Lee, received more votes than any of the other 53 candidates seeking the 18 seats in Legco. Lee said he believed the election showed "there is no doubt that the people wish to have democracy now, like any other people in the world."[2]

Before the election , Martin Lee was a popular figure in Hong Kong and a leader in the pro-democracy movement. A former chairman of the Hong Kong Bar Association, he was chosen in 1985 to represent the constituency of lawyers in the Legislative Council. Lee may have gotten some of his leadership qualities from his father, a Chinese general who led mainland troops against the Japanese invasion before World War II and later moved to Hong Kong to escape the Communist takeover.

When China criticized the British for plans to introduce direct voting in Hong Kong, Lee began criticizing Beijing for interfering in Hong Kong affairs. Through the late 1980s, he became even more outspoken in his belief that Hong Kong needed more democracy before the 1997 handover. After the June 1989 military crackdown in Beijing's Tiananmen Square, Lee and fellow pro-democracy advocate Szeto Wah, an educator, led hundreds of thousands of people in a march in Hong Kong to protest the violent suppression. Beijing responded by branding Lee as subversive. Even some of Hong Kong's appointed legislators cautioned Lee that his "confrontational" politics could upset Beijing and disturb their plans for "stability and prosperity."[3]

When asked about reasons for his public support, Lee said, "I am well liked here principally because I speak up for the people. They see I am bold enough to defend them, even from the Chinese government. I always represent Hong Kong interests—not Britain's interests, or China's, but Hong Kong's."[4]

Another analysis was made by Ian Scott, head of Hong Kong University's political science department: "Voters have been pretty emphatic in declaring they want more say in the policy-making process here." Scott called the election of 18 Legco members as "a triumph for the Hong Kong middle class, which has been excluded from power by traditional business elites [who usually receive government appointments]." Scott described the election winners as "a small, vocal opposition party whose members speak with moral authority." At the same time, reflecting much of Hong Kong's general sense of pragmatic acceptance, Scott said, "Everyone knows nothing much will change about the way Hong Kong is governed or the amount of democracy here until the leadership in China has changed."[5]

The Mall at Pacific Place on Queensway is filled with boutiques, shops, stores, restaurants and a movie complex.

Hong Kong's Legislative Council, in a surprising move of defiance, decided in December 1991 to allow the appointment of foreign judges to all five seats in the Court of Final Appeal, Hong Kong's highest court after July 1, 1997. Expressing its collective confidence following the first direct legislative elections, Legco voted 34 to 11 against limiting the number of foreign judges on tribunal.

The vote marked the first time ever that Legco had rejected a decision or colonial law by Britain, which had decided under pressure from Beijing that the post–1997 supreme court for Hong Kong should include only one foreign judge. Legislators argued that judges from Canada, Britain, United States and other common law countries on the Court of Final Appeal would be less influenced by political pressures in their decisions. At the same time, as some analysts noted, decisions of the Court of Final Appeal would not actually be final, but subject to review by the Standing Committee of China's National People's Congress.

The financial situation in Hong Kong remained uppermost in the minds and comments of international analysts, who apparently overlooked China's ancient attitude of maintaining total control of its territory and people before all other considerations. "Hong Kong is the prime driver of the greatest economic takeoff in world history," said William H. Overholt, executive director of Bankers Trust Company in Hong Kong. "It's much more important to China than New York is to the United States."[6] China's growing economic position in the world community in 1992 seemed almost dependent on Hong Kong's continued status as a financial center. As noted by Richard Y.C. Wong, head of the Hong Kong Center for Economic Research at Chinese University, "If Hong Kong were to disappear in an earthquake, China's economic activity would slowly grind to a half. There is no economic center in China."[7]

Emigration from Hong Kong continued at a high rate during 1990 and 1991, causing a serious labor shortage that in turn attracted large numbers of illegal immigrants from mainland China. Hong Kong officials reported returning some 33,000 Chinese to China in 1991, plus another 5,000 in January and February of 1992.

It was announced in late December 1991 that Hong Kong Governor David Wilson would soon be retiring and joining the British House of Lords. Wilson, who became governor following the death in 1986 of Edward Youde, had a precarious term, trying to defend the best interests of Hong Kong while at the same time trying to avoid upsetting China. Wilson had been heavily criticized by pro-democracy leaders for not working hard enough to guarantee more political freedom in Hong Kong before 1997. He also was under considerable pressure from China to suppress organized anti–Beijing activities in Hong Kong, especially following the June 1989 Tiananmen Square crackdown.

Wilson's replacement was announced in April 1992. Chris Patten, who as chairman of Britain's Conservative Party guided the successful re-election campaign of British Prime Minister John Major, would become governor of Hong Kong in July 1992.

CHAPTER 15

Changing of the Guard: Chris Patten Arrives in Hong Kong

"The new governor will bear an awesome responsibility for handing over, against its wishes, a free community, thriving under capitalism, to a Communist dictatorship."

Martin Ivens, political commentator (1992)[1]

Chris Patten stepped into one of the world's greatest political assignments when he agreed to become governor of Hong Kong at the request of British Prime Minister John Major. After spending a few days in France considering the offer, Patten decided to accept the job, perhaps as much for its challenges as for its perks—it made him Britain's highest-paid civil servant. At the same time, he needed a job. He spent so much time promoting the Conservative Party campaign to re-elect John Major that he lost re-election to his own seat in the House of Commons.

In accepting the post of governor, the 47-year-old Patten said he hoped "to demonstrate by the way I do the job in the next five years and by my commitment to the interests of the people of Hong Kong that I was the right appointment." He described the governorship as "immensely interesting" and "one of the most important jobs in the public service," promising to safeguard "the interests of the people of Hong Kong" and "first and foremost to uphold the interests of all the people of Hong Kong."[2]

Prime Minister John Major said Patten, as the twenty-eighth and newest governor of Hong Kong, "will have a vital job to do at a crucial time. No one could do it better. It is one of the government's highest priorities to manage the transition to 1997 so as to safeguard Hong

Kong's freedom, stability and prosperity."[3] Major also said Patten was "as tough as old boots," adding: "There are enormous advantages in having a governor of Chris Patten's political experience and seniority."[4]

In a brief congratulatory statement upon the appointment of Patten as governor of Hong Kong, the Chinese embassy in London said, "We hope that Mr. Patten will continue to maintain the close cooperation with the Chinese side to ensure the continued prosperity and stability of Hong Kong and the smooth transfer of power in 1997. This is where the common interests of China and Britain lie."[5]

Chris Patten's governorship of Hong Kong included a tax-free salary of 152,000 British pounds annually (then about $273,000 in American dollars), plus £2,800 monthly for expenses. In addition, he would have the use of a Rolls-Royce, two Daimlers, a 90-foot yacht, a helicopter, a weekend villa and Government House, the official residence of the governor, with its carefully landscaped gardens and remarkable view of the Hong Kong harbor and shoreside skyscrapers. The annual budget for the governor's residence, with its staff of 56, totaled nearly $1.5 million.

Most citizens of Hong Kong realized, at least inwardly, that Chris Patten would preside over the unraveling of the final protective threads of the silk barrier between China and Great Britain during the transition to full control by mainland China. Expectations were high, though guarded. One of the leading pro-democracy advocates, Emily Lau, elected to the Legislative Council in 1991, acknowledged the lack of political thinking in Hong Kong, which had been guided and protected by Great Britain for one and one-half centuries. "Most of my parents' generation were refugees, and thought they would one day go back to China," said Lau, a journalist in Hong Kong before accepting a position as assistant producer with the BBC in London. "Then, when they realized they couldn't, they were very grateful to the British for protecting them and looking after them. Many concentrated on making enough money to emigrate, which has always been a Hong Kong phenomenon, and means that nobody ever thinks anything is permanent."[6]

Lau said the problem also was affected by conflicting feelings. "On the one hand, they are scared by Communism," she said. "Most still have relatives in China and are keenly aware of the huge gap in freedom and living standards between the communist and capitalist systems. On the other hand, they are proud Chinese who do not want colonial rule." Some of the conflict could be attributed to education. "We were taught absolutely nothing about politics at school," she said. "We didn't know what communism and democracy meant."[7] Lau returned to Hong Kong after China and Britain signed the 1984 Joint Declaration, saying: "Hong Kong is not a country. The people in Hong Kong are not proud of saying 'I am a Hong Kong person.' There is no proper word for it. 'Hong Konger' sounds grotesque, but Hong Kong is my only real home. I had to be there when it was in trouble."[8]

Meanwhile, another sign of convergence occurred on April 22 when the British Army relinquished control over its 25-year assignment at the border of Hong Kong and China. The change, handing over border control to Hong Kong police, was held at Sandy Spur, a remote site overlooking Shenzhen, one of China's special economic zones.

China began trying to assert its influence on the new governor even before Chris Patten arrived in Hong Kong. In June, China cautioned the incoming governor against appointing any pro-democracy advocates to the Executive Council (Exco), which is responsible for policy-making. Guo Fengmin, head of China's delegation to the Sino-British Joint Liaison Group, said: "It is the view of the Chinese government that to appoint those who are opposed to the Basic Law and who openly advocate the subversion of the legitimate government of China is not in the interests of Hong Kong's prosperity and stability. Therefore, we are opposed to any such appointments."[9]

Patten responded a few days later in London, telling journalists that all appointments to Exco were matters for him alone to decide. Nevertheless, the Beijing-controlled Xinhua news agency in Hong Kong cautioned Patten against "unfavorable" appointments, saying one of his most crucial concerns would be handling "the relationship with China correctly, to reduce unnecessary impacts and ensure a smooth transition."[10]

Chris Patten arrived in Hong Kong on July 9, was greeted by a 17-gun salute and took the oath as the territory's twenty-eighth governor and the one appointed to preside over its transition from British to Chinese rule in 1997. The elaborate ceremonies for Patten began when he stepped from his yacht *The Lady Maureen* onto shore and walked to a podium to music from the Gurkha Rifles massed bands. There were officials wearing pith helmets, white gloves and swords and a cheering crowd of several thousand Chinese. The bands played "The Duke of York March" while Patten stepped up to the podium, watched proudly by his wife Lavender and their two daughters, 13-year-old Alice and 17-year-old Laura. Patten's first official speech in Hong Kong included all of his previous promises: "I pledge to devote all my energy to representing the interests of the people of Hong Kong as strongly and wisely as I can. I will stand up for Hong Kong as you would wish me to do, courteously and firmly. Good cooperation with China is my sincere aim and my profound wish. It is vital for the next years, vital for Hong Kong."[11]

Mainland China's state-operated television network failed to report on the swearing-in of Patten as Hong Kong governor. However, Wu Jianmin of China's Foreign Ministry issued a statement encouraging Patten to "make contributions to promoting continued development of the friendly relations of cooperation on the question of Hong Kong between China and Britain, to maintaining Hong Kong's long-term stability and prosperity and to guaranteeing Hong Kong's smooth transition and smooth transfer of government in 1997."[12]

Meanwhile, tensions between China and Britain climbed to new levels in mid–1992 during continued negotiations regarding preparations for the 1997 handover of Hong Kong to China. Although Beijing criticized spending plans for Hong Kong's new airport, most observers maintained that China was actually trying to undermine Britain's insistence on increasing democracy for the territory. China's endorsement of the spending was vital in attracting investors for the airport project.

Talks in Beijing on the airport financing dispute before Patten's arrival were at a stalemate, with the Chinese insisting "a large number of problems" had to be resolved and that their objections were in the best interests of Hong Kong. "At the moment, the Chinese side has no way of endorsing the financing arrangements, because we and all walks of life in Hong Kong society have doubts about it," said Chen Zuoer of Beijing's Hong Kong and Macau Affairs Office.[13] In another statement some days later, he said: "We cannot spend money lavishly which the Hong Kong people have accumulated over so many years, turning the new airport project into a tiger's mouth to swallow the wealth of the Hong Kong people."[14]

Beijing's constant stream of threats, warnings and statements regarding financing of the new airport finally forced David Ford, Hong Kong's chief secretary, to break a long-held secret in announcing that Hong Kong had reserves totaling $3.2 billion. However, the announcement had little impact on Beijing. Chen Zuoer's response was that "Britain has no right to say it is leaving [the reserves] to the future Hong Kong government as if it were charity."[15]

Pro-democracy leader Martin Lee said he believed "the Chinese are a little panicky as to whether the British government will adopt a different stance on China. They are making use of the airport to show the British who's the master." Lee said he hoped Britain would continue to support increased democracy in Hong Kong, stressing: "Once you kowtow to Beijing again and again, then Beijing expects you to be on your knees forever."[16]

CHAPTER 16

China Denounces Patten's Plans for Political Reforms

"I very much recognize we will have a number of tough and difficult problems to cope with in the next few years. The most important thing, I think, is to get to know each other."
Chris Patten, Governor of Hong Kong (1992)[1]

"Typhoon Chris," in his maiden speech as governor of the world's most prestigious colony, challenged the cooperation of China's leadership when he proposed increasing voter participation in Hong Kong. He drew immediate criticism from the Chinese leadership, who called his proposals "irresponsible and imprudent," warning that any changes before 1997 could be in violation of the 1984 Joint Declaration between China and Britain. The statement added that "the Chinese side will not be responsible for any arguments caused."[2] In addition, China said any proposals by Patten for reforms in Hong Kong should first be discussed with Beijing. The Chinese leadership had plenty of time to contemplate its response to Patten's proposals, since British Foreign Secretary Douglas Hurd gave a copy of his speech to senior Chinese officials in New York two weeks before Patten made them public in his appearance before Hong Kong's Legislative and Executive councils.

British officials had been hoping for support from China for possible changes in Hong Kong's immediate future but were pleased that the Chinese did not prematurely disclose the proposals. In his speech, Patten proposed a formula to widen Hong Kong's electorate, saying, "Democracy is more than just a philosophical idea. It is, for instance, an essential element in the pursuit of economic progress."[3] The *London Times* called Patten's two-hour address to Hong Kong's legislators "the most important speech of his career."[4]

Under Patten's proposed formula for the 1995 elections, 10 of the 60 available legislative seats would be appointed by the governor, while residents of Hong Kong would vote directly for 20 seats (up from 18 in 1991), leaving 30 "functional constituency" seats to be decided by voting from all working residents. The plan would raise voter participation for functional constituencies from 110,000 in 1992 to an estimated 2.7 million potential voters without increasing the number of legislative seats to be decided by direct election. He also called for lowering the voting age from 21 to 18 and proposed direct voting for all candidates of district and municipal boards in Hong Kong, positions which had always been filled by appointment. China's Foreign Ministry issued a statement calling Patten's proposals "major political changes" that could disrupt Hong Kong's transition in 1997.

In addition, Patten outlined new spending plans to improve welfare and social services for residents of Hong Kong. An editorial in *Ta Kung Pao*, a pro–Beijing newspaper in Hong Kong, criticized any new spending for social services: "Without China's support, the through train will not go through and the vast rose garden could be turned into ashes under the controversy stirred up by Patten."[5]

Patten delivered his speech to Hong Kong legislators on Thursday, October 7, arranging to discuss his proposals the same day during a two-hour live and phone-in appearance on Hong Kong radio. In addition, he scheduled four public forums—the first one on that same Thursday and the second one on Friday, with 1,400 free tickets available to each session. Tickets for the first two public sessions were gone within 20 minutes.

Patten wasted no time in testing his status with China, beginning a three-day official visit to Beijing on October 20. Following a six-hour discussion the next day with Lu Ping, the 65-year-old head of China's Hong Kong and Macau Affairs Office, Patten described the meeting as "very serious, very thoughtful and conducted—however vigorously—in a civilized manner."[6] He acknowledged that he gave considerable attention to explaining his proposals for political reform, which he said reflected a "broad balance of opinion" of Hong Kong residents. "I cannot say we reached a meeting of minds on what I put forward," Patten said. "There was progress in the sense that we spent six hours together and I think we got to know one another's positions and got to know one another a good deal better."[7]

Patten met on October 22 with Chinese Foreign Minister Qian Qichen, who accused him of trying to provoke the Beijing government with his proposals for more democracy in Hong Kong. "We want cooperation rather than confrontation," Qian said, describing Patten's democratic reform proposals as a "challenge to cooperation."[8] Even more bluntly, Qian said Patten's proposals "run counter to the provisions and spirit of the Joint Declaration"[9] and accused him of "jeopardizing the prosperity and stability of Hong Kong and placing obstacles before the smooth transition of Hong Kong in 1997."[10]

The question of China's support for financing development of Hong Kong's new airport also was touched on briefly during the talks, but without any reported progress. Patten said he hoped Beijing would eventually agree to the financing plans, but that he was prepared to proceed without it.

Immediately after Patten left Beijing, Lu Ping issued a strong statement warning that if Patten insisted on pursuing more democracy for Hong Kong, Beijing would disband its Legislative Council and establish a new one, with different member requirements, after the 1997 handover. Repeating the rhetoric of Chinese Foreign Minister Qian Qichen, Lu said: "The essence of our differences is not whether the pace of democracy should be accelerated. The essence is whether there should be cooperation or there should be confrontation. Of course, the Chinese side does not wish to seek confrontation. . . . Now we have to see if the British side has the sincerity to seek a smooth transfer."[11]

Lu also said any move by Patten to go ahead with the airport project without Beijing's consent would be in violation of the Memorandum of Understanding between China and Britain. He also suggested that the issue might lead to a decision by China against allowing airplanes using the Chek Lap Kok airport from entering Chinese airspace.

Included in the warnings directed at Patten by Lu was a surprising reference to a "secret" agreement for direct elections to Hong Kong's Legislative Council in 1995. Lu said plans for the 1995 elections were agreed upon secretly in 1990 by Chinese Foreign Minister Qian Qichen and British Foreign Secretary Douglas Hurd. The disclosure occurred when Lu said Patten's proposals for election reforms were in violation of that secret agreement. When questioned by Hong Kong legislators, Patten said there had been "diplomatic exchanges" regarding the 1995 elections, but no secret agreements. British officials confirmed there had been a "series of exchanges" in January and February of 1990 as part of Britain's diplomatic effort to conclude talks on the Basic Law.

Texts of the "diplomatic exchanges" were published on October 29,

first by Hong Kong and then by Beijing. Chris Patten said the 50 pages
of documents showed clearly that no secret arrangement had been
made to limit direct elections in 1995. "In view of the allegations that
were made, there was no choice but for me to make these documents
public," Patten said. Beijing maintained, however, that diplomats had
agreed on "key elements" on the 1995 elections and that making the
documents public would "enable the public to know the truth about the
understanding reached by the Chinese and British sides."[12]

In general, the series of diplomatic letters suggested that negotiators agreed only to continue studying certain key proposals regarding the election, without reaching any final agreement. One government official said: "In the end, the negotiations broke off because
China wouldn't agree to more directly elected seats." He summed up
the British view of the meetings by saying, "There's no agreement
here."[13]

Patten's "confrontational" approach to broaden democracy in the
territory received divided support during a six-hour debate on
November 11 by the Hong Kong Legislative Council. Legislators finally
voted 32–21 to approve a motion backing Patten's proposals in future
discussions with China, urging particular attention for "openness,
fairness and acceptability to the people of Hong Kong."[14]

One of the key sponsors of the motion, Jimmy McGregor, argued,
"We must not be frightened by China nor accept bullying by Chinese
officials. We have a strong case for reform and we must answer to our
consciences and ultimately to the people of Hong Kong."[15] Xinhua
downplayed the vote, saying the debate was conducted under pressure
from Britain and that the legislature was only "a consultative body to
the governor."[16]

Patten insisted that his plans for more democracy completely con-
formed with provisions of the Basic Law, but Lu Ping later disputed Patten's claim again: "Only the Standing Committee of the Chinese
National People's Congress has the right to interpret the Basic Law. The
British side has no such right."[17] Lu also threatened that if Patten continued to push for reforms, Beijing would ignore them and establish new
legislative, executive and judicial councils for Hong Kong.

Lu's warnings were strengthened in early November, when the
NPC's Standing Committee also cautioned Patten against proceeding
with his democratic reform proposals, saying it would have no choice
but to undo any changes in 1997. The Chinese view was stated by *Ta
Kung Pao*, which declared, "If the British side wants to give China

a 'stab in the back' during the remaining hours before sunset, the Chinese side will be forced to respond with a 'fatal weapon.'"[18] In an unusual personal attack on Patten, *Wen Wei Po*, another Beijing-supported publication, said: "Deep in his soul are all the deep-rooted bad habits of an extremely arrogant colonist who benefits himself at the expense of others."[19]

A Chinese official in London raised tensions further in mid-November by saying that continued efforts to increase the level of democracy in Hong Kong could force China to terminate the 1984 Joint Declaration. Chinese Deputy Prime Minister Zhu Rongji, quoted by Xinhua, said, "People cannot help but ask whether we still have to stick to the joint declaration. We regard it as a matter of principle, and the Chinese government and people have always been firm on matters of principle. We want cooperation, not confrontation, but no one should expect confrontation to force us into concessions."[20] Zhu's comments caused an immediate downward effect in Hong Kong's stock market; the Hang Seng Index of blue-chip stocks plunged 3 percent.

The Hong Kong government declined to respond to Zhu's remarks, though one official said: "It's a new ball game now, and quite a serious one."[21] Pro-democracy leader Martin Lee was much more vocal in his response: "Any threats made by the Chinese government not to honor the joint declaration will cause the international community to doubt China's commitment, not only to this agreement but to all its international agreements. Threats of this nature by the Chinese government often have a counter-effect, in that they serve only to encourage the people of Hong Kong to stand up for their interests."[22]

Chris Patten went to London in mid–November to meet with British Prime Minister John Major in an attempt to resolve the spiraling tension over Hong Kong and to encourage "calm and constructive and rational discussions" with China. At the same time, Patten said his democratic reform proposals had the support of Major. "We of course discussed our strategy for the weeks and months ahead and it remains our position that we are very happy to have discussions about positive proposals for the way forward with anyone, at any time, anywhere."[23]

Patten invited China to submit counter-proposals to his reforms, but said failure to reach any new agreement would cause him to proceed with the changes, despite objections by the Chinese. Responding to Patten's invitation, Chinese Prime Minister Li Peng said: "Any counter-proposal or any compromise plan on the basis of the Hong Kong governor's plan is unacceptable."[24] Li said China considered the issue "a matter of principle," adding: "The Chinese government will never compromise on matters of principle."[25]

Tensions escalated the next day when the Hong Kong government announced it would spend $1.2 billion for preparation work on its new airport, even though Beijing had refused to approve the financing. Officials said further postponement on the site preparation contract would mean costly delays in construction. Robert Broadfoot, director of Hong Kong's Political and Economic Risk Consultancy, said the action would certainly upset Beijing, but added: "If the government had done nothing, it would have been tantamount to admitting any decision in Hong Kong already rests with Beijing."[26]

The influence of China's threats against Chris Patten and his reforms was also being felt by business leaders in Hong Kong, who were concerned for their own financial futures after the 1997 handover. Vincent H.S. Lo, head of the Hong Kong Business and Professionals Federation, said his group believed Patten should withdraw some of his proposals. "To run the risk of developing a political system that will likely be dismantled in four and a half year's time is just not acceptable to us," Lo said.[27]

China turned its focus on the entire world in late November when the *People's Daily* in Beijing published a front-page story cautioning other countries against supporting Chris Patten's proposals for democratic reform in Hong Kong: "Foreign countries who support Patten's proposals are helping to wreak chaos and disaster on the people of Hong Kong," the story said. "Creating chaos will not only bring calamity to the people of Hong Kong, but will harm the interests of investors of every nationality."[28]

The article maintained that the issue of Hong Kong was a matter for Britain and China to resolve, warning other countries to refrain from involvement. Support for Patten and his proposals had already been given by the United States, Canada and Australia. The U.S. State Department characterized the reform proposals as a "constructive approach to the goal of the democratization of Hong Kong."

Tension in Hong Kong continued to heighten when China announced on November 30, 1992, that any contracts signed by Hong Kong but not approved by Beijing would be invalid on July 1, 1997, when Chinese rule assumed control over the territory.

The announcement, in retaliation against British efforts to broaden democracy in Hong Kong, said: "According to the Sino-British Joint Declaration, Britain's administrative power over Hong Kong will terminate on June 30, 1997, and it will then have no right to handle any affairs after the date. Accordingly, all contracts, leases and agreements signed or ratified by the Hong Kong British government will be valid until June 30, 1997." In addition, the statement said, "other contracts, lease and agreements signed and ratified by the Hong Kong British government which are not approved by the Chinese side will be invalid after June 30, 1997."[29]

Hong Kong officials issued an immediate response, maintaining that validity of thousands of contracts extending beyond 1997 was assured through 2047 by provisions of the 1984 Chinese-British Joint Declaration and the Basic Law. In a written statement issued November 30, the Hong Kong government said: "According to the Basic Law, contracts which are valid under Hong Kong's existing laws will continue to be valid and recognized and protected by the Hong Kong Special Administrative Region, provided that they do not contravene the Basic Law."[30]

Emily Lau, a Hong Kong legislator, described China's announcement as "horrific." She said Chinese officials were "intimidating the Hong Kong people. They're trying to bring Hong Kong to its knees. They will resort to anything."[31] One American businessman voiced the concerns of many: "If you've done business with the Hong Kong government, which is itself a large contractor, you have to ask yourself: What is the validity of that contract?"[32]

Pro-democracy leader Martin Lee said China had become accustomed to getting its way, noting that Patten was "suffering from that aftermath of a long period of British kowtowing to the Chinese."[33] A retired shop owner who fled from China in the early 1950s summed up the general feeling of most Hong Kongers: "We don't believe we have any control over events. So we just wait and see what happens."[34]

Hong Kong's stock market reflected the nervousness of investors raised by the barrage of warnings and responses between China and Hong Kong. The blue-chip Hang Seng Index plunged nearly 17 percent in four days, closing on December 3 at 4,978 – down 23 percent from its all-time high of 6,470 just three weeks earlier in November. Some analysts said many of the companies affected by the downturn were mainland Chinese, indicating that Beijing was placing political control above financial security.

CHAPTER 17

On the Road to Chinese Rule

> *"I think that it is sometimes the case that words mean different things to Chinese officials. I think what the word 'sincerity' means to some Chinese officials is—everybody else in the world must agree with us, otherwise they are not being sincere."*
> Chris Patten, Governor of Hong Kong (1993)[1]

Hong Kong's convergence with Chinese rule became more evident in 1993, especially involving money—its favorite commodity. New coins began circulating which featured Hong Kong's official flower, the bauhinia, instead of the profile of Queen Elizabeth II. Another sign was the announcement by the Bank of China that it had won approval from the Hong Kong government to issue bank notes beginning in May of 1994, joining two other commercial banks, Hongkong & Shanghai Banking Corporation and Standard Chartered Bank.

Still another sign was the introduction in Hong Kong schools of classes in Mandarin ("Putonghua"), encouraged in China as the universal language. Mandarin practice was encouraged by twice-daily television news programs ("Putonghua News") in Hong Kong, where the primary Chinese dialect was Cantonese. Perhaps most illuminating was a decision by Beijing to establish a "preparatory committee" for Hong Kong three years sooner than originally scheduled.

Hong Kong Governor Chris Patten began 1993 with his usual optimism and no indications of backing down under continued pressure from Beijing. The Legislative Council (Legco) also continued its support of the governor, defeating 35–2 a Beijing-backed proposal calling for Patten to end his efforts to increase democracy and consult with China before making any decisions affecting the future of Hong Kong. Political analysts said the lopsided vote (with 15 abstentions and 7 absences) indicated that legislators wanted to play a major role in the run-up to 1997.

Under terms of a 1991 "memorandum of understanding," foreign ministers of China and Britain were to meet twice a year to review transition progress for Hong Kong, but the talks became stalemated over disputed financing plans for Hong Kong's new airport. No statement was issued after the September 1992 meeting, and Beijing hinted in January 1993 that abandoning the proposed political reforms might be a condition for resuming the negotiations.

Lu Ping, head of the Hong Kong and Macau Affairs Office, said relations between China and Britain could improve if Patten would withdraw his proposals for democratic reform. "Hong Kong is not an independent political entity and is therefore hardly likely to survive if it confronts China," Lu said in a television interview. "If Hong Kong is to confront China, Hong Kong people may have to face a lot of hardship."[2]

Zhou Nan, head of the Xinhua branch in Hong Kong, told an interviewer in February that Chris Patten's announcement proposing political reforms was "completely unexpected." Zhou said agreements on political changes were already included in the Basic Law for Hong Kong, approved by China in 1990, adding that Patten's new proposals "violated the Joint Declaration, the Basic Law and Sino-British agreements."

Zhou also called for greater cooperation with Britain in the transition of Hong Kong to Chinese rule. "To better handle Sino-British relations and the question of Hong Kong, the British must clearly understand China's national conditions and its people's sentiments," he said. "To realize independence and reunification of our country has been a goal for which the Chinese people have fought for a long time, and the irresistible national sentiments of more than a billion Chinese people at home and abroad support this aim."[3]

Also in February, Hong Kong's Executive Council (Exco) offered its endorsement of Patten's democratic reform plans, backing up the previous endorsement by the Legislative Council. The action was taken about two weeks before Legco was scheduled to debate the proposals.

Patten Delays Election Reform Proposals

In early March, Patten advised the Legislative Council that he would delay formal publication and debate on his election reform proposals because of plans by China and Britain to resume negotiations on the transition of Hong Kong to Chinese rule. Increased diplomatic activity in Beijing ("talks about talks") during February indicated possible resumption of the talks, after which Patten said "we judge it best" to delay, for the third time, publishing the proposals and scheduling legislative debate. "We wished to give every opportunity for the Chinese side to respond," Patten said. "We received a positive response on the principle of talks."[4]

Martin Lee said Patten's delays appeared to represent manipulation by China. "I think the Hong Kong people welcome talks because they would like to see a democratic system being agreed between the two governments," Lee said. "But the impression we get, unfortunately, is that the governor is being led by the nose by the Chinese side even before they sit down at the conference table."[5]

When talks between China and Britain failed to begin by mid-March, Patten decided to publish his long-delayed reform legislation, clearing the way for debate by the Legislative Council. Patten told legislators, "Despite our hopes and our best endeavors right up until this afternoon, it has so far not proved possible to resolve the differences between the British and Chinese that stand in the way of talks getting under way."[6] The action brought a quick and angry response by Beijing, issued through Xinhua: "This means there is no way to continue talks, and it is all caused by Mr. Patten."[7] Patten's announcement was also reflected by a 3.1 percent plunge in the Hang Seng Index.

Chinese Prime Minister Li Peng raised tensions further in remarks to open the National People's Congress in Beijing. Li accused Patten of "perfidiously and unilaterally" violating Sino-British agreements by making changes in Hong Kong's political system. "The British government shall be held exclusively responsible for all serious consequences arising from its action," Li warned, without specifying the possible consequences.

Li also said Patten's plans for reform would "impede the smooth transfer of power," adding that China's resumption of sovereignty over Hong Kong was a fundamental right "which shall not be interfered with or sabotaged in any way."[8] Patten called Li Peng's outburst a "disap-

The Tian Tan Buddha at Po Lin Monastery on Hong Kong's Lantau Island is the world's largest bronze Buddha, standing seven stories high. Inaugurated in December 1993, it was financed entirely by donations.

pointing turn of events" and promised to continue working "positively and constructively" on the future of Hong Kong. "I want to work hard for Hong Kong, the Hong Kong government wants to work hard for the ordinary people of Hong Kong, " he said. "It is their interests we have in mind, and I am not sure why anyone would think their interests are served by excessive language."[9]

Xinhua director Zhou Nan also defended China's resumption of sovereignty over Hong Kong, calling it "a sacred right of China which brooks no interference or sabotage," adding: "Anyone who dreams of hindering this historical process will only eat their own bitter fruit in the end." More confusingly, Zhou said Patten's proposed reforms would "set up barriers for China's resumption of sovereignty over Hong Kong under the guise of democracy in an attempt to turn Hong Kong into a semi-independent political entity with a view to continuing, in another guise, Britain's colonial rule there after 1997."[10]

Jimmy McGregor, representing the Hong Kong Chamber of Commerce in the Legislative Council, said, "We have come to a crossroads, and China will have to decide whether it wants to take over a thoroughly good going concern, one of the economic miracles of the world, or whether it wants to continue to bash the Hong Kong government and governor all the way to 1997."[11] Commenting on Beijing-supported pressure against Patten, McGregor said: "I am aware many businessmen support Mr. Patten in principle and even in regard to some of his proposals, but they dare not say so publicly because they do substantial business in or with China. I am one of the few businessmen who do business with China who publicly support the governor. I think it is a very sad situation."[12]

The situation heated up in late March when Chinese Foreign Minister Qian Qichen announced he would not meet as scheduled with British Foreign Secretary Douglas Hurd and openly called for Britain to remove Chris Patten from his post as governor of Hong Kong. The announcement broke the pattern of twice-yearly sessions between China and Britain on the transition of Hong Kong. Qian also said, "If the package put forward by Mr. Patten is to be submitted to the Legislative Council for its deliberation in the form of draft legislation before the two sides reach agreement, it will not help with talks."[13]

Finally, a long-awaited agreement was announced in mid–April that negotiations would soon resume between China and Britain on rules for the 1995 elections in Hong Kong. The announcement, ending six months of diplomatic tension, was welcomed by Chris Patten as "a victory for common sense." Patten, in London to meet with British officials, said he was hopeful the negotiations would produce "an agreement on proposals which are fair and acceptable to the people of Hong Kong."[14] The announcement also implied that Beijing would stop insisting that Patten abandon his plans for election reforms. Patten had said previously he would delay submitting his proposals to the Legislative Council for debate if negotiations resumed between China and Britain.

The stalemate in talks between China and Britain eased in July when Chinese Foreign Minister Qian Qichen met in Beijing with British Foreign Secretary Douglas Hurd in their first diplomatic session since September of 1992. Hurd also met with Chinese President Jiang Zemin and secured approval by China to begin reclamation work on a project related to Hong Kong's new multi-billion-dollar airport.

Beijing's plan to set up an advisory committee for Hong Kong in 1993 instead of 1996, as originally scheduled, was announced in April in a rare news conference by Chinese Prime Minister Li Peng: "We should establish a preparatory committee in 1996, but time is pressing and there is a lot of work to be done," Li said. "The purpose of that preparatory body is to ensure a smooth transition and to ensure the long-term stability of Hong Kong."[15] Li also cautioned that the dispute over increased democracy in Hong Kong could lead to economic problems between China and Britain. "We hope the current Chinese-British dispute on the Hong Kong issue will not affect economic relations between the two countries," he said. "But if the current relationship should deteriorate, I'm afraid that it cannot be said that the economic relations will not be affected to a certain extent."[16]

Chinese President Jiang Zemin established the 57-member Preliminary Working Committee (including 30 from Hong Kong) as an advance group for the Preparatory Committee on Hong Kong, scheduled to begin work in 1996 on the "smooth transition" of Hong Kong. In effect, it was a preparatory committee for the Preparatory Committee. Foreign Minister Qian Qichen said one task of the group would be to resolve differences between Hong Kong laws and the Basic Law before 1997.

Hong Kong Governor Chris Patten, upset over continued delays in resolving proposals for the 1995 elections, announced in September that the absence of an agreement would force him to submit his reform plans to the Legislative Council, despite objections by Beijing. "Sooner or later," he said, "we will have to make the necessary administrative and legislative arrangements."[17] Patten's warning came on the eve of the tenth round of secret talks between China and Britain, and may have been designed to speed up progress towards an agreement, especially on a provision that would allow direct voting in 1995 by all of Hong Kong's working residents. "I hope it is still possible to build a bridge on which we can all happily stand," Patten said, "but the clock ticks on."[18]

Finally, in October, Patten acknowledged the failure of his yearlong effort to gain China's approval for plans to increase democracy in Hong Kong but said he would ask Legco to make the changes anyway. "I can say that we can only be as bold as you," Patten told legislators. "If we are not prepared to stand up for Hong Kong's way of life today, what chance of doing so tomorrow?"[19] Patten followed through with his promises in December, after 17 rounds of talks between China and Britain without any agreement on his election reform proposals, by formally submitting legislation that would increase democratic participation in Hong Kong.

The legislation, targeting municipal and legislative elections in 1994 and 1995, called for abolishing appointed members to local government groups, adjusting constituency representation in the legislature and lowering the voting age from 21 to 18. Beijing countered by declaring that after 1997 it would disband all elected bodies in Hong Kong, including the Legislative Council, and would determine if existing Hong Kong laws should remain in effect.

Chinese Foreign Minister Qian Qichen, in a well-publicized speech in New York, said Patten should abandon his efforts to increase democracy in Hong Kong, warning that results of the 1995 elections could be overturned by China in 1997. Qian said China could "change the existing government line-up" without a satisfactory resolution of the dispute. Patten described Qian's remarks as "neither accurate nor helpful."[20]

Meanwhile, the ongoing publicity surrounding Hong Kong, although upsetting to diplomats and government officials, contributed to increased interest by tourists in 1993. The Hong Kong Tourist Association reported that nearly 5 million foreign visitors came to Hong Kong between January and August, up 13 percent from the same period in 1992. The figures included more than 1 million from Taiwan and just under 1 million from mainland China. Travel agents said one significant reason for the upward trend in tourism was the publicity about the 1997 handover of Hong Kong to China. Visitors wanted to experience the city before its change to Chinese rule, and many expressed interest in experiencing the actual change. Despite repeated requests, however, all of Hong Kong's thousands of hotel rooms were booked up years in advance for the historic July 1, 1997, event.

CHAPTER 18

Hong Kong in 1997 and Beyond

"Hong Kong is a gyroscope. In order to remain balanced, it must maintain its incessant, dizzy motion. Only when it ceases to change will it have truly changed beyond recognition."
Simon Barnes, British journalist (1994)[1]

Governor Chris Patten, presiding over Hong Kong's building boom, volatile stock market, rising tourism and surplus budgets, continued to push for expanded democracy in 1994, despite repeated warnings from Beijing that any of his political reforms would be overturned in 1997. The "first phase" of Patten's proposed reforms, including a provision for lowering the voting age from 21 to 18, was approved in February by the Legislative Council after more than eight hours of debate. The bill also established single-member voting districts in the 1994 and 1995 local district council elections and give Hong Kong members of China's National People's Congress the right to seek political office in Hong Kong.

In the debate, unusual in its high level of emotion and confrontation among legislators, proponents of reforms argued with pro-business members who wanted to delay action until after China and Britain reached a negotiated settlement on election requirements. Patten said passage of the reforms could wait no longer, insisting they were needed to provide political security for Hong Kong after its 1997 handover to China.

Legislator Cheung Man-kwong, urging others to stand up against pressure from Beijing, argued, "Being a lonely fighter is bound to be painful, but the fruits to be enjoyed by Hong Kong people will be sweet because we will be winning democracy and a high degree of autonomy."[2]

Shen Guofeng, a spokesman for China's Foreign Ministry, responded to the Legislative Council's approval of Patten's "first phase" of election reforms by announcing that any political changes in Hong Kong "will definitely be terminated together with the end of the British administration. By that time," he said, "the political body of the Hong Kong Special Administrative Region will be formed according to the decisions of the Chinese National People's Congress and the relevant provisions of the Basic Law." Shen also blamed Britain for "the disruption of cooperation between China and the United Kingdom on Hong Kong's political system" and said, "the door to negotiations has now been closed by the British side."[3]

In a move which provoked the Chinese leadership in late 1993, Patten published a "White Paper" disclosing an account of 17 secret negotiating sessions on his proposed election reforms between China and Britain. He said the document, of which 140,000 copies were made in Chinese and 60,000 in English, demonstrated an attempt to "obtain truth from facts," showing that throughout 170 hours of talks between October 1992 and November 1993, it was Britain, not China, that offered to compromise. Beijing promptly accused London of violating diplomatic confidence in the disclosure, even though *People's Daily* in China had already published a long interview with an unnamed "relevant person" which reviewed the negotiations from China's point of view.[4]

Patten said Hong Kong's Legislative Council was being asked to consider "a system of free and fair elections." The proposals, he said, would allow "every working person" to vote in the 1994 and 1995 elections, producing an outcome that could not be predetermined by Beijing. He said the reforms were vital for Hong Kong's future stability, adding, "Her Majesty's government and the governor have said repeatedly that they will not go further, or less far, than the people of Hong Kong want them to go."[5]

In late February, encouraged by the Legislative Council's endorsement of his first phase of electoral reforms, Patten followed up with his second phase—providing for direct and indirect elections (by constituencies) for all legislators in 1995. In other words, none would be appointed, a situation sure to antagonize Chinese leaders already upset over the proposed "violations" of the Joint Declaration and Basic Law for Hong Kong.

The business climate in Hong Kong, already apprehensive about 1997 and the dissension between China and Britain, entered 1994 on a very optimistic note. The Hang Seng Index, which had been rising to new levels for several weeks, exploded past the 12,000 mark in January, nearly doubling its level in March 1993. Analysts were quick to offer praise, such as Peter Jones, research director at M&G Unit Trusts: "Over the past year, Hong Kong has come of age. I think it is now one of the world's genuine stock markets. It is also a very important route in and out of China."[6] Nick Train of GT Unit Managers remarked, "I think the whole of Asia could well blow out in '94. It will be a case of 'mind your eye in Hong Kong' and be aware that most of the other markets have doubled from a not especially cheap base."[7]

On the first trading day of 1994, the Hang Seng advanced 198 points to 12,086, with most of the interest in property stocks because of recent record land sales and planned asset re-evaluations by property companies. The following day, encouraged by an influx of overseas buying, the Hang Seng went up another 1 percent to a new high of 12,201, then dropped 793 points the following day to 11,374 – marking its largest single-day decline since the worldwide stock market crash in October 1987. It dropped another 343 points on the last day of the week, influenced by heavy selling, with a record trading volume of 15.2 billion shares.

A London analyst, Heath Manners of Henderson Investment Management, called the sharp decline "inevitable, given the pace and extent of the recent rise of the market."[8] Amsterdam analyst Fermin Da Costa Gomez of Pacific Asset Management compared the Hong Kong stock market to a jet fighter that "kept going straight up until it stalled and began to fall. There is a definite risk factor assigned to Hong Kong," he said, "which doesn't justify it trading at current levels. It needs to take a breather."[9]

A week later, the Hang Seng declined to 10,176 – nearly 17 percent below its record high ten days earlier. The lower level encouraged some international investors to again buy into the Hong Kong market, but by mid–March the Hang Seng slipped even further, dropping to 9,720. Analysts said the continued decline was caused by "weak sentiment, with a total lack of buying interest" combined with short-term money flowing into Japan instead of Hong Kong.[10] By late March, the Hang Seng had dropped below 9,000 to 8,412 – its lowest level since October 1993.

Lu Ping of China's Hong Kong and Macau Affairs Office said in March that Beijing was concerned about the economic situation in Hong Kong, and particularly about soaring property prices, which he admitted

Only a handful of rickshaw operators are still licensed in Hong Kong. Their activities now include short runs along the harbor or posing for photographs near the Star Ferry Pier.

were partly due to speculation by mainland-funded companies. He said the situation was unfair to potential investors because Chinese-funded companies were using state funds to realize profits. "They can push up the prices of property without having to bear any responsibility," he said, promising to take steps to halt the practice.[11]

Lu also focused on rising residential property prices in Hong Kong: "Many people cannot afford to buy their own flats. This is a big problem. It hinges upon people's livelihood. It hinges on whether Hong Kong will be able to maintain its status as an international financial center." He said a sub-group of the China's Preliminary Working Committee would be established to review the property market in Hong Kong. "We will give suggestions to the British side. It's a matter for them as to whether to accept it," he said. "We will also listen to people from all walks of life on effective ways to deal with the problem. We will do as much as we can."[12]

China also announced that the Preliminary Working Committee (pwc) would begin working in 1994 on a study of public institutions in Hong Kong, including the legislature, with a goal of reshaping them for the period after July 1, 1997. The pwc, an advance advisory group to the Preparatory Committee, was directed by Chinese Premier Li Peng to develop "concrete methods for forming the first Legislative Council of the future Hong Kong sar and solving other urged problems in accordance with the decisions of the National People's Congress and the Basic Law."[13]

Some political analysts suggested that China's action to study local institutions, in effect, was "the beginning of a unilateral takeover of Hong Kong," with Beijing "free to scrap in 1997 whatever arrangements Patten made on his own."[14]

Reports of Hong Kong media intimidation by China were criticized in early 1994 by Governor Chris Patten, who said a free press was "as important to our way of life as a fairly elected legislature and independent judiciary." He was especially critical about the arrest in Beijing of Hong Kong journalists accused of "stealing state secrets," about admissions of self-censorship on the part of local journalists and about increased pressure on print and electronic media to avoid subjects that might "offend" Beijing and lead to repercussions after 1997. He said the free press should be prevented "from being eroded by outside influence or outside pressure."[15]

In one highly publicized example of media intimidation, Hong Kong's Television Broadcasts Ltd. (tvb), the world's largest producer of

Chinese-language television programming,[16] acquired rights to a controversial British Broadcasting Company (BBC) documentary about Mao Zedong, but then decided not to show the film. Beijing had previously denounced the BBC for broadcasting "Chairman Mao, The Last Emperor," which featured an interview with his former doctor who discussed Mao's sexual appetite for young women."[17]

Hong Kong's tourist industry, already experiencing considerable growth by 1994, was expecting even more as visitors wanted to see Hong Kong before the 1997 handover. One of the newest attractions was the massive construction of the new Chek Lap Kok airport and nine other airport-related projects. The New Airport Projects Coordination Office was already promoting boat tours near the reclamation site, with plans to develop a major tourist center overlooking construction of the mile-long Tsing Ma suspension bridge. The center would include restaurants, bars, souvenir shops, working models, viewing areas and educational areas for visits by school children.

Meanwhile, Financial Secretary Hamish Macleod said Hong Kong could expect its government to approve more public spending during 1994-95 because of a $1.95 billion surplus during the fiscal year ending in 1994. He had projected a $440 million deficit, but unexpected windfalls from land sales and stamp duty from stock and property transactions produced the giant surplus. "Unlike many other societies, both Asian and Western," he said, "we have found the right budgetary balance."[18] Macleod said that about half of public spending was already devoted to housing and social welfare, but that he soon would propose increased spending for health, welfare, education and environment, possibly bringing the surplus down to just under $1 billion in 1995.[19]

Toward the 21st Century

Hong Kong's outlook for the late 1990s, heavily influenced by politics and economics, will be dependent largely on provisions of the Joint Declaration and the interpretation of that document by China and Britain. The Joint Declaration promises continued capitalism, unchanged legal and social systems, a high degree of autonomy and increased self-government. The Basic Law, effective July 1, 1997, is to serve as a constitution-like basis for judicial, social, economic and political systems in Hong Kong until June 30, 2047.

Looking to the past for a glimpse of a possible future, one finds the example of Weihai, a port city on the northeast coast of China. Weihai, once a British enclave, originally leased in 1898 along with the New Territories, was returned to Chinese rule in 1930 with assurances comparable to those given Hong Kong. Negotiations between China and Britain, without participation by local representatives, produced an agreement that Weihai would become a special administrative zone, with low tax rates, retention of civil servants and continued duty-free status. China also agreed to maintain local police services, sanitary regulation and building codes. The agreement, reached after eight years of negotiations, failed to include provisions for local self-government, as requested by Weihai officials.

Weihai's fortunes went into a steep decline soon after the handover. China, as agreed, designated the city of 128,000 a special administration zone, but sent in bureaucrats who raised taxes, ended the duty-free status and used forced labor to build roads. The city was occupied by Japan from 1938 to 1945, and in 1949, during the Communist revolution, became a military outpost and closed city.

Author Nien Cheng: A Different Hong Kong in the 21st Century

Author Nien Cheng, victimized during China's Cultural Revolution, predicts that Hong Kong will be "a very different place" in the twenty-first century. Cheng experienced firsthand the limits of suppression in China, where she was accused of being a British spy and spent six and one-half years (1966–73) in solitary confinement in a Shanghai prison. After her release and subsequent immigration to the United States, Cheng wrote of her experiences in "Life and Death in Shanghai," published in 1986.

During a lecture tour in 1990, Cheng stopped in Hong Kong, where she was pressed by journalists into describing a future under complete Chinese control. She said Hong Kong would no longer be a major financial center, it would suffer from repression and intimidation by corrupt officials, and its people would constantly confront a tense environment.

The reason, she said, was that the next generation of Chinese leaders would include many "very troublesome" men and women. "Many of these people were the Red Guards of the Cultural Revolution who left school and training to rampage through China," she said. "I think these people will trouble China in the future because they know only how to torture and destroy."[20]

Cheng said certain activities in Hong Kong might be permitted to continue under Chinese rule. "They will leave the race track, because all Chinese like to gamble. And they will leave the golf courses, because the top party people like the game. But they will not leave the Independent Commission Against Corruption. It's so inconvenient to have such an organization."[21]

Cheng called the optimism of some Hong Kong business leaders almost naïve, recalling one who said he hoped that "if many well-educated, prosperous people stay, they might be able to influence the Communists." She said it would be too much to hope for. "You can't influence the Communists. You see, that is too optimistic."[22]

Author Ross Terrill:
Two Possible Futures for Hong Kong

Writer Ross Terrill, a noted authority on China, offers two visions of Hong Kong's future. In one vision, Hong Kong would be a mere shell at the end of the twentieth century — "a ghost town in which the elevators do not move up the white skyscrapers because of power shortages, the hospitals have clerical staff but almost no doctors, the beautiful harbor is quiet because ships no longer wish to berth here."

Terrill's alternative vision, somewhat more optimistic, projects Hong Kong as "fundamentally unchanged," a territory "too far from Beijing to attract the fussiness of the Communist bureaucrats, too useful to Beijing to provoke gross interference, and too possessed of its own economic dynamic to be much influenced by the half-awake giant at its side."

Joint Declaration
of the Government of the People's Republic of China and the Government of the United Kingdom of Great Britain and Northern Ireland on the Question of Hong Kong

The Government of the People's Republic of China and the Government of the United Kingdom of Great Britain and Northern Ireland have reviewed with satisfaction the friendly relations existing between the two Governments and peoples in recent years and agreed that a proper negotiated settlement of the question of Hong Kong, which is left over from the past, is conducive to the maintenance of the prosperity and stability of Hong Kong and to the further strengthening and development of the relations between the two countries on a new basis. To this end, they have, after talks between the delegations of the two Governments, agreed to declare as follows:

1. The Government of the People's Republic of China declares that to recover the Hong Kong area (including Hong Kong Island, Kowloon and the New Territories, hereinafter referred to as Hong Kong) is the common aspiration of the entire Chinese people, and that it has decided to resume the exercise of sovereignty over Hong Kong with effect from 1 July 1997.

2. The Government of the United Kingdom declares that it will restore Hong Kong to the People's Republic of China with effect from 1 July 1997.

3. The Government of the People's Republic of China declares that the basic policies of the People's Republic of China regarding Hong Kong are as follows:

    (1) Upholding national unity and territorial integrity and taking account of the history of Hong Kong and its realities, the People's Republic of China has decided to establish, in accordance with the provisions of Article 31 of the Constitution of the People's Republic of China, a Hong Kong Special Administrative Region upon resuming the exercise of sovereignty over Hong Kong.

    (2) The Hong Kong Special Administrative Region will be directly under the authority of the Central People's Government of the People's Republic of China. The Hong Kong Special Administrative Region will enjoy a high degree of autonomy, except in foreign and defence affairs which are the responsibilities of the Central People's Government.

    (3) The Hong Kong Special Administrative Region will be vested with executive, legislative and independent judicial power, including that of

final adjudication. The laws currently in force in Hong Kong will remain basically unchanged.

(4) The Government of the Hong Kong Special Administrative Region will be composed of local inhabitants. The chief executive will be appointed by the Central People's Government on the basis of the results of elections or consultations to be held locally. Principal officials will be nominated by the chief executive of the Hong Kong Special Administrative Region for appointment by the Central People's Government. Chinese and foreign nationals previously working in the public and police services in the government departments of Hong Kong may also be employed to serve as advisers or hold certain public posts in government departments of the Hong Kong Special Administrative Region.

(5) The current social and economic systems in Hong Kong will remain unchanged, and so will the life-style. Rights and freedoms, including those of the person, of speech, of the press, of assembly, of association, of travel, of movement, of correspondence, of strike, of choice of occupation, of academic research and of religious belief will be ensured by law in the Hong Kong Special Administrative Region. Private property, ownership of enterprises, legitimate right of inheritance and foreign investment will be protected by law.

(6) The Hong Kong Special Administrative Region will retain the status of a free port and a separate customs territory.

(7) The Hong Kong Special Administrative Region will retain the status of an international financial centre, and its markets for foreign exchange, gold, securities and futures will continue. There will be free flow of capital. The Hong Kong dollar will continue to circulate and remain freely convertible.

(8) The Hong Kong Special Administrative Region will have independent finances. The Central People's Government will not levy taxes on the Hong Kong Special Administrative Region.

(9) The Hong Kong Special Administrative Region may establish mutually beneficial economic relations with the United Kingdom and other countries, whose economic interests in Hong Kong will be given due regard.

(10) Using the name of 'Hong Kong, China', the Hong Kong Special Administrative Region may on its own maintain and develop economic and cultural relations and conclude relevant agreements with states, regions and relevant international organisations.

The Government of the Hong Kong Special Administrative Region may on its own issue travel documents for entry into and exit from Hong Kong.

(11) The maintenance of public order in the Hong Kong Special Administrative Region will be the responsibility of the Government of the Hong Kong Special Administrative Region.

(12) The above-stated basic policies of the People's Republic of China regarding Hong Kong and the elaboration of them in Annex I to this Joint Declaration will be stipulated, in a Basic Law of the Hong Kong Special Administrative Region of the People's Republic of China, by

the National People's Congress of the People's Republic of China, and they will remain unchanged for 50 years.

4. The Government of the People's Republic of China and the Government of the United Kingdom declare that, during the transitional period between the date of the entry into force of this Joint Declaration and 30 June 1997, the Government of the United Kingdom will be responsible for the administration of Hong Kong with the object of maintaining and preserving its economic prosperity and social stability; and that the Government of the People's Republic of China will give its cooperation in this connection.

5. The Government of the People's Republic of China and the Government of the United Kingdom declare that, in order to ensure a smooth transfer of government in 1997, and with a view to the effective implementation of this Joint Declaration, a Sino-British Joint Liaison Group will be set up when this Joint Declaration enters into force; and that it will be established and will function in accordance with the provisions of Annex II to this Joint Declaration.

6. The Government of the People's Republic of China and the Government of the United Kingdom declare that land leases in Hong Kong and other related matters will be dealt with in accordance with the provisions of Annex III to this Joint Declaration.

7. The Government of the People's Republic of China and the Government of the United Kingdom agree to implement the preceding declarations and the Annexes to this Joint Declaration.

8. This Joint Declaration is subject to ratification and shall enter into force on the date of the exchange of instruments of ratification, which shall take place in Beijing before 30 June 1985. This Joint Declaration and its Annexes shall be equally binding.

Done in duplicate at Beijing on 19 December 1984 in the Chinese and English languages, both texts being equally authentic.

(Signed)	(Signed)
For the	For the
Government of the	Government of the United Kingdom
People's Republic of China	of Great Britain and Northern Ireland
Zhao Ziyang	Margaret Thatcher

EXCHANGE OF MEMORANDA

(A) UNITED KINGDOM MEMORANDUM

In connection with the Joint Declaration of the Government of the United Kingdom of Great Britain and Northern Ireland and the Government of the People's Republic of China on the Question of Hong Kong to be signed this day, the Government of the United Kingdom declares that, subject to the completion of the necessary amendments to the relevant United Kingdom legislation:

  (a) All persons who on 30 June 1997 are, by virtue of a connection with Hong Kong, British Dependent Territories Citizens (BDTCs) under the law in force in the United Kingdom will cease to be BDTCs with effect from 1 July 1997, but will be eligible to retain an appropriate status which, without conferring the right of abode in the United Kingdom, will entitle them to continue to use passports issued by the Government of the United Kingdom. This status will be acquired by such persons only if they hold or are included in such a British passport issued before 1 July 1997, except that eligible persons born on or after 1 January 1997 but before 1 July 1997 may obtain or be included in such as passport up to 31 December 1997.

(b) No person will acquire BDTC status on or after 1 July 1997 by virtue of a connection with Hong Kong. No person born on or after 1 July 1997 will acquire the status referred to as being appropriate in sub-paragraph (a).

(c) United Kingdom consular officials in the Hong Kong Special Administrative Region and elsewhere may renew and replace passports of persons mentioned in sub-paragraph *(a)* and may also issue them to persons, born before 1 July 1997 of such persons, who had previously been included in the passport of their parent.

(d) Those who have obtained or been included in passports issued by the Government of the United Kingdom under sub-paragraphs *(a)* and *(c)* will be entitled to receive, upon request, British consular services and protection when in third countries.

Beijing, 19 December 1984

(Stamp of the British Embassy)

(B) CHINESE MEMORANDUM
Translation

The Government of the People's Republic of China has received the memorandum from the Government of the United Kingdom of Great Britain and Northern Ireland dated 19 December 1984.

Under the Nationality Law of the People's Republic of China, all Hong Kong Chinese compatriots, whether they are holders of the "British Dependent Territories citizens' Passport" or not, are Chinese nationals.

Taking account of the historical background of Hong Kong and its realities, the competent authorities of the Government of the People's Republic of China will, with effect from 1 July 1997, permit Chinese nationals in Hong Kong who were previously called "British Dependent Territories citizens" to use travel documents issued by the government of the United Kingdom for the purpose of travelling to other states and regions.

The above Chinese nationals will not be entitled to British consular protection in the Hong Kong Special Administrative Region and other parts of the People's Republic of China on account of their holding the above-mentioned British travel documents.

Beijing, 19 December 1984

(Stamp of the Ministry of Foreign Affairs of the Central People's Government)

ANNEX I

Elaboration by the Government of
the People's Republic of China
of Its Basic Policies Regarding Hong Kong

The Government of the People's Republic of China elaborates the basic policies of
the People's Republic of China regarding Hong Kong as set out in paragraph 3 of
the Joint Declaration of the Government of the People's Republic of China and the
Government of the United Kingdom of Great Britain and Northern Ireland on the
Question of Hong Kong as follows:

I

The Constitution of the People's Republic of China stipulates in Article 31 that
'the state may establish special administrative regions when necessary. The systems
to be instituted in special administrative regions shall be prescribed by laws enacted
by the National People's Congress in the light of the specific conditions.' In accordance with this Article, the People's Republic of China shall, upon the resumption
of the exercise of sovereignty over Hong Kong on 1 July 1997, establish the Hong
Kong Special Administrative Region of the People's Republic of China. The National People's Congress of the People's Republic of China shall enact and promulgate a Basic Law of the Hong Kong Special Administrative Region of the People's
Republic of China (hereinafter referred to as the Basic Law) in accordance with the
Constitution of the People's Republic of China, stipulating that after the establishment of the Hong Kong Special Administrative Region the socialist system and
socialist policies shall not be practised in the Hong Kong Special Administrative
Region and that Hong Kong's previous capitalist system and life-style shall remain
unchanged for 50 years.

The Hong Kong Special Administrative Region shall be directly under the
authority of the Central People's Government of the People's Republic of China and
shall enjoy a high degree of autonomy. Except for foreign and defence affairs which
are the responsibilities of the Central People's Government, the Hong Kong Special
Administrative Region shall be vested with executive, legislative and independent
judicial power, including that of final adjudication. The Central People's Government shall authorise the Hong Kong Special Administrative Region to conduct on
its own those external affairs specific in Section XI of this Annex.

The government and legislature of the Hong Kong Special Administrative
Region shall be composed of local inhabitants. The chief executive of the Hong
Kong Special Administrative Region shall be selected by election or through consultations held locally and be appointed by the Central People's Government. Principal officials (equivalent to Secretaries) shall be nominated by the chief executive
of the Hong Kong Special Administrative Region and appointed by the Central People's Government. The legislature of the Hong Kong Special Administrative region
shall be constituted by elections. The executive authorities shall abide by the law
and shall be accountable to the legislature.

In addition to Chinese, English may also be used in organs of government and
in the courts in the Hong Kong Special Administrative Region.

Apart from displaying the national flag and national emblem of the People's Republic of China, the Hong Kong Special Administrative Region may use a regional flag and emblem of its own.

II

After the establishment of the Hong Kong Special Administrative Region, the laws previously in force in Hong Kong (i.e., the common law, rules of equity, ordinances, subordinate legislation and customary law) shall be maintained, save for any that contravene the Basic Law and subject to any amendment by the Hong Kong Special Administrative Region legislature.

The legislative power of the Hong Kong Special Administrative Region shall be vested in the legislature of the Hong Kong Special Administrative Region. The legislature may on its own authority enact laws in accordance with the provisions of the Basic Law and legal procedures, and report them to the Standing Committee of the National People's Congress for the record. Laws enacted by the legislature which are in accordance with the Basic Law and legal procedures shall be regarded as valid.

The laws of the Hong Kong Special Administrative Region shall be the Basic Law, and the laws previously in force in Hong Kong and laws enacted by the Hong Kong Special Administrative Region legislature as above.

III

After the establishment of the Hong Kong Special Administrative Region, the judicial system previously practised in Hong Kong shall be maintained except for those changes consequent upon the vesting in the courts of the Hong Kong Special Administrative Region of the power of final adjudication.

Judicial power in the Hong Kong Special Administrative Region shall be vested in the courts of the Hong Kong Special Administrative Region. The courts shall exercise judicial power independently and free from any interference. Members of the judiciary shall be immune from legal action in respect of their judicial functions. The courts shall decide cases in accordance with the laws of the Hong Kong Special Administrative Region and may refer to precedents in other common law jurisdictions.

Judges of the Hong Kong Special Administrative Region courts shall be appointed by the chief executive of the Hong Kong Special Administrative Region acting in accordance with the recommendation of an independent commission composed of local judges, persons from the legal profession and other eminent persons. Judges shall be chosen by reference to their judicial qualities and may be recruited from other common law jurisdictions. A judge may only be removed for inability to discharge the functions of his office, or for misbehaviour, by the chief executive of the Hong Kong Special Administrative Region acting in accordance with the recommendation of a tribunal appointed by the chief judge of the court of final appeal, consisting of not fewer than three local judges. Additionally, the appointment or removal of principal judges (i.e., those of the highest rank) shall be made by the chief executive with the endorsement of the Hong Kong Special Administrative Region legislature and reported to the Standing Committee of the National People's Congress for the record. The system of appointment and removal of judicial officers other than judges shall be maintained.

The power of final judgment of the Hong Kong Special Administrative Region shall be vested in the court of final appeal in the Hong Kong Special Administrative Region, which may as required invite judges from other common law jurisdictions to sit on the court of final appeal.

A prosecuting authority of the Hong Kong Special Administrative Region shall control criminal prosecutions free from any interference.

On the basis of the system previously operating in Hong Kong, the Hong Kong Special Administrative Region Government shall on its own make provision for local lawyers and lawyers from outside the Hong Kong Special Administrative Region to work and practise in the Hong Kong Special Administrative Region.

The Central People's Government shall assist or authorise the Hong Kong Special Administrative Region Government to make appropriate arrangements for reciprocal juridical assistance with foreign states.

IV

After the establishment of the Hong Kong Special Administrative Region, public servants previously serving in Hong Kong in all government departments, including the police department, and members of the judiciary may all remain in employment and continue their service with pay, allowances, benefits and conditions of service no less favourable than before. The Hong Kong Special Administrative Region Government shall pay to such persons who retire or complete their contracts, as well as to those who have retired before 1 July 1997, or to their dependants, all pensions, gratuities, allowances and benefits due to them on terms no less favourable than before, and irrespective of their nationality or place of residence.

The Hong Kong Special Administrative Region Government may employ British and other foreign nationals previously serving in the public service in Hong Kong, and may recruit British and other foreign nationals holding permanent identity cards of the Hong Kong Special Administrative region to serve as public servants at all levels, except as heads of major government departments (corresponding to branches or departments at Secretary level) including the police department, and as deputy heads of some of those departments. The Hong Kong Special Administrative Region Government may also employ British and other foreign nationals as advisers to government departments and, when there is a need, may recruit qualified candidates from outside the Hong Kong Special Administrative Region to professional and technical posts in government departments. The above shall be employed only in their individual capacities and, like other public servants, shall be responsible to the Hong Kong Special Administrative Region Government.

The appointment and promotion of public servants shall be on the basis of qualifications, experience and ability. Hong Kong's previous system of recruitment, employment, assessment, discipline, training and management for the public service (including special bodies for appointment, pay and conditions of service) shall, save for any provisions providing privileged treatment for foreign nationals, be maintained.

V

The Hong Kong Special Administrative Region shall deal on its own with financial matters, including disposing of its financial resources and drawing up its budgets and its final accounts. The Hong Kong Special Administrative Region shall report its budgets and final accounts to the Central People's Government for the record.

The Central People's Government shall not levy taxes on the Hong Kong Special Administrative Region. The Hong Kong Special Administrative Region shall use its financial revenues exclusively for its own purposes and they shall not be handed over to the Central People's Government. The systems by which taxation and public expenditure must be approved by the legislature, and by which there is accountability to the legislature for all public expenditure, and the system for auditing public accounts shall be maintained.

VI

The Hong Kong Special Administrative Region shall maintain the capitalist economic and trade systems previously practised in Hong Kong. The Hong Kong Special Administrative Region Government shall decide its economic and trade policies on its own. Rights concerning the ownership of property, including those relating to acquisition, use, disposal, inheritance and compensation for lawful deprivation (corresponding to the real value of the property concerned, freely convertible and paid without undue delay) shall continue to be protected by law.

The Hong Kong Special Administrative Region shall retain the status of a free port and continue a free trade policy, including the free movement of goods and capital. The Hong Kong Special Administrative Region may on its own maintain and develop economic and trade relations with all states and regions.

The Hong Kong Special Administrative Region shall be a separate customs territory. It may participate in relevant international organisations and international trade agreements (including preferential trade arrangements), such as the General Agreement on Tariffs and Trade and arrangements regarding international trade in textiles. Export quotas, tariff preferences and other similar arrangements obtained by the Hong Kong Special Administrative Region shall be enjoyed exclusively by the Hong Kong Special Administrative Region. The Hong Kong Special Administrative Region shall have authority to issue its own certificates of origin for products manufactured locally, in accordance with prevailing rules of origin.

The Hong Kong Special Administrative Region may, as necessary, establish official and semi-official economic and trade missions in foreign countries, reporting the establishment of such missions to the Central People's Government for the record.

VII

The Hong Kong Special Administrative Region shall retain the status of an international financial centre. The monetary and financial systems previously practised in Hong Kong, including the systems of regulation and supervision of deposit taking institutions and financial markets, shall be maintained.

The Hong Kong Special Administrative Region Government may decide its monetary and financial policies on its own. It shall safeguard the free operation of financial business and the free flow of capital within, into and out of the Hong Kong Special Administrative Region. No exchange control policy shall be applied in the Hong Kong Special Administrative Region. Markets for foreign exchange, gold, securities and futures shall continue.

The Hong Kong dollar, as the local legal tender, shall continue to circulate and remain freely convertible. The authority to issue Hong Kong currency shall be vested in the Hong Kong Special Administrative Region Government. The Hong Kong Special Administrative Region Government may authorise designated banks to issue or continue to issue Hong Kong currency under statutory authority, after satisfying itself that any issue of currency will be soundly based and that the arrangements for such issue are consistent with the object of maintaining the stability of the currency. Hong Kong currency bearing references inappropriate to the status of Hong Kong as a Special Administrative Region of the People's Republic of China shall be progressively replaced and withdrawn from circulation.

The Exchange Fund shall be managed and controlled by the Hong Kong Special Administrative Region Government, primarily for regulating the exchange value of the Hong Kong dollar.

VIII

The Hong Kong Special Administrative Region shall maintain Hong Kong's previous systems of shipping management and shipping regulation, including the system for regulating conditions of seamen. The specific functions and responsibilities of the Hong Kong Special Administrative Region Government in the field of shipping shall be defined by the Hong Kong Special Administrative Region Government on its own. Private shipping businesses and shipping-related businesses and private container terminals in Hong Kong may continue to operate freely.

The Hong Kong Special Administrative Region shall be authorised by the Central People's Government to continue to maintain a shipping register and issue related certificates under its own legislation in the name of 'Hong Kong, China'.

With the exception of foreign warships, access for which requires the permission of the Central People's Government, ships shall enjoy access to the ports of the Hong Kong Special Administrative Region in accordance with the laws of the Hong Kong Special Administrative Region.

IX

The Hong Kong Special Administrative Region shall maintain the status of Hong Kong as a centre of international and regional aviation. Airlines incorporated and having their principal place of business in Hong Kong and civil aviation related businesses may continue to operate. The Hong Kong Special Administrative Region shall continue the previous system of civil aviation management in Hong Kong, and keep its own aircraft register in accordance with provisions laid down by the Central People's Government concerning nationality marks and registration marks of aircraft. The Hong Kong Special Administrative Region shall be responsible on its own for matters of routine business and technical management of civil aviation, including the management of airports, the provision of air traffic services within the flight information region of the Hong Kong Special Administrative Region, and the discharge of other responsibilities allocated under the regional air navigation procedures of the International Civil Aviation Organisation.

The Central People's Government shall, in consultation with the Hong Kong Special Administrative Region Government, make arrangements providing for air services between the Hong Kong Special Administrative Region and other parts of the People's Republic of China for airlines incorporated and having their principal place of business in the Hong Kong Special Administrative Region and other airlines of the People's Republic of China. All Air Service Agreements providing for air services between other parts of the People's Republic of China and other states and regions with stops at the Hong Kong Special Administrative Region and air services between the Hong Kong Special Administrative Region and other states and regions with stops at other parts of the People's Republic of China shall be concluded by the Central People's Government. For this purpose, the Central People's Government shall take account of the special conditions and economic interests of the Hong Kong Special Administrative Region and consult the Hong Kong Special Administrative Region Government. Representatives of the Hong Kong Special Administrative Region Government may participate as members of delegations of the Government of the People's Republic of China in air service consultations with foreign governments concerning arrangements for such services.

Acting under specific authorisations from the Central People's Government, the Hong Kong Special Administrative Region Government may:

- renew or amend Air Service Agreements and arrangements previously in force; in principle, all such Agreements and arrangements may be renewed or amended with the rights contained in such previous Agreements and arrangements being as far as possible maintained;
- negotiate and conclude new Air Service Agreements providing routes for airlines incorporated and having their principal place of business in the Hong Kong Special Administrative Region and rights for overflights and technical stops; and
- negotiate and conclude provisional arrangements where no Air Service Agreement with a foreign state or other region is in force.

All scheduled air services to, from or through the Hong Kong Special Administrative Region which do not operate to, from or through the mainland of China shall be regulated by Air Service Agreements or provisional arrangements referred to in this paragraph.

The Central People's Government shall give the Hong Kong Special Administrative Region Government the authority to:

- negotiate and conclude with other authorities all arrangements concerning the implementation of the above Air Service Agreements and provisional arrangements;
- issue licences to airlines incorporated and having their principal places of business in the Hong Kong Special Administrative Region;
- designate such airlines under the above Air Service Agreements and provisional arrangements; and
- issue permits to foreign airlines for services other than those to, from or through the mainland of China.

X

The Hong Kong Special Administrative Region shall maintain the educational system previously practised in Hong Kong. The Hong Kong Special Administrative Region Government shall on its own decide policies in the fields of culture, education, science and technology, including policies regarding the educational system and its administration, the language of instruction, the allocation of funds, the examination system, the system of academic awards and the recognition of educational and technological qualifications. Institutions of all kinds, including those run by religious and community organisations, may retain their autonomy. They may continue to recruit staff and use teaching materials from outside the Hong Kong Special Administrative Region. Students shall enjoy freedom of choice of education and freedom to pursue their education outside the Hong Kong Special Administrative Region.

XI

Subject to the principle that foreign affairs are the responsibility of the Central People's Government, representatives of the Hong Kong Special Administrative Region Government may participate, as members of delegations of the Government of the People's Republic of China, in negotiations at the diplomatic level directly affecting the Hong Kong Special Administrative Region conducted by the Central People's Government. The Hong Kong Special Administrative Region may on its own, using the name 'Hong Kong, China', maintain and develop relations and conclude and implement agreements with states, regions and relevant international organisations in the appropriate fields, including the economic, trade, financial and monetary, shipping, communications, touristic, cultural and sporting fields. Representatives of the Hong Kong Special Administrative Region Government may participate, as members of delegations of the Government of the People's Republic of China, in international organisations or conferences in appropriate fields limited to states and affecting the Hong Kong Special Administrative Region, or may attend in such other capacity as may be permitted by the Central People's Government and the organisation or conference concerned, and may express their views in the name of 'Hong Kong, China'. The Hong Kong Special Administrative Region may, using the name 'Hong Kong, China', participate in international organisations and conferences not limited to states.

The application to the Hong Kong Special Administrative Region of international agreements to which the People's Republic of China is or becomes a party shall be decided by the Central People's Government, in accordance with the circumstances and needs of the Hong Kong Special Administrative Region, and after seeking the views of the Hong Kong Special Administrative Region Government. International agreements to which the People's Republic of China is not a party but which are implemented in Hong Kong may remain implemented in the Hong Kong Special Administrative Region. The Central People's Government shall, as necessary, authorise or assist the Hong Kong Special Administrative Region Government to make appropriate arrangements for the application to the Hong Kong Special Administrative Region of other relevant international agreements. The Central People's Government shall take the necessary steps to ensure that the Hong Kong Special Administrative Region shall continue to retain its status in an appropriate capacity in those international organisations of which the People's Republic of China is a member and in which Hong Kong participates in one capacity or another. The Central People's Government shall, where necessary, facilitate the continued participation of the Hong Kong Special Administrative Region in an appropriate capacity in those international organisations in which Hong Kong is a participant in one capacity or another, but of which the People's Republic of China is not a member.

Foreign consular and other official or semi-official missions may be established in the Hong Kong Special Administrative Region with the approval of the Central People's Government. Consular and other official missions established in Hong Kong by states which have established formal diplomatic relations with the People's Republic of China may be maintained. According to the circumstances of each case, consular and other official missions of states having no formal diplomatic relations with the People's Republic of China may either be maintained or changed to semi-official missions. States not recognised by the People's Republic of China can only establish non-governmental institutions.

The United Kingdom may establish a Consulate-General in the Hong Kong Special Administrative Region.

XII

The maintenance of public order in the Hong Kong Special Administrative Region shall be the responsibility of the Hong Kong Special Administrative Region Government. Military forces sent by the Central People's Government to be stationed in the Hong Kong Special Administrative Region for the purpose of defence shall not interfere in the internal affairs of the Hong Kong Special Administrative Region. Expenditure for these military forces shall be borne by the Central People's Government.

XIII

The Hong Kong Special Administrative Region Government shall protect the rights and freedoms of inhabitants and other persons in the Hong Kong Special Administrative Region according to law. The Hong Kong Special Administrative Region Government shall maintain the rights and freedoms as provided for by the laws previously in force in Hong Kong, including freedom of the person, of speech, of the press, of assembly, of association, to form and join trade unions, of correspondence, of travel, of movement, of strike, of demonstration, of choice of occupation, of academic research, of belief, inviolability of the home, the freedom to marry and the right to raise a family freely.

Every person shall have the right to confidential legal advice, access to the courts, representation in the courts by lawyers of his choice, and to obtain judicial remedies. Every person shall have the right to challenge the actions of the executive in the courts.

Religious organisations and believers may maintain their relations with religious organisations and believers elsewhere, and schools, hospitals and welfare institutions run by religious organisations may be continued. The relationship between religious organisations in the Hong Kong Special Administrative Region and those in other parts of the People's Republic of China shall be based on the principles of non-subordination, non-interference and mutual respect.

The provisions of the International Covenant on Civil and Political Rights and the International Covenant on Economic, Social and Cultural Rights as applied to Hong Kong shall remain in force.

XIV

The following categories of persons shall have the right of abode in the Hong Kong Special Administrative Region, and, in accordance with the law of the Hong Kong Special Administrative Region, be qualified to obtain permanent identity cards issued by the Hong Kong Special Administrative Region Government, which state their right of abode:

- all Chinese nationals who were born or who have ordinarily resided in Hong Kong before or after the establishment of the Hong Kong Special Administrative Region for a continuous period of 7 years or more, and persons of Chinese nationality born outside Hong Kong of such Chinese nationals;
- all other persons who have ordinarily resided in Hong Kong before or after the establishment of the Hong Kong Special Administrative Region for a continuous period of 7 years or more and who have taken Hong Kong as their place of permanent residence before or after the establishment of the Hong Kong Special Administrative Region, and persons under 21 years of age who were born of such persons in Hong Kong before or after the establishment of the Hong Kong Special Administrative Region;
- any other persons who had the right of abode only in Hong Kong before the establishment of the Hong Kong Special Administrative Region.

The Central People's Government shall authorise the Hong Kong Special Administrative Region Government to issue, in accordance with the law, passports of the Hong Kong Special Administrative Region of the People's Republic of China to all Chinese nationals who hold permanent identity cards of the Hong Kong Special Administrative Region, and travel documents of the Hong Kong Special Administrative Region of the People's Republic of China to all other persons lawfully residing in the Hong Kong Special Administrative Region. The above passports and documents shall be valid for all states and regions and shall record the holder's right to return to the Hong Kong Special Administrative Region.

For the purpose of travelling to and from the Hong Kong Special Administrative Region, residents of the Hong Kong Special Administrative Region may use travel documents issued by the Hong Kong Special Administrative Region Government, or by other competent authorities of the People's Republic of China, or of other states. Holders of permanent identity cards of the Hong Kong Special Administrative Region may have this fact stated in their travel documents as evidence that the holders have the right of abode in the Hong Kong Special Administrative Region.

Entry into the Hong Kong Special Administrative Region of persons from other parts of China shall continue to be regulated in accordance with the present practice.

The Hong Kong Special Administrative Region may apply immigration controls on entry, stay in and departure from the Hong Kong Special Administrative Region by persons from foreign states and regions.

Unless restrained by law, holders of valid travel documents shall be free to leave the Hong Kong Special Administrative Region without special authorisation.

The Central People's Government shall assist or authorise the Hong Kong Special Administrative Region Government to conclude visa abolition agreements with states or regions.

ANNEX II
Sino-British Joint Liaison Group

1. In furtherance of their common aim and in order to ensure a smooth transfer of government in 1997, the Government of the People's Republic of China and the Government of the United Kingdom have agreed to continue their discussions in a friendly spirit and to develop the cooperative relationship which already exists between the two Governments over Hong Kong with a view to the effective implementation of the Joint Declaration.

2. In order to meet the requirements for liaison, consultation and the exchange of information, the two Governments have agreed to set up a Joint Liaison Group.

3. The functions of the Joint Liaison Group shall be:
   (a) to conduct consultations on the implementation of the Joint Declaration;
   (b) to discuss matters relating to the smooth transfer of government in 1997;
   (c) to exchange information and conduct consultations on such subjects as may be agreed by the two sides.

Matters on which there is disagreement in the Joint Liaison Group shall be referred to the two Governments for solution through consultations.

4. Matters for consideration during the first half of the period between the establishment of the Joint Liaison Group and 1 July 1997 shall include:
   (a) action to be taken by the two Governments to enable the Hong Kong Special Administrative Region to maintain its economic relations as a separate customs territory, and in particular to ensure the maintenance of Hong Kong's participation in the General Agreement on Tariffs and Trade, the Multifibre Arrangement and other international arrangements; and
   (b) action to be taken by the two Governments to ensure the continued application of international rights and obligations affecting Hong Kong.

5. The two Governments have agreed that in the second half of the period between establishment of the Joint Liaison Group and 1 July 1997 there will be need for closer cooperation, which will therefore be intensified during that period. Matters for consideration during this second period shall include:
   (a) procedures to be adopted for the smooth transition in 1997;
   (b) action to assist the Hong Kong Special Administrative Region to maintain and develop economic and cultural relations and conclude agreements on these matters with states, regions and relevant international organisations.

6. The Joint Liaison Group shall be an organ for liaison and not an organ of power. It shall play no part in the administration of Hong Kong or the Hong Kong Special Administrative Region. Nor shall it have any supervisory role over that administration. The members and supporting staff of the Joint Liaison Group shall only conduct activities within the scope of the functions of the Joint Liaison Group.

7. Each side shall designate a senior representative, who shall be of Ambassadorial rank, and four other members of the group. Each side may send up to 20 supporting staff.

8. The Joint Liaison Group shall be established on the entry into force of the Joint Declaration. From 1 July 1988 the Joint Liaison Group shall have its

principal base in Hong Kong. The Joint Liaison Group shall continue its work until 1 January 2000.

9. The Joint Liaison Group shall meet in Beijing, London and Hong Kong. It shall meet at least once in each of the three locations in each year. The venue for each meeting shall be agreed between the two sides.

10. Members of the Joint Liaison Group shall enjoy diplomatic privileges and immunities as appropriate when in the three locations. Proceedings of the Joint Liaison Group shall remain confidential unless otherwise agreed between the two sides.

11. The Joint Liaison Group may by agreement between the two sides decide to set up specialist sub-groups to deal with particular subjects requiring expert assistance.

12. Meetings of the Joint Liaison Group and sub-groups may be attended by experts other than the members of the Joint Liaison Group. Each side shall determine the composition of its delegation to particular meetings of the Joint Liaison Group or sub-group in accordance with the subjects to be discussed and the venue chosen.

13. The working procedures of the Joint Liaison Group shall be discussed and decided upon by the two sides within the guidelines laid down in this Annex.

ANNEX III
Land Leases

The Government of the People's Republic of China and the Government of the United Kingdom have agreed that, with effect from the entry into force of the Joint Declaration, land leases in Hong Kong and other related matters shall be dealt with in accordance with the following provisions:

1. All leases of land granted or decided upon before the entry into force of the Joint Declaration and those granted thereafter in accordance with paragraph 2 or 3 of this Annex, and which extend beyond 30 June 1997, and all rights in relation to such leases shall continue to be recognised and protected under the law of the Hong Kong Special Administrative Region.

2. All leases of land granted by the British Hong Kong Government not containing a right of renewal that expire before 30 June 1997, except short term tenancies and leases for special purposes, may be extended if the lessee so wishes for a period expiring not later than 30 June 2047 without payment of an additional premium. An annual rent shall be charged from the date of extension equivalent to 3 per cent of the rateable value of the property at that date, adjusted in step with any changes in the rateable value thereafter. In the case of old schedule lots, village lots, small houses and similar rural holdings, where the property was on 30 June 1984 held by, or, in the case of small houses granted after that date, the property is granted to, a person descended through the male line from a person who was in 1898 a resident of an established village in Hong Kong, the rent shall remain unchanged so long as the property is held by that person or by one of his lawful successors in the male line. Where leases of land not having a right of renewal expire after 30 June 1997, they shall be dealt with in accordance with the relevant land laws and policies of the Hong Kong Special Administrative Region.

3. From the entry into force of the Joint Declaration until 30 June 1997, new leases of land may be granted by the British Hong Kong Government for terms expiring not later than 30 June 2047. Such leases shall be granted at a premium and nominal rental until 30 June 1997, after which date they shall not require payment of an additional premium but an annual rent equivalent to 3 per cent of the rateable value of the property at that date, adjusted in step with changes in the rateable value thereafter, shall be charged.

4. The total amount of new land to be granted under paragraph 3 of this Annex shall be limited to 50 hectares a year (excluding land to be granted to the Hong Kong Housing Authority for public rental housing) from the entry into force of the Joint Declaration until 30 June 1997.

5. Modifications of the conditions specified in leases granted by the British Hong Kong Government may continue to be granted before 1 July 1997 at a premium equivalent to the difference between the value of the land under the previous conditions and its value under the modified conditions.

6. From the entry into force of the Joint Declaration until 30 June 1997, premium income obtained by the British Hong Kong Government from land transactions shall, after deduction of the average cost of land production, be shared equally between the British Hong Kong Government and the future Hong Kong Special Administrative Region Government. All the income obtained by the British Hong Kong Government including the amount of the above-mentioned deduction, shall be put into the Capital Works Reserve Fund for the financing of land development and public works in Hong Kong. The Hong Kong Special Administrative Region Government's share of the premium income shall be deposited in banks incorporated in Hong Kong and shall not be drawn on except for the financing of land development and public works in Hong Kong in accordance with the provisions of paragraph 7 (d) of this Annex.

7. A Land Commission shall be established in Hong Kong immediately upon the entry into force of the Joint Declaration. The Land Commission shall be composed of an equal number of officials designated respectively by the Government of the People's Republic of China and the Government of the United Kingdom together with necessary supporting staff. The officials of the two sides shall be responsible to their respective governments. The Land Commission shall be dissolved on 30 June 1997.

The terms of reference of the Land Commission shall be:
- (a) to conduct consultations on the implementation of this Annex;
- (b) to monitor observance of the limit specified in paragraph 4 of this Annex, the amount of land granted to the Hong Kong Housing Authority for public rental housing, and the division and use of premium income referred to in paragraph 6 of this Annex;
- (c) to consider and decide on proposals from the British Hong Kong Government for increasing the limit referred to in paragraph 4 of this Annex;
- (d) to examine proposals for drawing on the Hong Kong Special Administrative Region Government's share of premium income referred to in paragraph 6 of this Annex and to make recommendations to the Chinese side for decision.

Matters on which there is disagreement in the Land Commission shall be referred to the Government of the People's Republic of China and the Government of the United Kingdom for decision.

8. Specific details regarding the establishment of the Land Commission shall be finalised separately by the two sides through consultations.

APPENDIX B

The Basic Law

of the Hong Kong Special Administrative Region of the People's Republic of China

Adopted April 4, 1990, by the Seventh National People's Congress of the People's Republic of China at its Third Session.

Chapter 1: General Principles

Article 1

The Hong Kong Special Administrative Region is an inalienable part of the People's Republic of China.

Article 2

The National People's Congress authorizes the Hong Kong Special Administrative Region to exercise a high degree of autonomy and enjoy executive, legislative and independent judicial power, including that of final adjudication, in accordance with the provisions of this Law.

Article 3

The executive authorities and legislature of the Hong Kong Special Administrative Region shall be composed of permanent residents of Hong Kong in accordance with the relevant provisions of this Law.

Article 4

The Hong Kong Special Administrative Region shall safeguard the rights and freedoms of the residents of the Hong Kong Special Administrative Region and of other persons in the region in accordance with law.

Article 5

The socialist system and policies shall not be practised in the Hong Kong Special Administrative Region, and the previous capitalist system and way of life shall remain unchanged for 50 years.

Article 6

The Hong Kong Special Administrative Region shall protect the right of private ownership of property in accordance with law.

Article 7

The land and natural resources within the Hong Kong Special Administrative

Region shall be State property. The Government of the Hong Kong Special Administrative Region shall be responsible for their management, use and development and for their lease or grant to individuals, legal persons or organizations for use or development. The revenues derived therefrom shall be exclusively at the disposal of the government of the Region.

Article 8

The laws previously in force in Hong Kong, that is, the common law, rules of equity, ordinances, subordinate legislation and customary law shall be maintained, except for any that contravene this Law, and subject to any amendment by the legislature of the Hong Kong Special Administrative Region.

Article 9

In addition to the Chinese language, English may also be used as an official language by the executive authorities, legislature and judiciary of the Hong Kong Special Administrative Region.

Article 10

Apart from displaying the national flag and national emblem of the People's Republic of China, the Hong Kong Special Administrative Region may also use a regional flag and regional emblem.

The regional flag of the Hong Kong Special Administrative Region is a red flag with a bauhinia highlighted by five star-tipped stamens.

The regional emblem of the Hong Kong Special Administrative Region is a bauhinia in the centre highlighted by five star-tipped stamens and encircled by the words 'Hong Kong Special Administrative Region of the People's Republic of China' in Chinese and 'HONG KONG' in English.

Article 11

In accordance with Article 31 of the Constitution of the People's Republic of China, the systems and policies practised in the Hong Kong Special Administrative Region, including the social and economic systems, the system for safeguarding the fundamental rights and freedoms of its residents, the executive, legislative and judicial systems, and the relevant policies, shall be based on the provisions of this Law.

No law enacted by the legislature of the Hong Kong Special Administrative Region shall contravene this Law.

Chapter II: Relationship between the Central Authorities and the Hong Kong Special Administrative Region

Article 12

The Hong Kong Special Administrative Region shall be a local administrative region of the People's Republic of China, which shall enjoy a high degree of autonomy and come directly under the Central People's Government.

Article 13

The Central People's Government shall be responsible for the foreign affairs relating to the Hong Kong Special Administrative Region.

The Ministry of Foreign Affairs of the People's Republic of China shall establish an office in Hong Kong to deal with foreign affairs.

The Central People's Government authorizes the Hong Kong Special Administrative Region to conduct relevant external affairs on its own in accordance with this Law.

Article 14

The Central People's Government shall be responsible for the defence of the Hong Kong Special Administrative Region.

The Government of the Hong Kong Special Administrative Region shall be responsible for the maintenance of public order in the Region.

Military forces stationed by the Central People's Government in the Hong Kong Special Administrative Region for defence shall not interfere in the local affairs of the Region. The Government of the Hong Kong Special Administrative Region may, when necessary, ask the Central People's Government for assistance from the garrison in the maintenance of public order and in disaster relief.

In addition to abiding by national laws, members of the garrison shall abide by the laws of the Hong Kong Special Administrative Region.

Expenditure for the garrison shall be borne by the Central People's Government.

Article 15

The Central People's Government shall appoint the Chief Executive and the principal officials of the executive authorities of the Hong Kong Special Administrative Region in accordance with the provisions of Chapter IV of this Law.

Article 16

The Hong Kong Special Administrative Region shall be vested with executive power. It shall, on its own, conduct the administrative affairs of the Region in accordance with the relevant provisions of this Law.

Article 17

The Hong Kong Special Administrative Region shall be vested with legislative power.

Laws enacted by the legislature of the Hong Kong Special Administrative Region must be reported to the Standing Committee of the National People's Congress for the record. The reporting for record shall not affect the entry into force of such laws.

If the Standing Committee of the National People's Congress, after consulting the Committee for the Basic Law of the Hong Kong Special Administrative Region under it, considers that any law enacted by the legislature of the Region is not in conformity with the provisions of this Law regarding affairs within the responsibility of the Central Authorities or regarding the relationship between the Central Authorities and the Region, the Standing Committee may return the law in question but shall not amend it. Any law returned by the Standing Committee of the National People's Congress shall immediately be invalidated. This invalidation shall not have retroactive effect, unless otherwise provided for in the laws of the Region.

Article 18

The laws in force in the Hong Kong Special Administrative Region shall be this Law, the laws previously in force in Hong Kong as provided for in Article 8 of this Law, and the laws enacted by the legislature of the Region.

National laws shall not be applied in the Hong Kong Special Administrative Region except for those listed in Annex III to this Law. The laws listed therein shall be applied locally by way of promulgation or legislation by the Region.

The Standing Committee of the National People's Congress may add to or delete from the list of laws in Annex III after consulting its Committee for the Basic Law of the Hong Kong Special Administrative Region and the government of the Region. Laws listed in Annex III to this Law shall be confined to those relating to defence and foreign affairs as well as other matters outside the limits of the autonomy of the Region as specified by this Law.

In the event that the Standing Committee of the National People's Congress decides to declare a state of war or, by reasons of turmoil within the Hong Kong Special Administrative Region which endangers national unity or security and is beyond the control of the government of the Region, decides that the Region is in a state of emergency, the Central People's Government may issue an order applying the relevant national laws in this Region.

Article 19

The Hong Kong Special Administrative Region shall be vested with independent judicial power, including that of final adjudication.

The courts of the Hong Kong Special Administrative Region shall have jurisdiction over all cases in the Region, except that the restrictions on their jurisdiction imposed by the legal system and principles previously in force in Hong Kong shall be maintained.

The courts of the Hong Kong Special Administrative Region shall have no jurisdiction over acts of state such as defence and foreign affairs. The courts of the Region shall obtain a certificate from the Chief Executive on questions of fact concerning acts of state such as defence and foreign affairs whenever such questions arise in the adjudication of cases. This certificate shall be binding on the courts. Before issuing such a certificate, the Chief Executive shall obtain a certifying document from the Central People's Government.

Article 20

The Hong Kong Special Administrative Region may enjoy other powers granted to it by the National People's Congress, the Standing Committee of the National People's Congress or the Central People's Government.

Article 21

Chinese citizens who are residents of the Hong Kong Special Administrative Region shall be entitled to participate in the management of state affairs according to law.

In accordance with the assigned number of seats and the selection method specified by the National People's Congress, the Chinese citizens among the residents of the Hong Kong Special Administrative Region shall locally elect deputies of the Region to the National People's Congress to participate in the work of the highest organ of state power.

Article 22

No department of the Central People's Government and no province, autonomous region, or municipality directly under the Central Government may interfere in the affairs which the Hong Kong Special Administrative Region administers on its own in accordance with this Law.

If there is a need for departments of the Central Government, or for provinces, autonomous regions, or municipalities directly under the Central Government to set up offices in the Hong Kong Special Administrative Region, they must obtain the consent of the government of the Region and the approval of the Central People's Government.

All offices set up in the Hong Kong Special Administrative Region by departments of the Central Government, or by provinces, autonomous regions, or municipalities directly under the Central Government, and the personnel of these offices shall abide by the laws of the Region.

For entry into the Hong Kong Special Administrative Region, people from other parts of China must apply for approval. Among them, the number of persons who enter the Region for the purpose of settlement shall be determined by the competent authorities of the Central People's Government after consulting the government of the Region. The Hong Kong Special Administrative Region may establish an office in Beijing.

Article 23

The Hong Kong Special Administrative Region shall enact laws on its own to prohibit any act of treason, secession, sedition or theft of state secrets.

Chapter III: Fundamental Rights and Duties of the Residents

Article 24

Residents of the Hong Kong Special Administrative Region ('Hong Kong residents') shall include permanent residents and non-permanent residents.

The permanent residents of the Special Administrative Region shall be:

(1) Chinese citizens born in Hong Kong before or after the establishment of the Hong Kong Special Administrative Region;

(2) Chinese citizens who have ordinarily resided in Hong Kong for a continuous period of not less than seven years before or after the establishment of the Hong Kong Special Administrative Region;

(3) Persons of Chinese nationality born outside Hong Kong of those residents listed in categories (1) and (2);

(4) Persons not of Chinese nationality who have entered Hong Kong with valid travel documents, have ordinarily resided in Hong Kong for a continuous period of not less than seven years and have taken Hong Kong as their place of permanent residence before or after the establishment of the Hong Kong Special Administrative Region;

(5) Persons under 21 years of age born in Hong Kong of those residents listed in category (4) before or after the establishment of the Hong Kong Special Administrative Region; and

(6) Persons other than those residents listed in categories (1) to (5), who, before the establishment of the Hong Kong Special Administrative Region, had the right of abode in Hong Kong only.

The above-mentioned residents shall have the right of abode in the Hong Kong Special Administrative Region and shall be qualified to obtain, in accordance with the laws of the Region, permanent identity cards which state their right of abode.

The non-permanent residents of the Hong Kong Special Administrative Region shall be persons who are qualified to obtain Hong Kong identity cards in accordance with the laws of the Region but have no right of abode.

Article 25

All Hong Kong residents shall be equal before the law.

Article 26

Permanent residents of the Hong Kong Special Administrative Region shall have the right to vote and the right to stand for election in accordance with law.

Article 27

Hong Kong residents shall have freedom of speech, of the press and of publication; freedom of association, of assembly, of procession and of demonstration; and the right and freedom to form and join trade unions, and to strike.

Article 28

The freedom of the person of Hong Kong residents shall be inviolable.

No Hong Kong resident shall be subjected to arbitrary or unlawful arrest, detention or imprisonment. Arbitrary or unlawful search of the body of any resident or deprivation or restriction of the freedom of the person shall be prohibited. Torture of any resident or arbitrary or unlawful deprivation of the life of any resident shall be prohibited.

Article 29

The homes and other premises of Hong Kong residents shall be inviolable. Arbitrary or unlawful search of, or intrusion into, a resident's home or other premises shall be prohibited.

Article 30

The freedom and privacy of communication of Hong Kong residents shall be protected by the law. No department or individual may, on any grounds, infringe upon the freedom and privacy of communication of residents except that the relevant authorities may inspect communication in accordance with legal procedures to meet the needs of public security or of investigation into criminal offences.

Article 31

Hong Kong residents shall have freedom of movement within the Hong Kong Special Administrative Region and freedom of emigration to other countries and regions. They shall have freedom to travel and to enter and to leave the Region. Unless restrained by law, holders of valid travel documents shall be free to leave the Region without special authorization.

Article 32

Hong Kong residents shall have freedom of conscience.

Hong Kong residents shall have freedom of religious belief and freedom to preach and to conduct and participate in religious activities in public.

Article 33

Hong Kong residents shall have freedom of choice of occupation.

Article 34

Hong Kong residents shall have freedom to engage in academic research, literary and artistic creation, and other cultural activities.

Article 35

Hong Kong residents shall have the right to confidential legal advice, access to the courts, choice of lawyers for timely protection of their lawful rights and interests or for representation in the courts, and to judicial remedies. Hong Kong residents shall have the right to social welfare in accordance with law. The welfare benefits and retirement security of the labour force shall be protected by law.

Article 36

Hong Kong residents shall have the right to social welfare as prescribed by law. The welfare benefits of the labour force shall be protected by law.

Article 37

The freedom of marriage of Hong Kong residents and their right to raise a family freely shall be protected by law.

Article 38

Hong Kong residents shall enjoy the other rights and freedoms safeguarded by the laws of the Hong Kong Special Administrative Region.

Article 39

The provisions of the International Covenant on Civil and Political Rights, the International Covenant on Economic, Social and Cultural Rights, and international labour conventions as applied to Hong Kong shall remain in force and shall be implemented through the laws of the Hong Kong Special Administrative Region.

The rights and freedoms enjoyed by Hong Kong residents shall not be restricted unless as prescribed by law. Such restrictions shall not contravene the provisions of the preceding paragraph of this Article.

Article 40

The lawful traditional rights and interests of the indigenous inhabitants of the 'New Territories' shall be protected by the Special Administrative Region.

Article 41

Persons in the Hong Kong Special Administrative Region other than Hong Kong residents shall, in accordance with law, enjoy the rights and freedoms of Hong Kong residents prescribed in this Chapter.

Article 42

Hong Kong residents and other persons in Hong Kong shall have the obligation to abide by the laws in force in the Hong Kong Special Administrative Region.

Chapter IV: Political Structure

Section 1: The Chief Executive

Article 43

The Chief Executive of the Hong Kong Special Administrative Region shall be the head of the Hong Kong Special Administrative Region and represent the Region.

The Chief Executive of the Hong Kong Special Administrative Region shall be accountable to the Central People's Government and the Hong Kong Special Administrative Region in accordance with the provisions of this Law.

Article 44

The Chief Executive of the Hong Kong Special Administrative Region shall be a Chinese citizen of not less than 40 years of age who is a permanent resident of the Region with no right of abode in any foreign country and has ordinarily resided in Hong Kong for a continuous period of not less than 20 years.

Article 45

The Chief Executive of the Hong Kong Special Administrative Region shall be selected by election or through consultations held locally and be appointed by the Central People's Government.

The method for selecting the Chief Executive shall be specified in the light of the actual situation in the Hong Kong Special Administrative Region and in accordance with the principle of gradual and orderly progress. The ultimate aim is the selection of the Chief Executive by universal suffrage upon nomination by a broadly representative nominating committee in accordance with democratic procedures.

The specific method for selecting the Chief Executive is prescribed in Annex I: 'Method for the Selection of the Chief Executive of the Hong Kong Special Administrative Region'.

Article 46
The term of office of the Chief Executive of the Hong Kong Special Administrative Region shall be five years. He or she may serve for not more than two consecutive terms.

Article 47
The Chief Executive of the Hong Kong Special Administrative Region must be a person of integrity, dedicated to his or her duties.

The Chief Executive, on assuming office, shall declare his or her assets to the Chief Justice of the Court of Final Appeal of the Hong Kong Special Administrative Region. This declaration shall be put on record.

Article 48
The Chief Executive of the Hong Kong Special Administrative Region shall exercise the following powers and functions:

(1) To lead the government of the Region;
(2) To be responsible for the implementation of this Law and other laws which, in accordance with this Law, apply in the Hong Kong Special Administrative Region;
(3) To sign bills passed by the Legislative Council and to promulgate laws; To sign budgets passed by the Legislative Council and report the budgets and final accounts to the Central People's Government for the record;
(4) To decide on government policies and to issue executive orders;
(5) To nominate and to report to the Central People's Government for appointment the following principal officials: Secretaries and Deputy Secretaries of Departments, Directors of Bureaux, Commissioner Against Corruption, Director of Audit, Commissioner of Police, Director of Immigration and Commissioner of Customs and Excise; and to recommend to the Central People's Government the removal of the above mentioned officials;
(6) To appoint or remove judges of the courts at all levels in accordance with legal procedures;
(7) To appoint or remove holders of public office in accordance with legal procedures;
(8) To implement the directives issued by the Central People's Government in respect of the relevant matters provided for in this Law;
(9) To conduct, on behalf of the Government of the Hong Kong Special Administrative Region, external affairs and other affairs as authorized by the Central Authorities;
(10) To approve the introduction of motions regarding revenues or expenditure to the Legislative Council;

(11) To decide, in the light of security and vital public interests, whether government officials or other personnel in charge of government affairs should testify or give evidence before the Legislative Council or its committees;

(12) To pardon persons convicted of criminal offences or commute their penalties; and

(13) To handle petitions and complaints.

Article 49

If the Chief Executive of the Hong Kong Special Administrative Region considers that a bill passed by the Legislative Council is not compatible with the overall interests of the Region, he or she may return it to the Legislative Council within three months for reconsideration. If the Legislative Council passes the original bill again by not less than a two-thirds majority of all the members, the Chief Executive must sign and promulgate it within one month, or act in accordance with the provisions of Article 50 of this Law.

Article 50

If the Chief Executive of the Hong Kong Special Administrative Region refuses to sign a bill passed the second time by the Legislative Council, or the Legislative Council refuses to pass a budget or any other important bill introduced by the government, and if consensus still cannot be reached after consultations, the Chief Executive may dissolve the Legislative Council.

The Chief Executive must consult the Executive Council before dissolving the Legislative Council. The Chief Executive may dissolve the Legislative Council only once in each term of his or her office.

Article 51

If the Legislative Council of the Hong Kong Special Administrative Region refuses to pass the budget introduced by the government, the Chief Executive may apply to the Legislative Council for provisional appropriations. If appropriation of public funds cannot be approved because the Legislative Council has already been dissolved, the Chief Executive may, prior to the election of the new Legislative Council, approve provisional short-term appropriations according to the level of expenditure of the previous fiscal year.

Article 52

The Chief Executive of the Hong Kong Special Administrative Region must resign under any of the following circumstances:

(1) When he or she loses the ability to discharge his or her duties as a result of serious illness or other reasons;

(2) When, after the Legislative Council is dissolved because he or she twice refuses to sign a bill passed by it, the new Legislative Council again passes by a two-thirds majority of all the members the original bill in dispute, but he or she still refuses to sign it; and

(3) When, after the Legislative Council is dissolved because it refuses to pass a budget or any other important bill, the new Legislative Council still refuses to pass the original bill in dispute.

Article 53

If the Chief Executive of the Hong Kong Special Administrative Region is not able to discharge his or her duties for a short period, such duties shall temporarily be assumed by the Administrative Secretary, Financial Secretary or Secretary of Justice in this order of precedence.

In the event that the office of Chief Executive becomes vacant, a new Chief Executive shall be selected within six months in accordance with the provisions of Article 45 of this Law. During the period of vacancy, his or her duties shall be assumed according to the provisions of the preceding paragraph.

Article 54

The Executive Council of the Hong Kong Special Administrative Region shall be an organ for assisting the Chief Executive in policy-making.

Article 55

Members of the Executive Council of the Hong Kong Special Administrative Region shall be appointed by the Chief Executive from among the principal officials of the executive authorities, members of the Legislative Council and public figures. Their appointment or removal shall be decided by the Chief Executive. The term of office of members of the Executive Council shall not extend beyond the expiry of the term of office of the Chief Executive who appoints them.

Members of the Executive Council of the Hong Kong Special Administrative Region shall be Chinese citizens who are permanent residents of the Region with no right of abode in any foreign country.

The Chief Executive may, as he or she deems necessary, invite other persons concerned to sit in on meetings of the Council.

Article 56

The Executive Council of the Hong Kong Special Administrative Region shall be presided over by the Chief Executive.

Except for the appointment, removal and disciplining of officials and the adoption of measures in emergencies, the Chief Executive shall consult the Executive Council before making important policy decisions, introducing bills to the Legislative Council, making subordinate legislation, or dissolving the Legislative Council.

If the Chief Executive does not accept a majority opinion of the Executive Council, he or she shall put the specific reasons on record.

Article 57

A Commission Against Corruption shall be established in the Hong Kong Special Administrative Region. It shall function independently and be accountable to the Chief Executive.

Article 58

A Commission of Audit shall be established in the Hong Kong Special Administrative Region. It shall function independently and be accountable to the Chief Executive.

Section 2: The Executive Authorities

Article 59

The Government of the Hong Kong Special Administrative Region shall be the executive authorities of the Region.

Article 60

The head of the Government of the Hong Kong Special Administrative Region shall be the Chief Executive of the Region.

A Department of Administration, a Department of Finance, a Department of Justice, and various bureaux, divisions and commissions shall be established in the Government of the Hong Kong Special Administrative Region.

Article 61

The principal officials of the Hong Kong Special Administrative Region shall be Chinese citizens who are permanent residents of the Region with no right of abode in any foreign country and have ordinarily resided in Hong Kong for a continuous period of not less than 15 years.

Article 62

The Government of the Hong Kong Special Administrative Region shall exercise the following powers and functions:

(1) To formulate and implement policies;
(2) To conduct administrative affairs;
(3) To conduct external affairs as authorized by the Central People's Government under this Law;
(4) To draw up and introduce budgets and final accounts;
(5) To draft and introduce bills, motions and subordinate legislation; and
(6) To designate officials to sit in on the meetings of the Legislative Council and to speak on behalf of the government.

Article 63

The Department of Justice of the Hong Kong Special Administrative Region shall control criminal prosecutions, free from any interference.

Article 64

The Government of the Hong Kong Special Administrative Region must abide by the law and be accountable to the Legislative Council of the Region: It shall implement laws passed by the Council and already in force; it shall present regular policy addresses to the Council; it shall answer questions raised by members of the Council; and it shall obtain approval from the Council for taxation and public expenditure.

Article 65

The previous system of establishing advisory bodies by the executive authorities shall be maintained.

Section 3: The Legislature

Article 66

The Legislative Council of the Hong Kong Special Administrative Region shall be the legislature of the Region.

Article 67

The Legislative Council of the Hong Kong Special Administrative Region shall be composed of Chinese citizens who are permanent residents of the Region with no right of abode in any foreign country. However, permanent residents of the Region who are not of Chinese nationality or who have the right of abode in foreign countries may also be elected members of the Legislative Council of the Region, provided that the proportion of such members does not exceed 20 per cent of the total membership of the Council.

Article 68

The Legislative Council of the Hong Kong Special Administrative Region shall be constituted by election.

The method for forming the Legislative Council shall be specified in the light of the actual situation in the Hong Kong Special Administrative Region and in accordance with the principle of gradual and orderly progress. The ultimate aim is the election of all the members of the Legislative Council by universal suffrage.

The specific method for forming the Legislative Council and its procedures for voting on bills and motions are prescribed in Annex II: 'Method for the Formation of the Legislative Council of the Hong Kong Special Administrative Region and Its Voting Procedures'.

Article 69

The term of office of the Legislative Council of the Hong Kong Special Administrative Region shall be four years, except the first term which shall be two years.

Article 70

If the Legislative Council of the Hong Kong Special Administrative Region is dissolved by the Chief Executive in accordance with the provisions of this Law, it must, within three months, be reconstituted by election in accordance with Article 68 of this Law.

Article 71

The President of the Legislative Council of the Hong Kong Special Administrative Region shall be elected by and from among the members of the Legislative Council.

The President of the Legislative Council of the Hong Kong Special Administrative Region shall be a Chinese citizen of not less than 40 years of age, who is a permanent resident of the Region with no right of abode in any foreign country and has ordinarily resided in Hong Kong for a continuous period of not less than 20 years.

Article 72

The President of the Legislative Council of the Hong Kong Special Administrative Region shall exercise the following powers and functions:

(1) To preside over meetings;
(2) To decide on the agenda, giving priority to government bills for inclusion in the agenda;
(3) To decide on the time of meetings;
(4) To call special sessions during the recess;
(5) To call emergency sessions on the request of the Chief Executive; and
(6) To exercise other powers and functions as prescribed in the rules of procedure of the Legislative Council.

Article 73

The Legislative Council of the Hong Kong Special Administrative Region shall exercise the following powers and functions:

(1) To enact, amend or repeal laws in accordance with the provisions of this Law and legal procedures;
(2) To examine and approve budgets introduced by the government;
(3) To approve taxation and public expenditure;

    (4) To receive and debate the policy addresses of the Chief Executive;

    (5) To raise questions on the work of the government;

    (6) To debate any issue concerning public interests;

    (7) To endorse the appointment and removal of the judges of the Court of Final Appeal and the Chief Judge of the High Court;

    (8) To receive and handle complaints from Hong Kong residents;

    (9) If a motion initiated jointly by one-fourth of all the members of the Legislative Council charges the Chief Executive with serious breach of law or dereliction of duty and if he or she refuses to resign, the Council may, after passing a motion for investigation, give a mandate to the Chief Justice of the Court of Final Appeal to form and chair an independent investigation committee. The committee shall be responsible for carrying out the investigation and reporting its findings to the Council. If the committee considers the evidence sufficient to substantiate such charges, the Council may pass a motion of impeachment by a two-thirds majority of all its members and report it to the Central People's Government for decision; and

  (10) To summon, as required when exercising the above-mentioned powers and functions, persons concerned to testify or give evidence.

Article 74

Members of the Legislative Council of the Hong Kong Special Administrative Region may introduce bills in accordance with the provisions of this Law and legal procedures. Bills which do not relate to public expenditure or political structure or the operation of the government may be introduced individually or jointly by members of the Council. The written consent of the Chief Executive shall be required before bills relating to government policies are introduced.

Article 75

The quorum for the meeting of the Legislative Council of the Hong Kong Special Administrative Region shall be not less than one half of all its members.

The rules of procedure of the Legislative Council shall be made by the Council on its own, provided that they do not contravene this Law.

Article 76

A bill passed by the Legislative Council of the Hong Kong Special Administrative Region may take effect only after it is signed and promulgated by the Chief Executive.

Article 77

Members of the Legislative Council of the Hong Kong Special Administrative Region shall be immune from legal action in respect of their statements at meetings of the Council.

Article 78

Members of the Legislative Council of the Hong Kong Special Administrative Region shall not be subjected to arrest when attending or on their way to a meeting of the Council.

Article 79

The President of the Legislative Council of the Hong Kong Special Administrative Region shall declare that a member of the Council is no longer qualified for the office under any of the following circumstances:

(1) When he or she loses the ability to discharge his or her duties as a result of serious illness or other reasons;

(2) When he or she, with no valid reason, is absent from meetings for three consecutive months without the consent of the President of the Legislative Council;

(3) When he or she loses or renounces his or her status as a permanent resident of the Region;

(4) When he or she accepts a government appointment and becomes a public servant;

(5) When he or she is bankrupt or fails to comply with a court order to repay debts;

(6) When he or she is convicted and sentenced to imprisonment for one month or more for a criminal offence committed within or outside the Region and is relieved of his or her duties by a motion passed by two-thirds of the members of the Legislative Council present; and

(7) When he or she is censured for misbehaviour or breach of oath by a vote of two-thirds of the members of the Legislative Council present.

Section 4: The Judiciary

Article 80

The courts of the Hong Kong Special Administrative Region at all levels shall be the judiciary of the Region, exercising the judicial power of the Region.

Article 81

The Court of Final Appeal, the High Court, district courts, magistrates' courts and other special courts shall be established in the Hong Kong Special Administrative Region. The High Court shall comprise the Court of Appeal and the Court of First Instance.

The judicial system previously practised in Hong Kong shall be maintained except for those changes consequent upon the establishment of the Court of Final Appeal of the Hong Kong Special Administrative Region.

Article 82

The power of final adjudication of the Hong Kong Special Administrative Region shall be vested in the Court of Final Appeal of the Region, which may as required invite judges from other common law jurisdictions to sit on the Court of Final Appeal.

Article 83

The structure, powers and functions of the courts of the Hong Kong Special Administrative Region at all levels shall be prescribed by law.

Article 84

The courts of the Hong Kong Special Administrative Region shall adjudicate cases in accordance with the laws applicable in the Region as prescribed in Article 18 of this Law and may refer to precedents of other common law jurisdictions.

Article 85

The courts of the Hong Kong Special Administrative Region shall exercise judicial power independently, free from any interference. Members of the judiciary shall be immune from legal action in the performance of their judicial functions.

Article 86
The principle of trial by jury previously practised in Hong Kong shall be maintained.

Article 87
In criminal or civil proceedings in the Hong Kong Special Administrative Region, the principles previously applied in Hong Kong and the rights previously enjoyed by parties to proceedings shall be maintained.

Anyone who is lawfully arrested shall have the right to a fair trial by the judicial organs without delay and shall be presumed innocent until convicted by the judicial organs.

Article 88
Judges of the courts of the Hong Kong Special Administrative Region shall be appointed by the Chief Executive on the recommendation of an independent commission composed of local judges, persons from the legal profession and eminent persons from other sectors.

Article 89
A judge of a court of the Hong Kong Special Administrative Region may only be removed for inability to discharge his or her duties, or for misbehaviour, by the Chief Executive on the recommendation of a tribunal appointed by the Chief Justice of the Court of Final Appeal and consisting of not fewer than three local judges.

The Chief Justice of the Court of Final Appeal of the Hong Kong Special Administrative Region may be investigated only for inability to discharge his or her duties, or for misbehaviour, by a tribunal appointed by the Chief Executive and consisting of not fewer than five local judges and may be removed by the Chief Executive on the recommendation of the tribunal and in accordance with the procedures prescribed in this Law.

Article 90
The Chief Justice of the Court of Final Appeal and the Chief Judge of the High Court of the Hong Kong Special Administrative Region shall be Chinese citizens who are permanent residents of the Region with no right of abode in any foreign country.

In the case of the appointment or removal of judges of the Court of Final Appeal and the Chief Judge of the High Court of the Hong Kong Special Administrative Region, the Chief Executive shall, in addition to following the procedures prescribed in Articles 88 and 89 of this Law, obtain the endorsement of the Legislative Council and report such appointment or removal to the Standing Committee of the National People's Congress for the record.

Article 91
The Hong Kong Special Administrative Region shall maintain the previous system of appointment and removal of members of the judiciary other than judges.

Article 92
Judges and other members of the judiciary of the Hong Kong Special Administrative Region shall be chosen on the basis of their judicial and professional qualities and may be recruited from other common law jurisdictions.

Article 93
Judges and other members of the judiciary serving in Hong Kong before the establishment of the Hong Kong Special Administrative Region may all remain in

employment and retain their seniority with pay, allowances, benefits and conditions of service no less favourable than before.

The Government of the Hong Kong Special Administrative Region shall pay to judges and other members of the judiciary who retire or leave the service in compliance with regulations, including those who have retired or left the service before the establishment of the Hong Kong Special Administrative Region, or to their dependants, all pensions, gratuities, allowances and benefits due to them on terms no less favourable than before, irrespective of their nationality or place of residence.

Article 94

On the basis of the system previously operating in Hong Kong, the Government of the Hong Kong Special Administrative Region may make provisions for local lawyers and lawyers from outside Hong Kong to work and practise in the Region.

Article 95

The Hong Kong Special Administrative Region may, through consultations and in accordance with law, maintain juridical relations with the judicial organs of other parts of the country, and they may render assistance to each other.

Article 96

With the assistance or authorization of the Central People's Government, the Government of the Hong Kong Special Administrative Region may make appropriate arrangements with foreign states for reciprocal juridical assistance.

Section 5: District Organizations

Article 97

District organizations which are not organs of political power may be established in the Hong Kong Special Administrative Region, to be consulted by the government of the Region or district administration and other affairs, or to be responsible for providing services in such fields as culture, recreation and environmental sanitation.

Article 98

The powers and functions of the district organizations and the method for their formation shall be prescribed by law.

Section 6: Public Servants

Article 99

Public servants serving in all government departments of the Hong Kong Special Administrative Region must be permanent residents of the Region, except where otherwise provided for in Article 101 of this Law regarding public servants of foreign nationalities and except for those below a certain rank as prescribed by law.

Public servants must be dedicated to their duties and be responsible to the Government of the Hong Kong Special Administrative Region.

Article 100

Public servants serving in all Hong Kong government departments, including the police department, before the establishment of the Hong Kong Special Administrative Region, may all remain in employment and retain their seniority with pay, allowances, benefits and conditions of service no less favourable than before.

Article 101

The Government of the Hong Kong Special Administrative Region may employ British and other foreign nationals previously serving in the public service in Hong Kong, or those holding permanent identity cards of the Region, to serve as public servants in government departments at all levels, but only Chinese citizens among permanent residents of the Region with no right of abode in any foreign country may fill the following posts: the Secretaries and Deputy Secretaries of Departments, Directors of Bureaux, Commissioner Against Corruption, Director of Audit, Commissioner of Police, Director of Immigration and Commissioner of Customs and Excise.

The Government of the Hong Kong Special Administrative Region may also employ British and other foreign nationals as advisers to government departments and, when required, may recruit qualified candidates from outside the Region to fill professional and technical posts in government departments. These foreign nationals shall be employed only in their individual capacities and shall be responsible to the government of the region.

Article 102

The Government of the Hong Kong Special Administrative Region shall pay to public servants who retire or who leave the service in compliance with regulations, including those who have retired or who have left the service in compliance with regulations before the establishment of the Hong Kong Special Administrative Region, or to their dependants, all pensions, gratuities, allowances and benefits due to them on terms no less favourable than before, irrespective of their nationality or place of residence.

Article 103

The appointment and promotion of public servants shall be on the basis of their qualifications, experience and ability. Hong Kong's previous system of recruitment, employment, assessment, discipline, training and management for the public service, including special bodies for their appointment, pay and conditions of service, shall be maintained, except for any provisions for privileged treatment of foreign nationals.

Article 104

When assuming office, the Chief Executive, principal officials, members of the Executive Council and of the Legislative Council, judges of the courts at all levels and other members of the judiciary in the Hong Kong Special Administrative Region must, in accordance with law, swear to uphold the Basic Law of the Hong Kong Special Administrative Region of the People's Republic of China and swear allegiance to the Hong Kong Special Administrative Region of the People's Republic of China.

Chapter V: Economy

Section 1: Public Finance, Monetary Affairs, Trade, Industry and Commerce

Article 105

The Hong Kong Special Administrative Region shall, in accordance with law, protect the right of individuals and legal persons to the acquisition, use, disposal and inheritance of property and their right to compensation for lawful deprivation of their property.

Such compensation shall correspond to the real value of the property concerned at the time and shall be freely convertible and paid without undue delay.

The ownership of enterprises and the investments from outside the Region shall be protected by law.

Article 106

The Hong Kong Special Administrative Region shall have independent finances.

The Hong Kong Special Administrative Region shall use its financial revenues exclusively for its own purposes, and they shall not be handed over to the Central People's Government.

The Central People's Government shall not levy taxes in the Hong Kong Special Administrative Region.

Article 107

The Hong Kong Special Administrative Region shall follow the principle of keeping expenditure within the limits of revenues in drawing up its budget, and strive to achieve a fiscal balance, avoid deficits and keep the budget commensurate with the growth rate of its gross domestic product.

Article 108

The Hong Kong Special Administrative Region shall practise an independent taxation system.

The Hong Kong Special Administrative Region shall, taking the low tax policy previously pursued in Hong Kong as reference, enact laws on its own concerning types of taxes, tax rates, tax reductions, allowances and exemptions, and other matters of taxation.

Article 109

The Government of the Hong Kong Special Administrative Region shall provide an appropriate economic and legal environment for the maintenance of the status of Hong Kong as an international financial centre.

Article 110

The monetary and financial systems of the Hong Kong Special Administrative Region shall be prescribed by law.

The Government of the Hong Kong Special Administrative Region shall, on its own, formulate monetary and financial policies, safeguard the free operation of financial business and financial markets, and regulate and supervise them in accordance with law.

Article 111

The Hong Kong dollar, as the legal tender in the Hong Kong Special Administrative Region, shall continue to circulate.

The authority to issue Hong Kong currency shall be vested in the Government of the Hong Kong Special Administrative Region. the issue of Hong Kong currency must be backed by a 100 per cent reserve fund. The system regarding the issue of Hong Kong currency and the reserve fund system shall be prescribed by law.

The Government of the Hong Kong Special Administrative Region may authorize designated banks to issue or continue to issue Hong Kong currency under statutory authority, after satisfying itself that any issue of currency will be soundly based and that the arrangements for such issue are consistent with the object of maintaining the stability of the currency.

Article 112

No foreign exchange control policies shall be applied in the Hong Kong Special Administrative Region. The Hong Kong dollar shall be freely convertible. Markets for foreign exchange, gold, securities, future and the like shall continue.

The Government of the Hong Kong Special Administrative Region shall safeguard the free flow of capital within, into and out of the Region.

Article 113

The Exchange Fund of the Hong Kong Special Administrative Region shall be managed and controlled by the government of the Region, primarily for regulating the exchange value of the Hong Kong dollar.

Article 114

The Hong Kong Special Administrative Region shall maintain the status of a free port and shall not impose any tariff unless otherwise prescribed by law.

Article 115

The Hong Kong Special Administrative Region shall pursue the policy of free trade and safeguard the free movement of goods, intangible assets and capital.

Article 116

The Hong Kong Special Administrative Region shall be a separate customs territory.

The Hong Kong Special Administrative Region may, using the name 'Hong Kong, China', participate in relevant international organizations and international trade agreements (including preferential trade arrangements), such as the General Agreement of Tariffs and Trade and arrangements regarding international trade in textiles.

Export quotas, tariff preferences and other similar arrangements, which are obtained or made by the Hong Kong Special Administrative Region or which were obtained or made and remain valid, shall be enjoyed exclusively by the Region.

Article 117

The Hong Kong Special Administrative Region may issue its own certificates of origin for products in accordance with prevailing rules of origin.

Article 118

The Government of the Hong Kong Special Administrative Region shall provide an economic and legal environment for encouraging investments, technological progress and the development of new industries.

Article 119

The Government of the Hong Kong Special Administrative Region shall formulate appropriate policies to promote and co-ordinate the development of various trades such as manufacturing, commerce, tourism, real estate, transport, public utilities, services, agriculture and fisheries, and pay regard to the protection of the environment.

Section 2: Land Leases

Article 120

All leases of land granted, decided upon or renewed before the establishment of the Hong Kong Special Administrative Region shall extend beyond 30 June 1997, and all rights in relation to such leases, shall continue to be recognized and protected under the law of the Region.

Article 121
As regards all leases of land granted or renewed where the original leases contain no right of renewal, during the period from 27 May 1985 to 30 June 1997, which extend beyond 30 June 1997 and expire not later than 30 June 2047, the lessee is not required to pay an additional premium as from 1 July 1997, but an annual rent equivalent to 3 per cent of the rateable value of the property at that date, adjusted in step with any changes in the rateable value thereafter, shall be charged.

Article 122
In the case of old schedule lots, village lots, small houses and similar rural holdings, where the property was on 30 June 1984 held by, or, in the case of small houses granted after that date, where the property is granted to, a lessee descended through the male line from a person who was in 1898 a resident of an established village in Hong Kong, the previous rent shall remain unchanged so long as the property is held by that lessee or by one of his lawful successors in the male line.

Article 123
Where leases of land without a right of renewal expire after the establishment of the Hong Kong Special Administrative Region, they shall be dealt with in accordance with laws and policies formulated by the Region on its own.

Section 3: Shipping

Article 124
The Hong Kong Special Administrative Region shall maintain Hong Kong's previous systems of shipping management and shipping regulation, including the system for regulating conditions of seamen.

The Government of the Hong Kong Special Administrative Region shall, on its own, define its specific functions and responsibilities in respect of shipping.

Article 125
The Hong Kong Special Administrative Region shall be authorized by the Central People's Government to continue to maintain a shipping register and issue related certificates under its legislation, using the name 'Hong Kong, China'.

Article 126
With the exception of foreign warships, access for which requires the special permission of the Central People's Government, ships shall enjoy access to the ports of the Hong Kong Special Administrative Region in accordance with the laws of the Region.

Article 127
Private shipping businesses and shipping-related businesses and private container terminals in the Hong Kong Special Administrative Region may continue to operate freely.

Section 4: Civil Aviation

Article 128
The Government of the Hong Kong Special Administrative Region shall provide

conditions and take measures for the maintenance of the status of Hong Kong as a centre of international and regional aviation.

Article 129
The Hong Kong Special Administrative Region shall continue the previous system of civil aviation management in Hong Kong and keep its own aircraft register in accordance with provisions laid down by the Central People's Government concerning nationality marks and registration marks of aircraft.

Access of foreign state aircraft to the Hong Kong Special Administrative Region shall require the special permission of the Central People's Government.

Article 130
The Hong Kong Special Administrative Region shall be responsible on its own for matters of routine business and technical management of civil aviation, including the management of airports, the provision of air traffic services within the flight information region of the Hong Kong Special Administrative Region, and the discharge of other responsibilities allocated to it under the regional air navigation procedures of the International Civil Aviation Organization.

Article 131
The Central People's Government shall, in consultation with the Government of the Hong Kong Special Administrative Region, make arrangements providing air services between the Region and other parts of the People's Republic of China for airlines incorporated in the Hong Kong Special Administrative Region and having their principal place of business in Hong Kong and other airlines of the People's Republic of China.

Article 132
All air service agreements providing air services between other parts of the People's Republic of China and other states and regions with stops at the Hong Kong Special Administrative Region and air services between the Hong Kong Special Administrative Region and other states and regions with stops at other parts of the People's Republic of China shall be concluded by the Central People's Government.

In concluding the air service agreements referred to in the first paragraph of this Article, the Central People's Government shall take account of the special conditions and economic interests of the Hong Kong Special Administrative Region and consult the government of the Region.

Representatives of the Government of the Hong Kong Special Administrative Region may, as members of the delegations of the Government of the People's Republic of China, participate in air service consultations conducted by the Central People's Government with foreign governments concerning arrangements for such services referred to in the first paragraph of this Article.

Article 133
Acting under specific authorizations from the Central people's Government, the Government of the Hong Kong Special Administrative Region may:

(1) renew or amend air service agreements and arrangements previously in force;

(2) negotiate and conclude new air service agreements providing routes for air lines incorporated in the Hong Kong Special Administrative Region and having their principal place of business in Hong Kong and providing rights for over-flights and technical stops; and

(3) negotiate and conclude provisional arrangements with foreign states or regions with which no air service agreements have been concluded.

All scheduled air services to, from or through Hong Kong, which do not operate to, from or through the mainland of China shall be regulated by the air service agreements or provisional arrangements referred to in this Article.

Article 134

The Central People's Government shall give the Government of the Hong Kong Special Administrative Region the authority to:

(1) negotiate and conclude with other authorities all arrangements concerning the implementation of the air service agreements and provisional arrangements referred to in Article 133 of this Law;

(2) issue licences to airlines incorporated in the Hong Kong Special Administrative Region and having their principal place of business in Hong Kong;

(3) designate such airlines under the air service agreements and provisional arrangements referred to in Article 133 of this Law; and

(4) issue permits to foreign airlines for services other than those to, from or through the mainland of China.

Article 135

Airlines incorporated and having their principal place of business in Hong Kong and businesses related to civil aviation functioning there prior to the establishment of the Hong Kong Special Administrative Region may continue to operate.

Chapter VI: Education, Science, Culture, Sports, Religion, Labour and Social Services

Article 136

On the basis of the previous educational system, the Government of the Hong Kong Special Administrative Region shall, on its own, formulate policies on the development and improvement of education, including policies regarding the educational system and its administration, the language of instruction, the allocation of funds, the examination system, the system of academic awards and the recognition of educational qualifications.

Community organizations and individuals may, in accordance with law, run educational undertakings of various kinds in the Hong Kong Special Administrative Region.

Article 137

Educational institutions of all kinds may retain their autonomy and enjoy academic freedom. They may continue to recruit staff and use teaching materials from outside the Hong Kong Special Administrative Region. Schools run by religious organizations may continue to provide religious education, including courses in religion.

Students shall enjoy freedom of choice of educational institutions and freedom to pursue their education outside the Hong Kong Special Administrative Region.

Article 138

The Government of the Hong Kong Special Administrative Region shall, on its own, formulate policies to develop Western and traditional Chinese medicine and to improve medical and health services. Community organizations and individuals may provide various medical and health services in accordance with law.

Article 139

The Government of the Hong Kong Special Administrative Region shall, on its own, formulate policies on science and technology and protect by law achievements in scientific and technological research, patents, discoveries and inventions.

The Government of the Hong Kong Special Administrative Region shall, on its own, decide on the scientific and technological standards and specifications applicable in Hong Kong.

Article 140

The Government of the Hong Kong Special Administrative Region shall, on its own, formulate policies on culture and protect by law the achievements and the lawful rights and interests of authors in their literary and artistic creation.

Article 141

The Government of the Hong Kong Special Administrative Region shall not restrict the freedom of religious belief, interfere in the internal affairs of religious organizations or restrict religious activities which do not contravene the laws of the Region.

Religious organizations shall, in accordance with law, enjoy the rights to acquire, use, dispose of and inherit property and the right to receive financial assistance. Their previous property rights and interests shall be maintained and protected.

Religious organizations may, according to their previous practice, continue to run seminaries and other schools, hospitals and welfare institutions and to provide other social services.

Religious organizations and believers in the Hong Kong Special Administrative Region may maintain and develop their relations with religious organizations and believers elsewhere.

Article 142

The Government of the Hong Kong Special Administrative Region shall, on the basis of maintaining the previous systems concerning the professions, formulate provisions on its own for assessing the qualifications for practice in the various professions.

Persons with professional qualifications or qualifications for professional practice obtained prior to the establishment of the Hong Kong Special Administrative Region may retain their previous qualifications in accordance with the relevant regulations and codes of practice.

The Government of the Hong Kong Special Administrative Region shall continue to recognize the professions and the professional organizations recognized prior to the establishment of the Region, and these organizations may, on their own, assess and confer professional qualifications.

The Government of the Hong Kong Special Administrative Region may, as required by developments in society and in consultation with the parties concerned, recognize new professions and professional organizations.

Article 143

The Government of the Hong Kong Special Administrative Region shall, on its own, formulate policies on sports. Non-governmental sports organizations may continue to exist and develop in accordance with law.

Article 144

The Government of the Hong Kong Special Administrative Region shall maintain the policy previously practised in Hong Kong in respect of subventions for non-governmental organizations in fields such as education, medicine and health, culture, art, recreation, sports, social welfare and social work. Staff members previously serving in subvented organizations in Hong Kong may remain in their employment in accordance with the previous system.

Article 145

On the basis of the previous social welfare system, the Government of the Hong Kong Special Administrative Region shall, on its own, formulate policies on the development and improvement of this system in the light of the economic conditions and social needs.

Article 146

Voluntary organizations providing social services in the Hong Kong Special Administrative Region may, on their own, decide their forms of service, provided that the law is not contravened.

Article 147

The Hong Kong Special Administrative Region shall on its own formulate laws and policies relating to labour.

Article 148

The relationship between non-governmental organizations in fields such as education, science, technology, culture, art, sports, the professions, medicine and health, labour, social welfare and social work as well as religious organizations in the Hong Kong Special Administrative Region and their counterparts on the mainland shall be based on the principles of non-subordination, non-interference and mutual respect.

Article 149

Non-governmental organizations in fields such as education, science, technology, culture, art, sports, the professions, medicine and health, labour, social welfare and social work as well as religious organizations in the Hong Kong Special Administrative Region may maintain and develop relations with their counterparts in foreign countries and regions and with relevant international organizations. They may, as required, use the name 'Hong Kong, China' in the relevant activities.

Chapter VII: External Affairs

Article 150

Representatives of the Government of the Hong Kong Special Administrative Region may, as members of delegations of the Government of the People's Republic of China, participate in negotiations at the diplomatic level directly affecting the Region conducted by the Central People's Government.

Article 151

The Hong Kong Special Administrative Region may on its own, using the name 'Hong Kong, China', maintain and develop relations and conclude and implement agreements with foreign states and regions and relevant international organizations in the appropriate fields, including the economic, trade, financial and monetary, shipping, communications, tourism, cultural and sports fields.

Article 152

Representatives of the Government of the Hong Kong Special Administrative Region may, as members of delegations of the People's Republic of China, participate in international organizations or conferences in appropriate fields limited to states and affecting the Region, or may attend in such other capacity as may be permitted by the Central People's Government and the international organization or conference concerned, and may express their views, using the name 'Hong Kong, China'.

The Hong Kong Special Administrative Region may, using the name 'Hong Kong, China', participate in international organizations and conferences not limited to states.

The Central People's Government shall take the necessary steps to ensure that the Hong Kong Special Administrative Region shall continue to retain its status in an appropriate capacity in those international organizations of which the People's Republic of China is a member and in which Hong Kong participates in one capacity or another.

The Central People's Government shall, where necessary, facilitate the continued participation of the Hong Kong Special Administrative Region in an appropriate capacity in those international organizations in which Hong Kong is a participant in one capacity or another, but of which the People's Republic of China is not a member.

Article 153

The application of the Hong Kong Special Administrative Region of international agreements to which the People's Republic of China is or becomes a party shall be decided by the Central People's Government, in accordance with the circumstances and needs of the Region, and after seeking the views of the government of the Region.

International agreements to which the People's Republic of China is not a party but which are implemented in Hong Kong may continue to be implemented in the Hong Kong Special Administrative Region. The Central People's Government shall, as necessary, authorize or assist the government of the Region to make appropriate arrangements for the application to the Region of other relevant international agreements.

Article 154

The Central People's Government shall authorize the Government of the Hong Kong Special Administrative Region to issue, in accordance with law, passports of the Hong Kong Special Administrative Region of the People's Republic of China to all Chinese citizens who hold permanent identity cards of the Region, and travel documents of the Hong Kong Special Administrative Region of the People's Republic of China to all other persons lawfully residing in the Region. The above passports and documents shall be valid for all states and regions and shall record the holder's right to return to the Region.

The Government of the Hong Kong Special Administrative Region may apply immigration controls on entry into, stay in and departure from the Region by persons from foreign states and regions.

Article 155
The Central People's Government shall assist to authorize the Government of the Hong Kong Special Administrative Region to conclude visa abolition agreements with foreign states or regions.

Article 156
The Hong Kong Special Administrative Region may, as necessary, establish official or semi-official economic and trade missions in foreign countries and shall report the establishment of such missions to the Central People's Government for the record.

Article 157
The establishment of foreign consular and other official or semi-official missions in the Hong Kong Special Administrative Region shall require the approval of the Central People's Government.

Consular and other official missions established in Hong Kong by states which have formal diplomatic relations with the People's Republic of China may be maintained.

According to the circumstances of each case, consular and other official missions established in Hong Kong by states which have no formal diplomatic relations with the People's Republic of China may be permitted either to remain or be changed to semi-official missions.

States not recognized by the People's Republic of China may only establish nongovernmental institutions in the Region.

Chapter VIII: Interpretation and Amendment of the Basic Law

Article 158
The power of interpretation of this Law shall be vested in the Standing Committee of the National People's Congress.

The Standing Committee of the National People's Congress shall authorize the courts of the Hong Kong Special Administrative Region to interpret on their own, in adjudicating cases, the provisions of this Law which are within the limits of the autonomy of the Region.

The courts of the Hong Kong Special Administrative Region may also interpret other provisions of this Law in adjudicating cases. However, if the courts of the Region, in adjudicating cases, need to interpret the provisions of this Law concerning affairs which are the responsibility of the Central People's Government, or concerning the relationship between the Central Authorities and the Region, and if such interpretation will affect the judgments on the cases, the courts of the Region shall, before making their final judgments which are not appealable, seek an interpretation of the relevant provisions from the Standing Committee of the National People's Congress through the Court of final Appeal of the Region. When the Standing Committee makes an interpretation of the provisions concerned, the courts of the Region, in applying those provisions, shall follow the interpretation of the Standing Committee. However, judgments previously rendered shall not be affected.

The Standing Committee of the National People's Congress shall consult its Committee for the Basic Law of the Hong Kong Special Administrative Region before giving an interpretation of this law.

Article 159

The power of amendment of this Law shall be vested in the National People's Congress.

The power to propose bills for amendments to this Law shall be vested in the Standing Committee of the National People's Congress, the State Council and the Hong Kong Special Administrative Region. Amendment bills from the Hong Kong Special Administrative Region shall be submitted to the National People's Congress by the delegation of the Region to the National People's Congress after obtaining the consent of two-thirds of the deputies of the Region to the National People's Congress, two-thirds of all the members of the Legislative Council of the Region, and the Chief Executive of the Region.

Before a bill for amendment to this Law is put on the agenda of the National People's Congress, the Committee for the Basic Law of the Hong Kong Special Administrative Region shall study it and submit its views.

No amendment to this Law shall contravene the established basic policies of the People's Republic of China regarding Hong Kong.

Chapter IX: Supplementary Provisions

Article 160

Upon the establishment of the Hong Kong Special Administrative Region, the laws previously in force in Hong Kong shall be adopted as laws of the Region except for those which the Standing Committee of the National People's Congress declares to be in contravention of this Law. If any laws are later discovered to be in contravention of this Law, they shall be amended or cease to have force in accordance with the procedure as prescribed by this Law.

Documents, certificates, contracts, and rights and obligations valid under the laws previously in force in Hong Kong shall continue to be valid and be recognized and protected by the Hong Kong Special Administrative Region, provided that they do not contravene this Law.

APPENDIX C

Hong Kong Bill of Rights

An Ordinance to provide for the incorporation into the law of Hong Kong of provisions of the International Covenant on Civil and Political Rights [ICCPR] as applied to Hong Kong; and for ancillary and connected matters.
(8 June 1991)
Enacted by the Governor of Hong Kong, with the advice and consent of the Legislative Council thereof.

PART I
Preliminary

1. Short title and commencement

(1) This Ordinance may be cited as the Hong Kong Bill of Rights Ordinance 1991.

(2) This Ordinance shall come into operation on 8 June 1991.

2. Interpretation

(1) In this Ordinance, unless the context otherwise requires—

"article" means an article of the Bill of Rights;
"Bill of Rights" means the Hong Kong Bill of Rights set out in Part II;
"commencement date" means the date on which this Ordinance comes into operation;
"legislation" means legislation that can be amended by an Ordinance;
"pre-existing legislation" means legislation enacted before the commencement date.

(2) The Bill of Rights is subject to Part III.

(3) In interpreting and applying this Ordinance, regard shall be had to the fact that the purpose of this Ordinance is to provide for the incorporation into the law of Hong Kong of provisions of the International Covenant on Civil and Political Rights as applied to Hong Kong, and for ancillary and connected matters.

(4) Nothing in this Ordinance shall be interpreted as implying for the Government or any authority, group or person any right to engage in any activity or perform any act aimed at the destruction of any of the rights and

169

freedoms recognized in the Bill of Rights or at their limitation to a greater extent than is provided for in the Bill.

[cf. ICCPR Art. 5.1]

(5) There shall be no restriction upon or derogation from any of the fundamental human rights recognized or existing in Hong Kong pursuant to law, conventions, regulations or existing in Hong Kong pursuant to law, conventions, regulations or custom on the pretext that the Bill of Rights does not recognize such rights or that it recognizes them to a lesser extent.

[cf. ICCPR Art. 5.2]

(6) A heading to any article does not have any legislative effect and does not in any way vary, limit or extend the meaning of the article.

3. Effect on pre-existing legislation
    (1) All pre-existing legislation that admits of a construction consistent with this Ordinance shall be given such a construction.
    (2) All pre-existing legislation that does not admit of a construction consistent with this Ordinance is, to the extent of the inconsistency, repealed.

4. Interpretation of subsequent legislation
All legislation enacted on or after the commencement date shall, to the extent that it admits of such a construction, be construed so as to be consistent with the International Covenant on Civil and Political Rights as applied to Hong Kong.

5. Public emergencies
    (1) In time of public emergency which threatens the life of the nation and the existence of which is officially proclaimed, measures may be taken derogating from the Bill of Rights to the extent strictly required by the exigencies of the situation, but these measures shall be taken in accordance with law.
    (2) No measure shall be taken under subsection (1) that—
        (a) is inconsistent with any obligation under international law that applies to Hong Kong (other than an obligation under the International Covenant on Civil and Political rights);
        (b) involves discrimination solely on the ground of race, colour, sex, language, religion or social origin; or
        (c) derogates from articles 2, 3, 4(1) and (2), 7, 12, 13 and 15.

[cf. ICCPR Art. 4]

6. Remedies for contravention of Bill of Rights
    1. A court or tribunal—
        (a) in proceedings within its jurisdiction in an action for breach of this Ordinance; and
        (b) in other proceedings within its jurisdiction in which a violation or threatened violation of the Bill of Rights is relevant,

may grant such remedy or relief, or make such order, in respect of such a breach, violation or threatened violation as it has power to grant or make in those proceedings and as it considers appropriate and just in the circumstances.

7. Binding effect of Ordinance
    (1) This Ordinance binds only—

(a) the Government and all public authorities; and

(b) any person acting on behalf of the Government or a public authority.

(2) In this section—

"person" includes any body of persons, corporate or unincorporate.

PART II
The Hong Kong Bill of Rights

8. Hong Kong Bill of Rights

The Hong Kong Bill of Rights is as follows.

Article 1
Entitlement to rights without distinction

(1) The Rights recognized in this Bill of Rights shall be enjoyed without distinction of any kind, such as race, colour, sex, language, religion, political or other opinion, national or social origin, property, birth, or other status.

(2) Men and women shall have an equal right to the enjoyment of all civil and political rights set forth in this Bill of Rights.

[cf. ICCPR Arts. 2 & 3]

Article 2
Right to life

(1) Every human being has the inherent right to life. This right shall be protected by law. No one shall be arbitrarily deprived of his life.

(2) Sentence of death may be imposed only for the most serious crimes in accordance with the law in force at the time of the commission of the crime and not contrary to the provisions of this Bill of Rights and to the Convention on the Prevention and Punishment of the Crime of Genocide. This penalty can only be carried out pursuant to a final judgment rendered by a competent court.

(3) When deprivation of life constitutes the crime of genocide, nothing in this article shall authorize the derogation in any way from any obligation assumed under the provisions of the Convention on the Prevention and Punishment of the Crime of Genocide.

(4) Anyone sentenced to death shall have the right to seek pardon or commutation of the sentence. Amnesty, pardon or commutation of the sentence of death may be granted in all cases.

(5) Sentence of death shall not be imposed for crimes committed by persons below 18 years of age and shall not be carried out on pregnant women.

(6) Nothing in this article shall be invoked to delay or to prevent the abolition of capital punishment in Hong Kong.

[cf. ICCPR Art. 6]

Article 3
No torture or inhuman treatment and no experimentation without consent

No one shall be subjected to torture or to cruel, inhuman or degrading treatment of punishment. In particular, no one shall be subjected without his free consent to medical or scientific experimentation.

[cf. ICCPR Art. 7]

Article 4
No slavery or servitude

(1) No one shall be held in slavery; slavery and the slave-trade in all their forms shall be prohibited.

(2) No one shall be held in servitude.

(3) *(a)* No one shall be required to perform forced or compulsory labor.

   (b) For the purpose of this paragraph the term "forced or compulsory labor" shall not include —

   (i) any work or service normally required of a person who is under detention in consequence of a lawful order of a court, or of a person during conditional release from such detention;

   (ii) any service of a military character and, where conscientious objection is recognized, any national service required by law of conscientious objectors;

   (iii) any service exacted in cases of emergency or calamity threatening the life or well-being of the community;

   (iv) any work or service which forms part of normal civil obligations.

[cf. ICCPR Art. 8]

Article 5
Liberty and security of person

(1) Everyone has the right to liberty and security of person. No one shall be subjected to arbitrary arrest or detention. No one shall be deprived of his liberty except on such grounds and in accordance with such procedure as are established by law.

(2) Anyone who is arrested shall be informed, at the time of arrest, of the reasons for his arrest and shall be promptly informed of any charges against him.

(3) Anyone arrested or detained on a criminal charge shall be brought promptly before a judge or other officer authorized by law to exercise judicial power and shall be entitled to trial within a reasonable time or to release. It shall not be the general rule that persons awaiting trial shall be detained in custody, but release may be subject to guarantees to appear for trial, at any other stage of the judicial proceedings, and, should occasion arise, for execution of the judgment.

(4) Anyone who is deprived of his liberty by arrest or detention shall be entitled to take proceedings before a court, in order that that court may decide without delay on the lawfulness of his detention and order his release if the detention is not lawful.

(5) Anyone who has been the victim of unlawful arrest or detention shall have an enforceable right to compensation.

[cf. ICCPR Art. 9]

Article 6
Rights of persons deprived of their liberty

(1) All persons deprived of their liberty shall be treated with humanity and with respect for the inherent dignity of the human person.

(2) *(a)* Accused persons shall, save in exceptional circumstances, be segregated from convicted persons and shall be subject to separate treatment appropriate to their status as unconvicted persons.

(b) Accused juvenile persons shall be separated from adults and brought as speedily as possible for adjudication.

(3) The penitentiary system shall comprise treatment of prisoners the essential aim of which shall be their reformation and social rehabilitation. Juvenile offenders shall be segregated from adults and be accorded treatment appropriate to their age and legal status.

[cf. ICCPR Art. 10]

Article 7
No imprisonment for breach of contract
No one shall be imprisoned merely on the ground of inability to fulfil a contractual obligation.

[cf. ICCPR Art. 11]

Article 8
Liberty of movement
(1) Everyone lawfully within Hong Kong shall, within Hong Kong, have the right to liberty of movement and freedom to choose his residence.
(2) Everyone shall be free to leave Hong Kong.
(3) The above-mentioned rights shall not be subject to any restrictions except those which are provided by law, are necessary to protect national security, public order *(ordre public)*, public health or morals or the rights and freedoms of others, and are consistent with the other rights recognized in this Bill of Rights.
(4) No one who has the right of abode in Hong Kong shall be arbitrarily deprived of the right to enter Hong Kong.

[cf. ICCPR Art. 12]

Article 9
Restrictions on expulsion from Hong Kong
A person who does not have the right of abode in Hong Kong but who is lawfully in Hong Kong may be expelled therefrom only in pursuance of a decision reached in accordance with law and shall, except where compelling reasons of national security otherwise require, be allowed to submit the reasons against his expulsion and to have his case reviewed by, and be represented for the purpose before, the competent authority or a person or persons especially designated by the competent authority.

[cf. ICCPR Art. 13]

Article 10
Equality before courts and right to fair and public hearing
All persons shall be equal before the courts and tribunals. In the determination of any criminal charge against him, or of his rights and obligations in a suit at law, everyone shall be entitled to a fair and public hearing by a competent, independent and impartial tribunal established by law. The press and the public may be excluded from all or part of a trial for reasons of morals, public order *(ordre public)* or national security in a democratic society, or when the interest of the private lives of the parties so requires, or to the extent strictly necessary in the opinion of the court in special circumstances where publicity would prejudice the interests of justice; but any judgment rendered in a criminal case or in a suit at law shall be made public

except where the interest of juvenile persons otherwise requires or the proceedings concern matrimonial disputes or the guardianship of children.

[cf. ICCPR Art. 14.1]

Article 11
Rights of persons charged with or convicted of criminal offence

(1) Everyone charged with a criminal offence shall have the right to be presumed innocent until proved guilty according to law.

(2) In the determination of any criminal charge against him, everyone shall be entitled to the following minimum guarantees, in full equality—

   (a) to be informed promptly and in detail in a language which he understands of the nature and cause of the charge against him;

   (b) to have adequate time and facilities for the preparation of his defence and to communicate with counsel of his own choosing;

   (c) to be tried without undue delay;

   (d) to be tried in his presence, and to defend himself in person or through legal assistance of his own choosing; to be informed, if he does not have legal assistance, of this right; and to have legal assistance assigned to him, in any case where the interests of justice so require, and without payment by him in any such case if he does not have sufficient means to pay for it;

   (e) to examine, or have examined, the witnesses against him and to obtain the attendance and examination of witnesses on his behalf under the same conditions as witnesses against him;

   (f) to have the free assistance of an interpreter if he cannot understand or speak the language used in court;

   (g) not to be compelled to testify against himself or to confess guilt.

(3) In the case of juvenile persons, the procedure shall be such as will take account of their age and the desirability of promoting their rehabilitation.

(4) Everyone convicted of a crime shall have the right to his conviction and sentence being reviewed by a higher tribunal according to law.

(5) When a person has by a final decision been convicted of a criminal offence and when subsequently his conviction has been reversed or he has been pardoned on the ground that a new or newly discovered fact shows conclusively that there has been a miscarriage of justice, the person who has suffered punishment as a result of such conviction shall be compensated according to law, unless it is proved that the non-disclosure of the unknown fact in time is wholly or partly attributable to him.

(6) No one shall be liable to be tried or punished again for an offence for which he has already been finally convicted or acquitted in accordance with the law and penal procedure of Hong Kong.

[cf. ICCPR Art. 14.2 to 7]

Article 12
No retrospective criminal offences or penalties

(1) No one shall be held guilty of any criminal offence on account of any act or omission which did not constitute a criminal offence, under Hong Kong or international law, at the time when it was committed. Nor shall a heavier penalty be imposed than the one that was applicable at the time

when the criminal offence was committed. If, subsequent to the commission of the offence, provision is made by law for the imposition of a lighter penalty, the offender shall benefit thereby.

(2) Nothing in this article shall prejudice the trial and punishment of any person for any act or omission which, at the time when it was committed, was criminal according to the general principles of law recognized by the community of nations.

[cf. ICCPR Art. 15]

Article 13
Right to recognition as person before law

Everyone shall have the right to recognition everywhere as a person before the law.

[cf. ICCPR Art. 16]

Article 14
Protection of privacy, family, home, correspondence, honour and reputation

(1) No one shall be subjected to arbitrary or unlawful interference with his privacy, family, home or correspondence, nor to unlawful attacks on his honour and reputation.

(2) Everyone has the right to the protection of the law against such interference or attacks.

[cf. ICCPR Art. 17]

Article 15
Freedom of thought, conscience and religion

(1) Everyone shall have the right to freedom of thought, conscience and religion. This right shall include freedom to have or to adopt a religion or belief of his choice, and freedom, either individually or in community with others and in public or private, to manifest his religion or belief in worship, observance, practice and teaching.

(2) No one shall be subject to coercion which would impair his freedom to have or to adopt a religion or belief of his choice.

(3) Freedom to manifest one's religion or beliefs may be subject only to such limitations as are prescribed by law and are necessary to protect public safety, order, health, or morals or the fundamental rights and freedoms of others.

(4) The liberty of parents and, when applicable, legal guardians to ensure the religious and moral education of their children in conformity with their own convictions shall be respected.

[cf. ICCPR Art. 18]

Article 16
Freedom of opinion and expression

(1) Everyone shall have the right to hold opinions without interference.

(2) Everyone shall have the right to freedom of expression; this right shall include freedom to seek, receive and impart information and ideas of all kinds, regardless of frontiers, either orally, in writing or in print, in the form of art, or through any other media of his choice.

(3) The exercise of the rights provided for in paragraph (2) of this article carries with it special duties and responsibilities. It may therefore be subject to certain restrictions, but these shall only be such as are provided by law and are necessary —

    (a) for respect of the rights or reputations of others; or

    (b) for the protection of national security or of public order *(ordre public)*, or of public health or morals.

[cf. ICCPR Art. 19]

Article 17
Right of peaceful assembly

The right of peaceful assembly shall be recognized. No restrictions may be placed on the exercise of this right other than those imposed in conformity with the law and which are necessary in a democratic society in the interests of national security or public safety, public order *(ordre public)*, the protection of public health or morals or the protection of the rights and freedoms of others.

[cf. ICCPR Art. 21]

Article 18
Freedom of association

(1) Everyone shall have the right to freedom of association with others, including the right to form and join trade unions for the protection of his interests.

(2) No restrictions may be placed on the exercise of this right other than those which are prescribed by law and which are necessary in a democratic society in the interests of national security or public safety, public order *(ordre public)*, the protection of public health or morals or the protection of the rights and freedoms of others. This article shall not prevent the imposition of lawful restrictions on members of the armed forces and of the police in their exercise of this right.

(3) Nothing in this article authorizes legislative measures to be taken which would prejudice, or the law to be applied in such a manner as to prejudice, the guarantees provided for in the International Labour Organization Convention of 1948 concerning Freedom of Association and Protection of the Right to Organize as it applies to Hong Kong.

[cf. ICCPR Art. 22]

Article 19
Rights in respect of marriage and family

(1) The family is the natural and fundamental group unit of society and is entitled to protection by society and the State.

(2) The right of men and women of marriageable age to marry and to found a family shall be recognized.

(3) No marriage shall be entered into without the free and full consent of the intending spouses.

(4) Spouses shall have equal rights and responsibilities as to marriage, during marriage and at its dissolution. In the case of dissolution, provision shall be made for the necessary protection of any children.

Article 20
Rights of children

(1) Every child shall have, without any discrimination as to race, colour, sex, language, religion, national or social origin, property or birth, the right to such measures of protection as are required by his status as a minor, on the part of his family, society and the State.

(2) Every child shall be registered immediately after birth and shall have a name.

[cf. ICCPR Art. 24]

Article 21
Right to participate in public life

Every permanent resident shall have the right and the opportunity, without any of the distinctions mentioned in article 1 (1) and without unreasonable restrictions —

(a) to take part in the conduct of public affairs, directly or through freely chosen representatives;

(b) to vote and to be elected at genuine periodic elections which shall be by universal and equal suffrage and shall be held by secret ballot, guaranteeing the free expression of the will of the electors;

(c) to have access, on general terms of equality, to public service in Hong Kong.

[cf. ICCPR Art. 25]

Article 22
Equality before and equal protection of law

All persons are equal before the law and are entitled without any discrimination to the equal protection of the law. In this respect, the law shall prohibit any discrimination and guarantee to all persons equal and effective protection against discrimination on any ground such as race, colour, sex, language, religion, political or other opinion, national or social origin, property, birth or other status.

[cf. ICCPR Art. 26]

Article 23
Rights of minorities

Persons belonging to ethnic, religious or linguistic minorities shall not be denied the right, in community with the other members of their group, to enjoy their own culture, to profess and practise their own religion, or to use their own language.

[cf. ICCPR Art. 27]

PART III

Exceptions and Savings

9. Armed forces and persons detained in penal establishments

Members of and persons serving with the armed forces of the government responsible for the foreign affairs of Hong Kong and persons lawfully detained in penal establishments of whatever character are subject to such restrictions as may from time to time be authorized by law for the preservation of service and custodial discipline.

10. Juveniles under detention

Where at any time there is a lack of suitable prison facilities or where the mixing of adults and juveniles is mutually beneficial, article 6(2)(b) and (3) does not require juveniles who are detained to be accommodated separately from adults.

11. Immigration legislation

As regards persons not having the right to enter and remain in Hong Kong, this Ordinance does not affect any immigration legislation governing entry into, stay in and departure from Hong Kong, or the application of any such legislation.

12. Persons not having the right of abode

Article 9 does not confer a right of review in respect of a decision to deport a person not having the right of abode in Hong Kong or a right to be represented for this purpose before the competent authority.

13. Executive and Legislative Councils

Article 21 does not require the establishment of an elected Executive or Legislative Council in Hong Kong.

14. Temporary savings

(1) For a period of 1 year beginning on the commencement date, this Ordinance is subject to the Ordinances listed in the Schedule.

(2) This Ordinance does not affect—

(a) any act done (including any act done in the exercise of a discretion); or

(b) any omission authorized or required, or occurring in the exercise of a discretion,

before the first anniversary of the commencement date, under or by any Ordinance listed in the Schedule.

(3) The Legislative Council may before the first anniversary of the commencement date by resolution amend this section for all or any of the following purposes—

(a) to provide that, for a period of 1 year beginning on the first anniversary of the commencement date, this Ordinance is subject to such of the Ordinances listed in the Schedule as are specified in the amendment;

(b) to provide that this Ordinance does not affect—

(i) any act done (including any act done in the exercise of a discretion); or

(ii) any omission authorized or required, or occurring in the exercise of a discretion,

before the second anniversary of the commencement date, under or by any Ordinance listed in the Schedule that is specified in the amendment; and

(c) to repeal this subsection.

(4) In this section, a reference to an Ordinance includes a reference to any subsidiary legislation made under that Ordinance.

(5) This section operates notwithstanding section 3.

SCHEDULE [S. 14]
Provisions to which Section 14(1) and (2) applies

Immigration Ordinance (Cap. 115)
Societies Ordinance (Cap. 151)
Crimes Ordinance (Cap. 200)
Prevention of Bribery Ordinance (Cap. 201)
Independent Commission against Corruption Ordinance (Cap. 204)
Police Force Ordinance (Cap. 232)

APPENDIX D

"Current Events in China"
(Statement by British Foreign Secretary Geoffrey Howe, June 5, 1989)

Policy statement by British Foreign Secretary Geoffrey Howe to Britain's House of Commons one day after the June 4, 1989, Tiananmen Square crackdown in Beijing, addressing current events in China and their implications for Hong Kong.

During the last few days, units of the Chinese Army have been engaged in the violent suppression of peaceful and popular demonstrations in the streets of Peking. The indiscriminate and unprovoked use of military force has caused the death or injury of thousands of students and other innocent civilians. I am sure that all members of the House will share that sense of horror and join in the international condemnation of the slaughter of innocent people.

I summoned the Chinese Charge d'Affaires yesterday. I told him that the British Government and people were united in condemning the merciless treatment of peaceful demonstrators, and deeply deplored the use of force to suppress the democratic aspirations of the Chinese people.

I told him that the British Government looked to the Chinese authorities to fulfil their obligations to Hong Kong in the Joint Declaration of 1984.

I reminded him of the responsibilities of the Chinese Government to ensure the safety of British citizens and Hong Kong residents. I expressed concern at the maltreatment of British journalists, particularly Michael Fathers of *The Independent* and Jonathan Mirksey of *The Observer*. We have since seen disturbing reports of the ill treatment of Kate Adie of the BBC.

Our Ambassador in Peking and his staff have been working round the clock to ensure the safety of British citizens and Hong Kong residents in Peking and, as far as possible, in other parts of China. The Embassy have advised those who are concerned about their safety and have no pressing need to remain in China to leave immediately.

Since the Cultural Revolution, there has been a substantial improvement in relations between the United Kingdom and the People's Republic of China as the Chinese Government has sought to broaden its contacts with the international community and to introduce economic and other reforms. Friends of China in this House and around the world must share the hope that sane and balanced government will be swiftly and securely restored in Peking. In present circumstances, however, there can be no question of continuing normal business with the Chinese authorities.

Her Majesty's Government have, therefore, decided on the following action:

- All scheduled ministerial exchanges between Britain and China have been suspended. The visit of the Chinese Minister of Justice, who was due to arrive here tomorrow, has been canceled. My Right Honourable Friend, the Minister of Agriculture, Fisheries and Food, has also canceled his forthcoming visit to China.
- The proposed visit of Their Royal Highness The Prince and Princess of Wales to China in November clearly cannot take place so long as those responsible for the atrocities over the past weekend remain in control of the Chinese Government.
- All high-level military contacts with China have been suspended.
- All arms sales to China have been banned.

At the same time, the Government are examining how we can respond to any requests for humanitarian assistance from non-governmental organizations.

The whole House will share the Government's special concern about the implications for Hong Kong of what has been happening in Peking. The Government understand and share the grave concern felt by the people of Hong Kong. We have all been deeply impressed by the strength and restraint of their response to what has happened.

Everything that has been accomplished in Hong Kong has been achieved in the unique context of the geography and history of the Territory, and by the talent and enterprise of its people. All that underlines the extent to which the future prosperity of Hong Kong must depend upon a successful and secure partnership with the government and people of China. That objective is enshrined in the commitments made by the British Government and the Government of China under the Joint Declaration.

Those commitments were reaffirmed by the Charge d'Affaires when he called on me yesterday. But it is self-evident that if we are to have confidence in the commitment of the Chinese Government to their obligations, there must be a stable and responsible government in Peking. The British Government will stand by its obligations under the Joint Declaration. The Government and the House look to the Government of the People's Republic of China to live up to that international commitment as well.

The events in Peking must affect the prospects and procedure for implementation of the Joint Declaration. Consultations about the second draft of the Basic Law for Hong Kong have been suspended. It is also difficult to see how our contacts with the Chinese Government about the future of Hong Kong can continue in present circumstances.

Meanwhile, I can assure the House that we shall be conducting a thorough examination of the programme for advancing and consolidating effective democracy in Hong Kong. We are considering urgently what further steps can be taken to enshrine and protect Hong Kong's freedoms and way of life after 1997.

All of us in this House are acutely conscious of the wish of the people of Hong Kong to secure some form of assurance for themselves and their families. I know that this has been one of the issues studied by the Select Committee on Foreign Affairs. Some commentators have recommended that a right of abode in this country should be given to the 3 1/4 million people in Hong Kong who hold British nationality. We share the desire of the House to do everything we can to enhance the security of the people of Hong Kong. On that basis, the Government are looking urgently and sympathetically at the scope for flexibility. But the House will appreciate the reason why we could not easily contemplate a massive new immigration commitment which could more than double the ethnic minority population of the United Kingdom—a possibility that cannot be disregarded. Our overriding aim must be to do everything possible to secure the continuation of those conditions in Hong Kong that have led to its outstanding success over the last century.

I hope the House will send a message to the people of Hong Kong, reaffirming our commitment to their secure, stable, and prosperous future.

The Chinese people are seeking from their Communist leadership rights and liberties which are taken for granted in the free world. The slaughter in Peking is a tragic setback to the campaign for democracy, but I hope this House will send a united message.

China cannot ignore the lessons which are being learned elsewhere in the World. Economic prosperity and personal liberty go hand in hand. People will not forever tolerate government by repression.

Chronology of Political Events
Relating to Hong Hong

1841
January 20

Convention of Chuanpi (ceding Hong Kong Island to Great Britain) is signed by Chinese Imperial Commissioner Qishan and British Captain Charles Elliot. Document is later repudiated by both China and Britain.

1841–42

Britain occupies Hong Kong Island during First Opium War. Possession is formalized in first of what China calls "unequal treaties" – the Treaty of Nanking.

1842
August 29

Treaty of Nanking (ceding Hong Kong Island to Great Britain "in perpetuity") is signed by Imperial Commissioner Qishan and Sir Henry Pottinger. Treaty is ratified June 26, 1843, by an exchange of documents between China and Britain.

1860
October 24

Second Opium War ends. Under first Convention of Peking, China cedes tip of Kowloon peninsula and Stonecutters Island, expanding Hong Kong's size and security.

1898

New Territories added to Hong Kong under second Convention of Peking. This time the land is not ceded outright but leased for 99 years (until July 1, 1997).

1900

Boxer Rebellion in China.

1911

Manchu dynasty overthrown in China; republic established.

1925–26

Nationalist fervor grows in Hong Kong. General strike and boycott express popular indignation at privileged status of foreigners.

1926–27

Hong Kong Governor Cecil Clementi, prodded by investors, asks London to demand permanent cession of New Territories in order to resolve questions about leases extending past 1997.

1941
Mark Young appointed governor of Hong Kong.

1941–45
Japanese occupy Hong Kong.

August
Japan surrenders. Franklin Gimson, Colonial Secretary of Hong Kong when Second World War began, raises Union Jack and proclaims himself "Officer Administering the Government in Hong Kong."

September
Local Japanese commanders formally surrender In Hong Kong.

November
Hong Kong reopens to normal trading.

1946
May
Mark Young returns to Hong Kong as governor, restores civil government and announces Britain's intention to give local inhabitants more voice in management of their own affairs.

1947
July
Alexander Grantham arrives as new governor of Hong Kong.

1949
January
The Hong Kong Reform Club is formed. Later petitions governor for, among other things, a directly-elected Legislative Council.

July
The Hong Kong Chinese Reform Association, Chinese Manufacturers Union, Kowloon Chamber of Commerce, Kowloon Chinese Chamber of Commerce and 138 other Chinese organizations petition Hong Kong governor for constitutional changes at both the central and municipal levels.

September
Mao Zedong proclaims establishment of the People's Republic of China in Peking.

October
Communists capture Chinese mainland. Chiang Kai-shek flees to Taiwan. Peking seals China's border with Hong Kong.

1950
January
United Kingdom recognizes the People's Republic of China.

June
Governor Alexander Grantham goes to London for meetings with British ministers and officials about constitutional changes in Hong Kong. Korean War begins.

October
China enters the Korean War.

December
United States imposes embargo on selected exports from China, depriving Hong Kong of its single-most important trading partner.

1952
February
Governor Alexander Grantham requests permission from Colonial Office to resume preparations for constitutional reform in Hong Kong.

May
British Cabinet approves Grantham's 1950 proposals for reform.

June
Grantham sends a telegram to the Colonial Office to express "fear" of constitutional reform on the part of unofficial members of Hong Kong's Legislative Council.

July
Grantham, in London, urges British Cabinet to withdraw its approval of reforms.

September
British Cabinet agrees to drop all major reforms for Hong Kong.

October
British Foreign Secretary determines that reform in Hong Kong would be limited to the Urban Council, and any major reform would be "inopportune."

1950s to mid–1960s
Immigrants from People's Republic of China flood into Hong Kong, almost doubling the population.

1963
March 8
People's Daily article reiterates China's stand on Hong Kong: Issue will be settled peacefully through negotiations "when conditions are ripe," with status quo to be maintained until that time.

1967
Cultural Revolution spills over into Hong Kong. There are riots against British rule.

1969
American Chamber of Commerce established in Hong Kong, with 212 members (grows to become the largest American Chamber of Commerce outside United States).

1971
Murray MacLehose appointed governor of Hong Kong.

1972
March 8
China tells United Nations Special Committee on Decolonization that "settlement of the questions of Hong Kong and Macau is entirely within China's sovereign right." Asks U.N. to remove Hong Kong and Macau from list of colonial territories. Document says "the Chinese government has consistently held that [questions of Hong Kong and Macau] should be settled in an appropriate way when conditions are ripe."

March 13
China and Britain announce resumption of diplomatic relations.

1973
April 17
Chinese government wants "representative organ" in Hong Kong. Proposal first made in 1956, rejected in 1957. Raised again several times in later years.

1974
Portugal offers to return Macau to China. China declines.

1975
Beijing signs agreement with Lisbon allowing Portugal to continue rule over Macau.

1977
October 25
Senior Chinese official Liao Chengzhi tells Hong Kong–Macau delegation in Beijing that Mao Zedong once said recovery of Hong Kong shouldn't precede "liberation" of Taiwan.

1978
November–December
Chinese Communist Party meets in Beijing, supports Deng Xiaoping as top Party leader and endorses his proposed "reforms." Members discuss question of Hong Kong, urging its reunification with "motherland" China and characterizing residents of Hong Kong as "patriots belonging to one family."

1979
March 24–April 4
Hong Kong Governor Murray MacLehose visits Beijing, marking first official visit to mainland China by a Hong Kong governor since Communists won power in 1949. MacLehose asks Deng Xiaoping whether British-issued sub-leases in New Territories will be allowed to continue beyond 1997. Deng withholds approval, but advises MacLehose: "Tell your investors to put their hearts at ease."

April 6
MacLehose, in Hong Kong, says Chinese leaders stressed Hong Kong's future importance. He repeats assurances: "Vice Premier Deng Xiaoping formally requested me to ask investors in Hong Kong to put their hearts at ease."

May 7
Chinese Deputy Foreign Minister Song Zhiguang says "Hong Kong is part of China," adding that "when the lease expires, an appropriate attitude would be adopted in settling the question."

September
Great Britain is formally advised by China's Foreign Ministry that changes in the terms of New Territories land leases are "unnecessary."

October 7
Chinese Premier Hua Guofeng says China's position is "very clear" on future of Hong Kong in twenty-first century. "At present, our relationship with both the United Kingdom and the British authority in Hong Kong is quite good. We think that, through negotiations, a satisfactory way can be sought to settle the question of Hong Kong, Kowloon and the New Territories. But I can say, no

matter how the question is resolved, we would take into consideration the interests of the investors there."

1980
July 30

Britain releases White Paper on proposed British Nationality Bill changing 2.6 million Hong Kong Chinese from their status as British subjects to "citizens of the British dependent territory of Hong Kong." Under the bill, these people would become stateless when Hong Kong ceases to be a British dependent territory.

October

Chinese Foreign Minister Huang Hua, in London, rebuffs British request to discuss extending Hong Kong leases after 1997.

1981

Under Britain's new Nationality Act, Hong Kong British passport holders (British Dependent Territories Citizens) do not have the right of abode in Britain (unlike residents in colonies of Gibraltar and Falkland Islands).

April 1

Hong Kong Governor Murray MacLehose and British Foreign Secretary Lord Carrington caution that China may resist efforts to allow direct elections for seats in Hong Kong's Legislative Council.

April 3

British Foreign Secretary Lord Carrington visits Deng Xiaoping in Beijing. Deng refuses to talk at length about the future of Hong Kong. However, Carrington later says Deng again assured Hong Kong investors to "put their hearts at ease," adding that he believes investor interests probably wouldn't be affected by any changes in Hong Kong, either before or after 1997.

September 30

China's National People's Congress Chairman Ye Jianying proposes a "Nine-Point Plan" to reunify Taiwan with China. Some elements are similar to the "one country, two systems" philosophy promoted during negotiations over Hong Kong between China and Britain.

1982
January 6

British Foreign Office Minister Humphrey Atkins meets with Chinese Prime Minister Zhao Ziyang in Beijing to prepare for September visit by Prime Minister Thatcher. Zhao assures Atkins that Hong Kong will continue to be a free port, but must be returned to the sovereignty of China.

April 6

Deng Xiaoping meets in Beijing with former British Prime Minister Edward Heath, who later says China is insistent about recovering sovereignty, but intends to allow self-government in Hong Kong. He says China's new Constitution provides for continuing existing systems in Hong Kong as a "Special Administrative Region." Heath also says Deng wonders if Britain would agree to a Hong Kong settlement similar to Nine-Point Plan proposed for Taiwan by National People's Congress Chairman Ye Jianying.

April

Murray MacLehose retires as governor of Hong Kong.

May 20

Edward Youde, former British ambassador in Beijing, becomes Hong Kong governor.

June 15

Deng Xiaoping asks for suggestions on Hong Kong's future from delegation of twelve visiting businessmen, but sets two criteria: sovereignty by China and continued prosperity.

July 16

National People's Congress Vice Chairman Peng Zhen says new China Constitution will provide for "Special Administrative Regions," which could benefit Hong Kong, Macau and Taiwan. Peng also says China's efforts for reunification are based on principles of "respect history, respect the reality, and look forward to the future."

September 5–6

Hong Kong Governor Edward Youde and Hong Kong Executive Council members meet with Prime Minister Thatcher in London before her visit to Beijing.

September 22

British Prime Minister Margaret Thatcher arrives in Beijing to open formal talks with China on the question of Hong Kong's future. She encourages "cooperation, confidence and commitment" in resolving question of Hong Kong. She also upsets her hosts by insisting on validity of the treaties ceding Hong Kong to Britain.

September 23

Prime Minister Thatcher meets with Chinese Premier Zhao Ziyang, who reaffirms China's demand to "recover" sovereignty over Hong Kong.

September 24

Prime Minister Thatcher meets with Deng Xiaoping for two and one-half hours. Agreement is reached to begin negotiations to resolve question of Hong Kong, but her proposal to continue British administration in Hong Kong after 1997 is rejected.

September 26–28

Prime Minister Thatcher, in Hong Kong, declares: "If a country will not stand by one treaty, it will not stand by another treaty." Her comments anger China's leaders, who issue strongly worded statement cautioning against clinging to "unequal treaties." She also voices confidence that China and Britain will "reconcile their differences" over Hong Kong.

September 30

Editorial by Xinhua (China's official news agency) calls Britain's treaties involving Hong Kong are "illegal, and therefore null and void."

October

Formal Sino-British talks on Hong Kong begin, but soon deadlocked on issue of sovereignty by China.

October 7

Chinese Foreign Ministry leaders say priority issue regarding Hong Kong is China's recovery of sovereignty, assuring that China also wants continued "stability and prosperity."

October 11

London's *Financial Times* quotes senior Chinese official as saying China's recovery of Hong Kong would not lessen its current degree of freedom.

October 14

Britain's House of Lords is formally advised that Beijing and London have differing views on sovereignty of Hong Kong. Lord Belstead says the most important consideration for Great Britain is Hong Kong's continued stability and prosperity.

November 1

National People's Congress Vice Chairman Xi Zhongxun tells Hong Kong Trade Development Council members that talks over "the next one or two years" should produce a plan to maintain stability, prosperity and confidence in Hong Kong.

November 20

China's Hong Kong and Macau Affairs Office director Liao Chengzhi "Hong Kong people will rule Hong Kong" after 1997. Liao says Hong Kong will continue as a free port and financial center, with little change in its lifestyle.

December 4

China's National People's Congress adopts new China Constitution, providing for "Special Administrative Regions" where capitalism is permitted and encouraged.

1983

January 26

Hong Kong Government leaders propose that the Executive Council be consulted on negotiations between China and Britain.

January–June

"Talks about talks" continue between China and Britain regarding future of Hong Kong.

February 10

Chinese Foreign Minister Wu Xueqian says China and Britain have not yet begun talking about substantive issues involving Hong Kong, explaining that negotiations are stalled on procedural matters.

March 9

Prime Minister Thatcher, hoping to end stalled negotiations, sends letter to Chinese Premier Zhao Ziyang offering to "recommend" that British Parliament accept China's demand for sovereignty over Hong Kong.

April 11

China's Hong Kong and Macau Affairs Office director Liao Chengzhi assures group of academic leaders that Hong Kong will have its own constitution after 1997 under provisions of a "Special Administrative Region."

May 12

Liao Chengzhi tells businessmen and industrialists from New Territories that China cannot accept a "three-stool" situation by allowing Hong Kong a voice in the talks, maintaining that only China and Britain can negotiate towards an agreement.

May

Chinese and British diplomatic representatives hold two rounds of meetings in Beijing, finally setting agenda and establishing framework for formal negotiations.

June 6

Chinese Premier Zhao Ziyang tells Sixth National People's Congress that China will "recover" sovereignty over Hong Kong "at an opportune moment, and take appropriate measures to maintain its prosperity."

June 17

Xu Jiatun, new director of Xinhua in Hong Kong, says issue of Chinese sovereignty over Hong Kong isn't negotiable, but certain measures will be in place to maintain its prosperity during transition and afterwards.

June 22

Queen Elizabeth II opens new session of British Parliament by stating that the British government "will continue talks with China with the aim of reaching a solution acceptable to this Parliament, to China and to the people of Hong Kong."

June 24

Hong Kong Governor Edward Youde maintains that current negotiations on Hong Kong are genuine, rather than just "talks about talks." Youde also says he expects soon to begin taking part in the negotiations.

July 1

China and Britain issue joint statement announcing that the second phase of formal negotiations on the future of Hong Kong will begin July 12th in Beijing.

July 5

Delegations to the Sino-British negotiations are announced by the Chinese Foreign Ministry. The Chinese delegation is headed by Vice Foreign Minister Yao Guang. Britain's group is led by Percy Cradock, the British ambassador to Beijing. Group also includes Hong Kong Governor Edward Youde.

July

Prime Minister Thatcher assures Britain's House of Commons that "the view of the people of Hong Kong will continue to be taken into account at all stages."

July 7

Hong Kong Governor Edward Youde, upon return from London, tells reporters he represents the people of Hong Kong in the talks, stressing that he will emphasize the need for continuing certain freedoms now enjoyed in the territory.

July 8

Chinese Foreign Ministry issues a statement clarifying that Youde is taking part in the talks as member of British delegation, not as representative of Hong Kong.

July 12–13

Formal negotiations on Hong Kong resume in Beijing. Britain proposes continued British administration of Hong Kong after 1997. A very brief joint statement is issued, describing the talks as "useful and constructive."

July 25–26

Second round of talks in Beijing are characterized as "useful" in a joint statement.

August 2–3

Third round of talks in Beijing, during which China advises it won't accept British administration in Hong Kong after 1997. A statement is issued, saying little about progress and omitting phrase "useful and constructive."

August 15

China's Communist Party General Secretary Hu Yaobang says China plans to "recover" Hong Kong on July 1, 1997. It marks the first time a Chinese official has publicly mentioned the date.

September 10

Deng Xiaoping tells former British Prime Minister Edward Heath that settlement of Hong Kong issue will be satisfactory to both China and Britain, and again affirms China's demand to assume sovereignty over Hong Kong in 1997.

September 13

Heath walks out of a dinner given for him by Hong Kong's Legislative and Executive councils after some members accuse him of supporting China's demands for sovereignty over Hong Kong.

September 16

Xinhua criticizes Hong Kong government for encouraging local public support for British presence after 1997. Chinese Deputy Foreign Minister Zhou Nan says "sovereignty and administration are inseparable" in regards to Hong Kong.

September 22–23

Fourth round of talks in Beijing stalled over Britain's demand to continue administration over post–1997 Hong Kong. Prime Minister Thatcher concedes existence of "great financial and political uncertainty" in Hong Kong's future. Unrest sends Hang Seng Index into decline and drops Hong Kong dollar to new low (US$1 = HK$9.50).

September 27

Hong Kong Governor Edward Youde and Executive Council meet with Percy Cradock (head of Britain's negotiating team). Cradock advises more concessions from Britain to keep talks from collapsing.

September 30

Ji Pengfei, director of China's Hong Kong and Macau Affairs Office, says an agreement about Hong Kong must be reached in one year or the Chinese government will declare its own position.

October 7–8

British Prime Minister Thatcher, Foreign Minister Sir Geoffrey Howe and Percy Cradock meet in London with Hong Kong Governor Edward Youde and members of Hong Kong's Executive Council. Agreement is reached to permit Britain to "conditionally" set aside demands for continuing its administration over Hong Kong after 1997 and to "explore" proposals by China.

October 15

Hong Kong Financial Secretary John Brembridge announces that the Hong Kong dollar will be fixed at US$1 = HK$7.75 beginning October 17.

October 19–20

Fifth round of talks in Beijing. British ambassador to Beijing delivers letter from

Prime Minister Thatcher that generally accepts Chinese claim to sovereignty over Hong Kong after 1997. Statement issued after the talks again includes the words "useful and constructive."

October 21

Hong Kong Governor Edward Youde says "informal" contacts between China and Britain will be made before the next formal round of negotiations.

November 2

Chinese Vice Foreign Minister Qian Qichen assures that negotiations will continue until an agreement is reached, even if it means going past China's deadline of September 1984.

November 5

China reaffirms earlier intention to make a unilateral statement on Hong Kong's future if no agreement is reached by September 1984.

November 8

Britain announces the appointment of Richard Evans as ambassador to Beijing and chairman of the British negotiating team.

November 14–15

Sixth round of formal talks in Beijing includes British concession of "no links of authority" over post–1997 Hong Kong. Joint statement says both sides "continued useful and constructive talks" and that informal contacts would continue.

November 15

Ji Pengfei, head of China's Hong Kong and Macau Affairs Office, says Hong Kong's legal, financial and political systems will continue unchanged for 50 years after 1997.

December 7–8

Seventh round of formal talks in Beijing includes discussion of Hong Kong's government structure and legal system after 1997. Joint statement says negotiations were "useful and constructive," adding that China and Britain "reviewed the course of the talks and the progress made so far."

1984

January

China Daily publishes interview with Ji Pengfei, who says post–1997 Hong Kong will enjoy "a high degree of autonomy."

January 7

Ji Pengfei outlines proposed makeup of Hong Kong Legislature after 1997: one-third pro–China membership, one-third pro–British and one-third neutral.

January 13

Thousands of rioters rampage through Kowloon during evening hours, taking advantage of a dispute between Hong Kong government and striking taxi drivers, marking the worst riots since 1967.

January 25–26

Eighth round of talks in Beijing is followed by joint statement describing the session as "useful and constructive."

February 22–23

Ninth round of talks in Beijing is again described as "useful and constructive."

February 25

Hong Kong Chief Secretary Philip Haddon-Cave announces slight shift towards more democracy in Hong Kong. One proposal increases elected members to Hong Kong's 18-district board from one-third to two-thirds of each board's membership. Second proposal establishes regional councils in New Territories to supervise hygiene, recreational and cultural programs.

March 14

Hong Kong's Legislative Council unanimously approves a resolution declaring as "essential that any proposal for the future of Hong Kong should be debated in this Council before any final agreement is reached."

March 16–17

Tenth round of talks is followed by a statement describing session as "useful and constructive," and scheduling next round in ten days (instead of one month).

March 26–27

Eleventh round of talks is again called "useful and constructive."

March 28

Hong Kong's oldest company, Jardine Matheson, announces plans to move its headquarters to Bermuda. Another major trading company, Hutchison Whampoa, announces plans to issue large bonus dividends instead of reinvesting its profits (widely interpreted as an indication of lack of confidence in Hong Kong).

April

Jardine Matheson moves headquarters to Bermuda, after 150 years in Hong Kong.

April 11–12

Twelfth round of talks ends with familiar statement describing the session as "useful and constructive."

April 15–18

British Foreign Secretary Geoffrey Howe, in Beijing, discusses future of Hong Kong with Chinese Premier Zhao Ziyang. Joint statement says they "reviewed the course of the talks and agreed valuable progress had been made and negotiations would continue."

April 18–20

Howe, in Hong Kong, affirms that Britain will concede sovereignty of Hong Kong to China, saying "it would not be realistic to think of an agreement that provides for British administration after 1997." He also reaffirms British intentions of preserving for Hong Kong (after 1997) a high degree of autonomy, the essentials of the existing system and the current lifestyle. Hong Kong stock market drops 46 points.

April 27–28

Thirteenth round of talks in Beijing.

May 9

Fourteenth round of talks in Beijing.

May 25

Deng Xiaoping announces that China will station troops in Hong Kong after 1997. Hang Seng Index drops 30 points before midday.

May 30
Fifteenth round of talks in Beijing.

June 7
Burton Levin, U.S. consul-general in Hong Kong, speaking to Asia Society in New York City, says: "We believe [Hong Kong residents] deserve a secure future."

June 12–13
Sixteenth round of talks in Beijing.

July
Hong Kong government publishes Green Paper ("The Further Development of Local Representation in Hong Kong") proposing local elections for some seats in Legislative Council (Legco). Public comment is invited to develop a system of government "which is more directly accountable to the people of Hong Kong."

July
Prime Minister Thatcher sends Foreign Secretary Geoffrey Howe to work out differences in Hong Kong question with Chinese Premier Zhao Ziyang.

July 16
Chinese propose a Joint Liaison Group to monitor the Hong Kong's transition period before 1997. Hang Seng Index sinks to its lowest point of the year.

July 31
Chinese Foreign Minister Wu Xueqian notes significant progress towards an agreement on Hong Kong after meeting with Geoffrey Howe in Beijing.

August 1
Howe, in Hong Kong, outlines draft agreement of Joint Declaration. Hang Seng Index gains 67 points.

September 5–6
Final (twenty-second) round of talks in Beijing.

September
Britain's two houses of Parliament debate resolution to approve Draft Joint Declaration for Hong Kong, both passing it without division.

September 26
Draft agreement of Sino-British Joint Declaration on Hong Kong is initialed in Beijing. Assessment Office in Hong Kong is to receive views of local residents.

September 26
Publication of "The Draft Agreement Between the Government of the United Kingdom of Great Britain and Northern Ireland and the Government of the People's Republic of China on the Future of Hong Kong." All available copies are snapped up quickly by Hong Kong residents kept in the dark for two years.

September 26
Acting U.S. Department of State spokesman Alan Romberg says the United States "welcomes the successful conclusion" of talks, offering to "provide any assistance" to "maintain Hong Kong's appropriate participation in international bodies."

September 27

Hong Kong Governor Edward Youde says China accepts principle of an elected legislature after 1997.

October 15

Hong Kong's Legislative Council debates the Joint Declaration. Most members are resigned to it, but there is some opposition.

November 29

Hong Kong Government publishes White Paper "The Further Development of Representative Government in Hong Kong" (formal version of previous Green Paper). Proposes shift from previous appointive system to an elective system through several steps over three years. Paper acknowledges that "the bulk of public response from all sources suggested a cautious approach with a gradual start by introducing a very small number of directly elected members in 1988 and building up to a significant number of directly elected members by 1997."

December 5

British House of Commons debates and accepts Joint Declaration on Hong Kong.

December 19

Joint Declaration on Hong Kong is formally signed in Beijing by British Prime Minister Margaret Thatcher and Chinese Premier Zhao Ziyang.

December 21

Thatcher, in Hong Kong, is questioned about "morality" of handing Hong Kong and its millions of residents to China. She responds with a question: "What do you think would have happened if we had not attempted to get an agreement?"

1985

January

Draft Joint Declaration for Hong Kong is presented to British Parliament in London, briefly acknowledging transfer of Hong Kong sovereignty to China in 1997.

April

British Parliament passes bill approving Joint Declaration for Hong Kong.

May 27

Britain and China ratify Joint Declaration, exchanging documents of ratification.

June

China establishes Basic Law Drafting Committee (BLDC), comprised of 59 members (23 from Hong Kong) to develop constitution-like document for post–1997 Hong Kong.

June 19

Hong Kong beats China 2–1 (big upset) in run-up to the World Cup. Riots follow. One Hong Kong soccer player is cut by a flying bottle. Reports show 30 policemen were beaten, 127 people detained and 25 vehicles damaged (including 5 taxis and 11 buses).

November 21

Spokesman for Xinhua in Hong Kong cautions against formation of political parties and broadening of voting rights in Hong Kong before 1997. (Warning brings decline in political activities in Hong Kong.) He says Britain may be violating terms of the Joint Declaration by attempting to introduce political reforms in Hong Kong.

December

China establishes the Basic Law Consultative Committee (BLCC), comprising 180 members (all from Hong Kong) as "advisers" commissioned to gather public opinion on provisions of the post–1997 Basic Law for Hong Kong.

1986

January

Lu Ping, head of the Hong Kong and Macau Affairs Office, says the concept of "Hong Kong ruled by the Hong Kong people" is unscientific, because it hadn't been proposed by China. Phrase soon fades from use.

April 22

BLDC develops Basic Law framework.

June

Talks begin between China and Portugal over return of Macau to China.

September

Third meeting of BLDC, with "substantial progress on major aspects."

October

Queen Elizabeth II and husband Prince Philip visit China; they are given warm reception.

December 4

Edward Youde dies of heart attack in Beijing. His full title was "His Excellency the 26th Governor of the Crown Colony of Hong Kong." Circumstances stimulated superstitions in Hong Kong: He was the first Hong Kong governor to die in office; he died in Beijing while on Hong Kong business; he died on the fourth (a "bad" day).

1987

March 26

After four rounds of talks, agreement is announced between Beijing and Lisbon on return of Macau to China. Joint Declaration is signed, returning sovereignty of Macau to China in 1999.

April

David Wilson becomes Hong Kong's twenty-seventh governor.

May

Hong Kong government publishes Green Paper inviting public comment on options for political reform. Survey Office receives comments and commissions two polls on options. Most interest concerns question of direct elections.

November

Hong Kong Governor David Wilson denies "brain drain," insisting that "the level of emigration has been much the same as it now for more than twenty years."

1988

February

Hong Kong government publishes White Paper ("The Development of Representative Government: The Way Forward"), announcing several political revisions. The most controversial is the decision to delay direct elections until 1991, after China has approved the Basic Law. Protesters burn copies of the White Paper outside the Central Government Offices.

April

Hong Kong Governor David Wilson admits "brain drain" is a problem and says his government will investigate. First draft of the Basic Law is released.

October

American Chamber of Commerce sends delegation to Beijing to seek increased freedoms in the Basic Law for residents of Hong Kong. Its purpose is to stem the "brain drain."

December

Some 5,000 march in a pro-democracy rally outside Xinhua office in Hong Kong.

1989
February

China releases the second draft of the Basic Law for Hong Kong.

May

People of Hong Kong hold public marches (very large) in support of "Beijing Spring" pro-democracy demonstrations in Tiananmen Square.

June 3–4

Chinese crack down on pro-democracy demonstrations in Tiananmen Square in Beijing, killing hundreds of demonstrators. Thousands of dissidents and suspected pro-democracy sympathizers are arrested throughout China. More than 1 million Hong Kong residents march in peaceful protest.

June 5

British Foreign Secretary Geoffrey Howe issues policy statement on "Current Events in China." In his statement, issued one day after Tiananmen Square crackdown, Howe says Britain "could not easily contemplate a massive new immigration commitment" to Hong Kong.

October

U.S. Consulate General in Hong Kong issues report "Impact of the Brain Drain on Hong Kong's Economy." Report is subsequently published in magazine of the American Chamber of Commerce in Hong Kong.

October 4

Hong Kong government announces $16 billion port-and-airport development to restore international confidence in Hong Kong.

December

The British begin forcible repatriation of Vietnamese refugees in Hong Kong back to Hanoi. As a result, world sympathy for Hong Kong is greatly reduced.

1990
January

Beijing drafts Basic Law that would limit to 18 the number of elected seats in Hong Kong's 60-member legislature, with more than two-thirds to be approved by China.

February

London and Beijing agree to raise number of directly elected members of Hong Kong's Legislative Council to one-third (20) in 1995 elections.

April

Britain announces plans to grant 50,000 passports to select Hong Kong families. National People's Congress in Beijing ratifies Basic Law, which pro-democracy forces say is incompatible with the 1984 Joint Declaration.

April 2

The Basic Law for Hong Kong is approved by the National People's Congress.

June

Beijing continues to attack plans for new multi-billion-dollar airport, fearing the project will strip Hong Kong of its reserves. The airport become a major political issue and test of Britain's commitment to Hong Kong.

1991

June

Britain issues "Memorandum of Understanding: The New Airport in Hong Kong," giving China a voice in awarding of contracts.

September

Landmark direct elections in Hong Kong. Pro-democracy candidates (led by Martin Lee) win all but 2 of 18 seats contested (of Legislative Council's 60 seats). No pro–China candidate wins.

November

Britain returns another group of Vietnamese boat people to Vietnam, in an effort to empty the camps within 2–3 years.

December

Hong Kong legislators, defying recommendations of China and Britain to allow only one foreign judge on the Court of Final Appeal, approves 34–11 a plan to allow foreign judges for all five seats on the "supreme court" effective July 1, 1997.

December 31

Hong Kong's Exchange Fund (foreign exchange reserves) totals $30.54 billion, twelfth largest reserve of foreign currency in the world.

1992

January

Hong Kong Governor David Wilson announces plans to retire.

March

Hong Kong's Provisional Airport Authority awards $70 million contract to develop design for passenger terminal at new Chek Lap Kok Airport.

March 8

Hang Seng Index hits 4,964 – its sixth record high in seven trading sessions.

March 17

Midland Bank of Britain announces merger with Hongkong and Shanghai Banking Corp., creating tenth largest bank in the world.

April

Prime Minister John Major offers Hong Kong governorship to Chris Patten.

April 22

British Army hands over control of Hong Kong's border with China to local police.

April 24
>Chris Patten accepts post of governor of Hong Kong.

June 11
>Hong Kong announces plans to raze Kowloon's Walled City (world's largest slum).

June 18
>Beijing cautions incoming Governor Chris Patten against appointing pro-democratic proponents to his policy-making Executive Council.

July 8
>Beijing issues warning (on day before governor's inaugural) that Patten won't have the flexibility to establish a democratic system in Hong Kong.

July 9
>Chris Patten becomes twenty-eighth governor of Hong Kong, succeeding David Wilson.

July 16
>Hang Seng Index hits record high 6,162 points.

August
>Construction on new airport halted pending Chinese endorsement of airport financing plans.

October 7
>Patten outlines democratic reform proposals: lowering voting age from 21 to 18, expanding voter base to include all working persons and direct elections (instead of appointments) for local district boards.

October 8
>Beijing accuses Patten of violating Joint Declaration with his proposed reforms.

October 20
>Patten arrives in Beijing for three-day visit to discuss reform proposals. Chinese Foreign Minister Qian Qichen accuses Patten of trying to provoke Beijing, saying: "We want cooperation rather than confrontation."

October 25
>Hang Seng Index hits new record high of 6,329 points. Price of seat in Hong Kong's stock exchange rises to $115,000, up from $51,000 a year earlier.

October 28
>Patten issues texts of secret diplomatic exchanges between China and Britain on his proposed election reforms, to disprove Beijing's claim of a "deal."

November 7
>Beijing announces plans to dismantle democratic reforms in Hong Kong after 1997.

November 11
>Legislative Council endorses Patten's plans to increase democracy in Hong Kong.

November 12
>Beijing accuses Britain of pressuring Legislative Council to support Patten's reforms.

November 16

Beijing claims Patten's reform proposals are contrary to the 1984 Joint Declaration.

November 17

Patten challenges Beijing to submit alternatives to his proposals for election reform. Hang Seng Index hits record high 6,447 points.

November 23

Beijing rules out "any counter-proposal or any compromise plan" as alternative to Patten's democratic reform proposals.

November 30

Hong Kong awards $1.17 billion contract for site preparation at new airport, despite lack of agreement from Beijing on financing arrangements.

December 1

Britain advises China that it supports Patten's reform proposals for Hong Kong.

December 2

Hang Seng Index falls to 5,411 points, down 16 percent from mid–November's record, reacting to escalating verbal exchanges between China and Hong Kong.

December 3

Beijing threatens to abandon Joint Declaration if Patten goes ahead with reforms. Hang Seng Index falls to 4,978, down 22 percent from mid–November record high, reacting to escalating verbal exchanges between China and Hong Kong.

December 4

Former U.S. President Richard Nixon endorses Patten's reform proposals.

December 9

Former British Prime Minister Margaret Thatcher endorses Patten's proposals to increase democracy in Hong Kong.

1993

January 3

Beijing threatens "a lot of hardship" for Hong Kong residents unless Patten withdraws his proposed political reforms.

January 13

Legislative Council, on 35–2 vote, rejects proposal urging Patten to withdraw his plans for democratic reform in Hong Kong.

February 3

Patten undergoes heart operation to clear two coronary arteries.

February 7

Beijing warns that government employees in Hong Kong could lose their jobs in 1997 if they support Patten's proposals for political reforms. Hong Kong's Executive Council endorses Patten's plans for democratic reforms.

February 24

Hong Kong warns Beijing that Patten's reform proposals will be considered by legislators unless talks resume between China and Britain.

March 5

Patten delays submitting reform plans to Legislative Council because of pending talks between China and Britain.

March 11

Patten gives Beijing 24 hours to agree to resumption of talks with Britain or he will submit reform proposals for debate in the Legislative Council.

March 12

Patten publishes democratic reform bill, clearing the way for legislative debate.

March 15

Beijing accuses Britain of a "perfidious act" in allowing Patten to publish his proposals for democratic reform in Hong Kong.

March 17

Beijing declares Patten "will stand condemned as a criminal for all eternity" for trying to introduce more democracy in Hong Kong before 1997.

March 18

Beijing threatens trade boycott with Britain if Patten goes ahead with reforms.

March 21

Sixteen "rickshaw boys" (average age 70) are licensed in Hong Kong, compared with hundreds in the early 1960s.

March 23

Razing begins at Kowloon's Walled City, to be replaced by a park.

March 31

Beijing announces establishment of an advisory preparatory committee, three years before originally scheduled, to plan for "smooth transition" of Hong Kong to China.

April 6

Patten urges Beijing to resume talks with Britain or he will submit his reform proposals to the Legislative Council for debate.

April 13

Beijing agrees to resume talks with Britain on election reforms for Hong Kong.

April 14

Hang Seng Index rises to record high 6,784 points after announcement that China and Britain will resume talks on election reform proposals for Hong Kong.

April 22

China and Britain resume talks on proposed democratic reforms for Hong Kong.

May 27

Hang Seng Index rises to record high 7,447 points.

June 4

China and Britain resume talks on financing arrangements for new Hong Kong airport.

July 9

British Foreign Minister Douglas Hurd meets in Beijing with Chinese Foreign Minister Qian Qichen to discuss Patten's reform proposals for Hong Kong.

July 16

China's Preliminary Working Committee, an advance advisory group for the Preparatory Committee, begins work on "smooth transition" of Hong Kong.

July 31
Tourist Association reports nearly 5 million visitors to Hong Kong during January through July, up 13 percent from same period in 1992.

August 19
Hang Seng Index tops record 7,600 level, gaining 38 percent during 1993.

September 3
Patten warns Beijing that lack of an agreement soon in Sino-British talks will force him to go ahead with his election reforms.

September 29
Beijing warns that results of the 1995 Hong Kong legislative elections will be revoked and replaced with new elections in 1997 unless Patten abandons his democratic reform proposals.

October 6
Patten announces plans to submit his reform proposals to Hong Kong's Legislative Council, admitting failure of yearlong effort to gain Beijing's approval.

October 8
Hang Seng Index rises to record high 8,005 points.

October 11
Beijing threatens to terminate any elected political bodies in Hong Kong in 1997 if proposed election changes are carried out in 1994 and 1995.

October 18
Hang Seng Index breaks 9,000 level, hitting record high 9,031—marking sixth record high in as many trading days.

December 2
Patten announces plans to submit proposed reforms to the Legislative Council this month, despite lack of approval by Beijing.

December 10
Patten publishes reform plans, clearing the way for submission to legislators.

December 27
Beijing announces plans to disband Hong Kong's Legislative Council in 1997 and review Hong Kong laws to determine if they should remain in force.

1994
January 3
Hang Seng Index soars past 12,000 to new record high 12,086 points.

January 4
Hang Seng Index rises again to new record, hitting 12,201 points.

January 5
Patten voices concern about Chinese intimidation of Hong Kong journalists.

January 6
Hang Seng Index falls to 11,374, marking its largest single-day point decline since the October 1987 worldwide stock market crash.

January 7
Hang Seng Index declines 9.6 percent (to 10,283) after sellers trade a record 15.2 billion shares.

January 13
Hang Seng Index closes at 10,176 points, or 17 percent below January 4 high.

January 23
Hong Kong legislators approve $216 million in financing for new airport, defying Chinese objections against funding without their approval.

February 24
Hong Kong's Legislative Council endorses "first phase" of Patten's democratic reform proposals, calling for lowering the voting age from 21 to 18 and introducing single-member voting districts (instead of appointments) in 1994-95 elections. Beijing criticizes Hong Kong legislators for approving "first phase" of Patten's reforms, threatening again to dismantle the Legislative Council in 1997 if it is chosen through democratic elections.

February 27
Patten publishes "second phase" of his proposed reforms, extending voter eligibility to all working residents for electing special constituency legislators and, in effect, allowing voters to elect all 60 members of the Legislative Council.

March 2
Hong Kong reports $1.95 billion budget surplus for 1993-94 fiscal year, with cash reserves of $40 billion. Plans are announced for more public spending in 1994-95, which could reduce budget surplus to less than $1 billion.

March 18
Hang Seng Index falls below 10,000 level, ending the trading week at 9,720.

March 19
Commissioned survey determines that 80 percent of Hong Kong residents have not read the Basic Law, the constitution-like blueprint for post–1997 Hong Kong. Hong Kong Legislative Council endorses report suggesting that council salaries be raised from $5,545 to $13,430 per month, with retirement benefits for members serving two or more four-year terms.

March 21
Hang Seng Index falls to 8,667 points—its lowest level since mid–October 1993.

March 26
Beijing criticizes soaring property values in Hong Kong, but admits Chinese-funded companies contributed to the problem through speculation in the property market.

April
Governor Chris Patten meets with British Foreign Secretary Douglas Hurd in London to review progress in transition talks with China.

May
China begins issuing Hong Kong currency through the Bank of China, becoming Hong Kong's third note-issuing institution.

September
District and local council elections in Hong Kong.

1995

Legislative Council elections (four-year terms) are held for the last time before Hong Kong's handover to China in 1997.

1997
June 30

Britain's 99-year colonial lease ends at midnight, after which China assumes sovereignty of Hong Kong, Kowloon, Stonecutters Island, the New Territories and 235 adjacent islands. The historical transition brings to an end more than 150 years of British rule in Hong Kong.

2047
June 30

Expiration of the Basic Law for Hong Kong, a constitutional document in which China guaranteed 50 years of autonomy, capitalism and continued fundamental rights after taking effect on July 1, 1997.

Notes

Introduction

    1. Rafferty, p. 48.

Chapter 1

    1. Cottrell, p. 9.
    2. Ibid., p. 10.
    3. McGurn, p. 26.
    4. Cottrell, p. 13.
    5. Ibid., p. 21.
    6. Ibid., p. 23.
    7. Ibid., p. 24.

Chapter 2

    1. Cheng, Joseph Y.S., p. 61.
    2. Adley, p. 26.
    3. Scott, p. 112.
    4. *London Times,* April 28, 1978.
    5. Cottrell, p. 33.
    6. Ibid., p. 37.

Chapter 3

    1. Adley, p. 21.
    2. Lethbridge, p. 232.
    3. Ibid., p. 106.
    4. Cheng, Joseph Y.S., p. 29.
    5. Ibid., p. 38.
    6. Cottrell, p. 68.
    7. Ibid.
    8. *Far Eastern Economic Review,* June 21, 1982, p. 23.
    9. Ibid.

10. Ibid.
11. Cottrell, p. 70.
12. *Business Week*, July 19, 1982, p. 80.
13. Cheng, p. 16.
14. Ibid.
15. Cottrell, p. 73.
16. Ibid., p. 74.
17. Cheng, Joseph Y.S., p. 70.

Chapter 4

1. Cottrell, p. 83.
2. Ibid.
3. Ibid., p. 85.
4. *Mao-tai* is a Chinese sorghum liquor. Clive James, a member of the press party with Mrs. Thatcher, said *mao-tai* "has the same effect as inserting your head in a cupboard and asking a large male friend to slam the door." Cottrell, p. 85.
5. Cottrell, p. 86.
6. Benton, p. 10.
7. Cottrell, p. 86.
8. *New York Times*, September 4, 1982.
9. Cottrell, p. 88.
10. McGurn, p. 35.
11. *Time*, October 11, 1982, p. 32.
12. *New York Times*, September 25, 1982.
13. Ibid., p. 2.
14. Cottrell, p. 90.
15. *New York Times*, September 25, 1982, p. 2.
16. Cottrell, p. 91.
17. Ibid.
18. *New York Times*, September 26, 1982, p. 10.
19. Cottrell, p. 92.
20. *New York Times*, September 26, 1982, p. 10.
21. Ibid.
22. *New York Times*, September 22, 1982, p. 3.
23. Cheng, Joseph Y.S., p. 40.

Chapter 5

1. Cottrell, p. 95.
2. Ibid., p. 96.
3. William McGurn called the intense Chinese propaganda "classic united-front agitprop, calculated to appeal to the latent Chinese nationalism of the Hong Kong public." McGurn, p. 41.
4. Cottrell, p. 96.
5. Ibid.
6. Ibid., p. 97.

7. Ibid.
8. Ibid., p. 99.
9. Ibid.
10. Ibid., p. 100.
11. Ibid., p. 101.

Chapter 6

1. *New York Times*, December 23, 1983, p. D9.
2. Adley, p. 49.
3. *Newsweek*, June 27, 1983, p. 59.
4. Benton, p. 62.
5. Browning, p. 212.
6. *New York Times*, July 14, 1983, p. 4.
7. *New York Times*, October 16, 1983, p. D4.
8. Adley, p. 24.
9. McGurn, p. 45.
10. Adley, p. 68.
11. Hungdau Chiu, p. 187.
12. Ibid., p. 188.
13. Ibid.
14. Domes, p. 89.
15. *Newsweek*, August 13, 1984, p. 48.
16. *New York Times*, September 27, 1984, p. 1.
17. Following traditional British fashion, the government issues a "Green Paper" which outlines a certain proposed policy, requesting public opinion on the proposal. Reaction is then considered for inclusion in a subsequent "White Paper," a more detailed explanation which follows adoption of the proposed policy.

Chapter 7

1. *New York Times*, September 27, 1984, p. 12.
2. *New York Times*, September 26, 1984, p. 10.
3. Ibid.
4. McGurn, p. 64.
5. *New York Times*, September 27, 1984, p. 1.
6. Ibid.
7. Cottrell, p. 173.
8. *New York Times*, September 27, 1984, p. 12.
9. *New York Times*, October 2, 1984, p. 30.
10. Cottrell, p. 174.
11. Ibid.
12. Ibid.
13. Patrikeeff, p. 136.
14. McGurn, p. 55.

Chapter 8

1. *New York Times,* January 7, 1986, p. 2.
2. *London Times,* May 22, 1985.
3. *New York Times,* May 21, 1984, p. 3.
4. *New York Times,* May 26, 1985, p. D2.
5. Scott, p. 286.
6. Ibid., p. 287.
7. Ibid.
8. Ibid., p. 290.
9. Ibid., p. 291.
10. *London Times,* October 14, 1986, p. 1.
11. Ibid.
12. Ibid.
13. Ibid.
14. *New York Times,* December 14, 1986, p. 19.
15. Ibid.
16. *New York Times,* December 8, 1986, p. 4.

Chapter 9

1. *New York Times,* April 26, 1987, p. 20.
2. *New York Times,* January 23, 1987, p. 4.
3. *London Times,* January 17, 1987, p. 1.
4. Ibid.
5. *London Times,* January 17, 1987, p. 6.
6. Ibid.
7. *New York Times,* April 26, 1987, p. 1.
8. *New York Times,* September 21, 1987.
9. Scott, p. 288.
10. Ibid., p. 291.
11. Ibid.
12. *New York Times,* April 26, 1987, p. 20.
13. Ibid.
14. Cottrell, p. 184.
15. Scott, p. 289.

Chapter 10

1. *New York Times,* May 15, 1989, p. 4.
2. *New York Times,* March 5, 1988, p. 4.
3. Ibid.
4. Ibid.
5. *New Book of World Rankings 1991* (figures from 1988).
6. *New York Times,* April 29, 1988, p. 5.
7. Ibid.
8. Ibid.

9. *New York Times,* May 8, 1988, p. 15.
10. *New York Times,* February 12, 1989, p. 3.
11. Ibid.
12. *New York Times,* May 15, 1989, p. 4.
13. *New York Times,* March 6, 1989, p. D12.

Chapter 11

1. *New York Times,* June 30, 1989, p. 6.
2. McGurn, p. 90.
3. *New York Times,* June 10, 1989, p. 7.
4. *New York Times,* July 3, 1989, p. 6.
5. *New York Times,* July 4, 1989, p. 4.
6. Ibid.
7. *United Press International,* July 5, 1989.
8. *King Features Syndicate,* August 2, 1989.
9. *Los Angeles Times,* December 21, 1989, p. 19.
10. Ibid.
11. Ibid.
12. *New York Times,* January 10, 1990, p. 1.
13. *New York Times,* December 21, 1989, p. 3.
14. Ibid.
15. Ibid.
16. Ibid.
17. *Los Angeles Times,* December 21, 1989, p. 19.
18. *New York Times,* December 21, 1989, p. 3.
19. Ibid.
20. Ibid.
21. *New York Times,* December 31, 1989, p. 16.
22. Ibid.
23. *London Times,* January 1, 1990, p. 2.
24. Ibid., p. 8.
25. *New York Times,* January 10, 1990, p. 1.
26. Ibid.
27. *New York Times,* January 13, 1990, p. 8.
28. *New York Times,* March 3, 1990, p. 3.
29. *Wall Street Journal,* March 2, 1990, p. 10.
30. Ibid.
31. *New York Times,* March 22, 1990, p. 4.

Chapter 12

1. *Beijing Review,* April 16, 1990, p. 17.
2. *New York Times,* April 23, 1990, p. 3.
3. Ibid.
4. *New York Times,* April 23, 1990, p. 6.
5. Ibid., p. 3.

6. Ibid.
7. *New York Times*, January 22, 1990, p. 3.
8. Ibid.
9. Ibid.
10. *New York Times*, April 5, 1990, p. 6.
11. Ibid.
12. *Beijing Review*, April 30, 1990, p. 10.
13. *New York Times*, July 29, 1990, p. 4.
14. *New York Times*, May 16, 1990, p. 12.
15. *New York Times*, October 7, 1990, p. 19.
16. Ibid.
17. *New York Times*, November 13, 1990, p. 6.

Chapter 13

1. *New York Times*, July 5, 1991, p. 3.
2. *New York Times*, October 16, 1989, p. D10.
3. Ibid.
4. *New York Times*, June 12, 1991, p. 15.
5. Ibid.
6. *New York Times*, January 21, 1991, p. 3.
7. *New York Times*, June 12, 1991, p. 15.
8. Ibid.
9. *New York Times*, January 21, 1991, p. 3.
10. *New York Times*, September 1991, p. 5.
11. *New York Times*, September 4, 1991, p. 5.
12. *New York Times*, March 1, 1991, p. 3.
13. Ibid.

Chapter 14

1. *New York Times*, October 7, 1991, p. 4.
2. *New York Times*, September 17, 1991, p. 1.
3. *New York Times*, October 7, 1991, p. 4.
4. Ibid.
5. *New York Times*, September 17, 1991, p. 1.
6. *New York Times*, April 12, 1992, p. 20.
7. Ibid.

Chapter 15

1. *London Times*, April 16, 1992, p. 16.
2. *London Times*, April 25, 1992, p. 1.
3. Ibid.
4. *New York Times*, April 26, 1992, p. 11.
5. *London Times*, April 25, 1992, p. 1.
6. *London Times*, April 22, 1992, p. LT5.

7. Ibid.
8. Ibid.
9. *London Times,* June 19, 1992, p. 11.
10. *London Times,* July 1, 1992, p. 12.
11. *London Times,* July 10, 1992, p. 11.
12. Ibid.
13. *London Times,* July 7, 1992, p. 14.
14. *London Times,* July 22, 1992, p. 9.
15. Ibid.
16. *New York Times,* July 3, 1992, p. 4.

Chapter 16

1. *New York Times,* October 21, 1992, p. 4.
2. *New York Times,* October 8, 1992, p. 11.
3. *London Times,* October 8, 1992, p. 1.
4. Ibid., p. 15.
5. *London Times,* October 9, 1992, p. 13.
6. *London Times,* October 22, 1992, p. 15.
7. Ibid.
8. *London Times,* October 23, 1992, p. 12.
9. Ibid.
10. *Beijing Review,* November 2, 1992, p. 10.
11. *London Times,* October 24, 1992, p. 10.
12. *New York Times,* October 29, 1992, p. 14.
13. Ibid.
14. *London Times,* November 12, 1992, p. 16.
15. Ibid.
16. *London Times,* November 13, 1992, p. 15.
17. *Beijing Review,* November 2, 1992, p. 10.
18. *New York Times,* November 11, 1992, p. 1.
19. Ibid.
20. *London Times,* November 17, 1992, p. 1.
21. *New York Times,* November 18, 1992, p. 1.
22. Ibid.
23. *New York Times,* November 19, 1992, p. 1.
24. *New York Times,* November 24, 1992, p. 8.
25. *Maclean's,* December 7, 1992, p. 28.
26. *New York Times,* November 20, 1992, p. 6.
27. *New York Times,* November 11, 1992, p. 1.
28. *London Times,* November 21, 1992, p. 11.
29. *New York Times,* December 1, 1992, p. 4.
30. Ibid.
31. Ibid.
32. Ibid.
33. *New York Times,* December 3, 1992, p. 1.
34. *Maclean's,* December 7, 1992, p. 28.

Chapter 17

1. *New York Times*, December 11, 1993, p. 3.
2. *London Times*, January 5, 1993, p. 9.
3. *Beijing Review*, February 15, 1993, p. 9.
4. *London Times*, March 6, 1993, p. 13.
5. *London Times*, March 12, 1993, p. 13.
6. *London Times*, March 13, 1993, p. 10.
7. Ibid.
8. *London Times*, March 16, 1993, p. 1.
9. *London Times*, March 17, 1993, p. 19.
10. *London Times*, March 19, 1993, p. 14.
11. Ibid.
12. *London Times*, March 24, 1993, p. 12.
13. Ibid.
14. *London Times*, April 14, 1993, p. 4.
15. *London Times*, April 1, 1993, p. 11.
16. *New York Times*, April 1, 1993, p. 1.
17. *London Times*, September 4, 1993, p. 10.
18. *London Times*, September 5, 1993, p. 1.
19. *New York Times*, October 7, 1993, p. 3.
20. *London Times*, September 30, 1993, p. 15.

Chapter 18

1. *London Times Magazine*, January 8, 1994, p. 5.
2. *New York Times*, February 2, 1994, p. 9.
3. *New York Times*, February 25, 1994, p. 1.
4. *London Times*, February 25, 1994, p. 5.
5. *New York Times*, February 25, 1994, p. 1.
6. *London Times*, January 1, 1994, p. B1.
7. Ibid.
8. *Wall Street Journal*, January 7, 1994, p. C1.
9. Ibid.
10. *South China Morning Post*, March 19, 1994, p. B8.
11. *South China Morning Post*, March 26, 1994, p. 4.
12. Ibid.
13. *Beijing Review*, December 20, 1993, p. 4.
14. *Asiaweek*, January 5, 1994, p. 19.
15. *London Times*, January 6, 1994, p. 2.
16. *Wall Street Journal*, December 1, 1993.
17. *London Times*, January 6, 1994, p. 2.
18. *Wall Street Journal*, March 3, 1994, p. C2.
19. Ibid.
20. *Wall Street Journal*, November 9, 1990, p. 4.
21. Ibid.
22. Ibid.

Bibliography

Books

Adley, Robert. *All Change Hong Kong.* Blandford Press, Poole, Dorset, United Kingdom, 1984

Atwell, Pamela. *British Mandarins and Chinese Reformers.* Oxford University Press, Hong Kong, 1985.

Beazer, William F. *The Commercial Future of Hong Kong.* Praeger Publishers, New York, 1978.

Benton, Gregor. *The Hongkong Crisis.* Pluto Press, London, 1983.

Bih-jaw Lin (Editor). *The Aftermath of the 1989 Tiananmen Crisis in Mainland China.* Westview Press Inc., Boulder, Colo., 1992.

Black, George and Munro, Robin. *Black Hands of Beijing: Lives of Defiance in China's Democracy Movement.* John Wiley & Sons, New York, 1993.

Browning, Graeme. *If Everybody Bought One Shoe: American Capitalism in Communist China.* Hill and Wang, New York, 1989.

Bueno de Mesquita, Bruce; Newman, David; Rabushka, Alvin. *Forecasting Political Events: The Future of Hong Kong.* Yale University Press, New Haven, Conn., 1985.

Chan, Ming K. and Clark, David J. (Editors) *The Hong Kong Basic Law: Blueprint for "Stability and Prosperity" Under Chinese Sovereignty?* M.E. Sharpe Inc., Armonk, N.Y., 1991.

Cheng, Chu-yuan. *Behind the Tiananmen Massacre.* Westview Press, Boulder, Colo., 1990.

Cheng, Joseph Y.S. (editor). *Hong Kong: In Search of a Future.* Oxford University Press, Hong Kong, 1984.

Clark, Cumberland. *The Crown Colonies and Their History.* Mitre Press, London, 1939.

Clavell, James. *Noble House: A Novel of Contemporary Hong Kong.* Delacorte Press, New York, 1981.

_____. *Tai-Pan: A Novel of Hong Kong.* Atheneum, New York, 1966.

Coates, Austin. *Prelude to Hongkong.* Routledge & Kegan Paul, London, 1966.

Cohen, Joan Lebold. *The New Chinese Painting, 1949–1986.* Harry N. Abrams, New York, 1987.

Congressional Quarterly. *China: U.S. Policy Since 1945.* Congressional Quarterly, Washington, D.C., 1980.

Cooper, John. *Colony in Conflict: The HK Disturbances May 1967–January 1968.* Swindon Book Co., Hong Kong, 1970.

Cottrell, Robert. *The End of Hong Kong: The Secret Diplomacy of Imperial Retreat.* John Murray Ltd., London, 1993.

Davis, Michael C. *Constitutional Confrontation in Hong Kong.* The Macmillan Press Ltd., London, 1989.

Domes, Jurgen and Shaw, Yu-ming (editors). *Hong Kong: A Chinese and International Concern.* Westview Press, London, 1988.

Faligot, Roger and Kauffer, Remi. *The Chinese Secret Service.* William Morrow, New York, 1987.

Franz, Uli. *Deng Xiaoping.* Harcourt Brace Jovanovich, Boston, 1988.

Hachten, William A. *The Growth of Media in the Third World.* Iowa State University Press, Ames, Iowa, 1992.

Harding, Harry. *A Fragile Relationship: The US & China Since 1972.* Brookings Institution, Washington, D.C., 1992.

Harris, Kenneth. *Thatcher.* Little, Brown & Co., Boston, 1988.

Heath, Edward. *Edward Heath Travels: People & Places in My Life.* Griffin Press Ltd., Toronto, 1977.

Hicks, George L. *Hong Kong Countdown.* Writers' & Publishers' Cooperative, Hong Kong, 1988.

Hillman, Judy and Clarke, Peter. *Geoffrey Howe: A Quiet Revolutionary.* Weidenfeld & Nicolson, London, 1988.

Hughes, Richard. *Hong Kong: Borrowed Place – Borrowed Time.* Frederick A. Praeger, New York, 1968.

Hungdah Chiu. *The Future of Hong Kong: Toward 1997 and Beyond.* Quorum Books, New York, 1987.

Hurd, Douglas and Osmond, Andrew. *The Smile on the Face of the Tiger.* Macmillan, New York, 1970.

Junior, Penny. *Margaret Thatcher: Wife – Mother – Politician.* Sidgwick & Jackson, London, 1983.

Kelly, Ian. *Hong Kong: A Political-Geographic Analysis.* Macmillan, London, 1987.

Kotkin, Joel. *Tribes: How Race, Religion and Identity Determine Success in the New Global Economy.* Random House, New York, 1993.

Lau Siu-Kaiand Kuan Hsin-Chi. *The Ethos of the Hong Kong Chinese.* The Chinese University Press, Hong Kong, 1988.

Lethbridge, David G. (editor). *The Business Environment in Hong Kong*, 2nd edition. Oxford University Press, Hong Kong, 1984.

Leung, Benjamin K.P. (editor). *Social Issues in Hong Kong.* Oxford University Press, Hong Kong, 1990.

Lo, T. Wing. *Corruption and Politics in Hong Kong and China.* Open University Press, Buckingham, England, 1993.

McGurn, William. *Perfidious Albion: The Abandonment of Hong Kong 1997.* Ethics & Public Policy Center, Washington, D.C., 1992.

Miners, Norman. *The Government and Politics of Hong Kong*, 5th edition. Oxford University Press, Hong Kong, 1991.

Morris, Jan. *Hong Kong.* Random House, New York, 1988.

Mushkat, Miron. *The Economic Future of Hong Kong.* Lynne Rienner Publishers, Boulder, Colo., 1990.

Ogden, Chris. *Maggie: An Intimate Portrait of a Woman in Power.* Simon & Schuster, New York, 1990.

Patrikeeff, Felix. *Mouldering Pearl: Hong Kong at the Crossroads.* George Philip Ltd., London, 1989.

Petersen, Gwenn Boardman. *Across the Bridge to China.* Elsevier-Nelson, New York, 1979.

Posner, Gerald L. *Warlords of Crime: Chinese Secret Societies – The New Mafia.* McGraw-Hill, New York, 1988.

Rafferty, Kevin. *City on the Rocks: Hong Kong's Uncertain Future.* Viking, New York, 1990.

Roberts, Elfed Vaughan. *Historical Dictionary of Hong Kong & Macau.* Scarecrow Press, Metuchen, N.J., 1992.

Scott, Ian. *Political Change and the Crisis of Legitimacy in Hong Kong.* Hurst & Co., London, 1989.

Segal, Gerald. *The Fate of Hong Kong.* St. Martin's, New York, 1993.

Sung, Yun-Wing. *The China–Hong Kong Connection.* Cambridge University Press, Cambridge, 1991.

Terrill, Ross. *China in Our Time.* Simon & Schuster, New York, 1992.

Thatcher, Margaret. *Margaret Thatcher: The Downing Street Years.* HarperCollins, New York, 1993.

Thomas, Gordon. *Chaos Under Heaven: The Shock Story of China's Search for Democracy.* Carol Publishing Group, Secaucus, N.J., 1991.

Tsai, Jung-fang. *Hong Kong in Chinese History.* Columbia University Press, New York, 1993.

Tsang, Steve Yui-Sang. *Democracy Shelved: Great Britain, China, and Attempts at Constitutional Reform in Hong Kong, 1945–1952.* Oxford University Press, Hong Kong, 1988.

Viviano, Frank. *Dispatches from the Pacific Century.* Addison-Wesley, Reading, Mass., 1993.

Wacks, Raymond (editor). *Human Rights in Hong Kong.* Oxford University Press, New York, 1992.

Wesley-Smith, Peter. *Unequal Treaty 1898–1997: China, Great Britain and Hong Kong's New Territories.* Oxford University Press, Oxford, 1980.

White, Jo Ann (editor). *Impact! Asian Views of the West.* Julian Messner, New York, 1971.

Wickman, Michael (editor). *Living in Hong Kong.* Amcham Publications, Hong Kong, 1973.

Wilson, Dick. *Hong Kong! Hong Kong!* Unwin Hyman, London, 1990.

Young, Hugo. *The Iron Lady: A Biography of Margaret Thatcher.* Farrar, Straus & Giroux, New York, 1989.

Youngson, A.J. *Hong Kong: Economic Growth and Policy.* Oxford University Press, Hong Kong, 1982.

Yufan Hao and Guocang Huan (editors). *The Chinese View of the World.* Pantheon, New York, 1989.

Zang Zhong Mei. *Hu Yaobang.* M.E. Sharpe Inc., Armonk, N.Y., 1988.

Periodicals

Asian Outlook

Asiaweek

Associated Press

Aviation Week

Beijing Review
Business Week
Economist
Far Eastern Economic Review
International Herald Tribune
London Times
Los Angeles Times
Maclean's
National Review

New York Times
Newsweek
Reuters
South China Morning Post
Time
United Press International
U.S. News & World Report
Wall Street Journal

Index